THE WHEEL OF FORTUNE:

The History of a Poor Community in Jakarta

LEA JELLINEK

UNIVERSITY OF HAWAII PRESS
Honolulu

Published in North America by
University of Hawaii Press
2840 Kolowalu Street
Honolulu, Hawaii 96822

First published in 1991 by
Allen & Unwin in association with
the Asian Studies Association of Australia

ISBN 0 8248 1381 2

Library of Congress Cataloguing-in-Publication Data

Jellinek, Lea.
The wheel of fortune: the history of a poor community in
Jakarta
by Lea Jellinek.
    p.   cm.
Includes bibliographical references and index.
ISBN 0-8248-1381-2
1. Community development, Urban—Indonesia—Jakarta. 2.
Poor— Indonesia—Jakarta. 3. Jakarta (Indonesia)—Social conditions.
4. Jakarta (Indonesia)—Economic conditions. 5. Jakarta (In-
donesia) —Politics and government. I. Title.
HN704.J45 1991
306'.08598'22—dc20   89-46274
                    CIP

Typeset by Vera-Reyes Inc., Manila

Printed in Singapore by Kim Hup Lee Printer

THE WHEEL OF FORTUNE

To my beloved mother and father, Eva and Fred

Acknowledgements

My greatest debt is to the kampung dwellers, and especially Bud, who invited me into her life and made this story possible. The late Ir Duddy Soegoto (Head of Planning and Feasibility at Perumnas) gave me faith in the idealism, goodwill and ability of Indonesian officials. It was Indonesia, the kampung dwellers', his family's and my loss that he died whilst still young and before completing the rehousing project. Dr Howard Dick helped this book come to fruition by having faith in the kampung dwellers' story and my ability to write it. I am also indebted to Professor Merle Ricklefs and Dr Susan Abeyasekere.

Contents

Preface

This research started from curiosity as to how the poor survive. Its beginning is difficult to pin-point. From the time when I first visited Jakarta in the early 1970s, it evolved gradually over fifteen years and my initially unstructured observations of many individual lives became a study of the birth, evolution and death of one neighbourhood which was part of the rapidly expanding metropolis of Jakarta.

While teaching at the University of Indonesia as an Australian Volunteer in 1972–1973, I developed a passion for the hand-made ice-creams and hot lemon juice sold by the petty traders of Jakarta. Bud, a trader at whose stall I regularly ate, invited me to her home. Initially my study focused upon her life and later expanded to encompass her immediate neighbours whom she met on a daily basis. Eventually it included all 77 households that made up Bud's neighbourhood. Ten years later my horizons extended beyond the neighbourhood to encompass many other households which were affected by the kampung's demolition.

The more frequently I visited Bud and the longer I stayed in her neighbourhood, the more I was accepted by the kampung dwellers. Even those who in the beginning were reluctant to talk increasingly wanted to do so. Many confided their deepest worries and major concerns. I provided a sympathetic ear. Some turned to me for help to pay for food, the education of their children or medical attention. Others asked me to help them find jobs as cooks, drivers, cleaners or gardeners. On a few occasions I travelled with them back to their home villages. At other times I attended festivities where the community gathered to talk and celebrate. When the community was threatened by demolition many sought my advice and assistance. I, however, only played a marginal role in their lives. Ultimately they each battled on as best they could in a very harsh and trying environment.

Having come into the kampung as a stranger with the desire to understand the lives of people that were totally different from my own, I stood midway between the kampung and the outside world. I looked at the community and its inhabitants with all the curiosity of an outsider. I wanted to be part of the community and share the kampung dwellers' experiences and values but was encumbered by my preconceived ideas and stable background as a middle-class Australian. Without actually living through the turmoil of kampung dwellers' lives and personally experiencing their joys and sorrow, I could never know precisely how they felt. I could, however, observe, discuss and become involved and eventually hope to understand some aspects of their lives.

After ten years, I was no longer just an observer but had become an occasional member of the community. When I arrived in the narrow pathways after a period of absence, the kampung's children would call "Lea, Lea, Lea" and run to tell their parents that I had returned. Eagerly awaited presents—clothes, sweets, toy koala bears—were distributed and there was endless chatter about what had transpired whilst I had been away. Children had been born, a person had died, a wife had beaten her husband for chasing another woman, a neighbour had lost a job and a trader had lost all his wares in a trader-clearing campaign, a house had burnt down and nearly set the entire community alight. My life seemed static compared to the perpetually changing scenerio of the kampung dwellers' lives.

Unlike the kampung dwellers who had to labour each day to keep themselves alive, I had the time, resources and desire to record their stories. After writing a number of kampung dwellers' life stories, I desired an over-view.[1] Every individual's life seemed so different. Each case seemed to show the diversity of human experience. Between 1978 and 1984, professional involvement with the World Bank and United Nations encouraged me to try and grapple with the more general features of urban poverty.

My intellectual journey evolved almost of its own accord with little intellectual framework. Curiosity and friendship gradually evolved into scholarship. My initial findings surprised me: dire poverty was not the dominant feature. All around me were small-scale entrepreneurs battling to improve their lives. I soon discovered, however, that the findings of one visit were overturned by the next. Unpredictability and uncertainty were the only constant feature of kampung dwellers' lives. A period of upward mobility was rapidly followed by decline. Human relationships and jobs were in flux. Government which had seemed irrelevant, suddenly became all-powerful. During the final shattering experience of the kampung's demolition, I tried to make use of my position midway between the community and outside world to serve as a channel of communication. With the kampung's imminent demise I became interested in how it came into being in the first place. Where did its inhabitants come from and to where did they go?

My position in the community was ambiguous. In the eyes of officialdom, my status was unclear because I had not come into the community with the official permission of the headman. Rather, like most kampung guests, I had been introduced to the kampung and its local headman by my host, Bud. Some years later, Bud confided that an official had made enquiries as to what I was doing in the neighbourhood. Without my knowing, Bud and other kampung dwellers had supported and protected me against such enquiries. They explained that I was a teacher at the university who was only seeking companionship and a home in their neighbourhood.

When I first met Bud her spirits were high and her life seemed atypical. I had come to study poverty and instead befriended a prosperous cooked-food seller. Since 1967 her trade had boomed. She had an entourage of assistants—her husband, his second wife and some villagers who worked for food, accommodation, clothing and a little pocket money. Bud proudly oversaw her stall from late evening to the early hours of the morning. She had a beaming moon-like face with poorly fitting large false teeth. Military officers, policeman and civil servants patronized her well stocked stall. She served banana fritters, fried chicken, beef, fish, cashew nuts, beer and numerous other delicacies. Bud was able to renovate her shanty and buy numerous consumer goods. She dreamed of obtaining a permanent trade stall and her baby daughter becoming a doctor.

By 1976, Bud's good fortune had started to turned sour. Her trade stall was being squeezed out of the city centre by multi-storey buildings, highways, traffic and the city's authorities who were keen to make Jakarta a modern metropolis. By 1978 Bud no longer had a large mobile stall or strategic central-city location but was carting her wares on hip and head around the streets of Jakarta. Her numerous assistants had fled. Only her aged mother and young daughter remained. She felt poor, confused and depressed. To feed them she had been forced to sell all her newly acquired possessions. By 1979 Bud's cooked-food trade was no longer viable and, with my assistance, she reluctantly became a domestic servant. Although her new job provided greater security and a regular monthly income, she had lost the pride, freedom and independence of petty trade.

In 1981 Bud's home, like that of her kampung neighbours, was threatened with demolition. The city's authorities viewed Kebun

Kacang as an eye-sore in the middle of modern Jakarta. The inhabitants were offered rehousing in central-city flats where the kampung had formerly been. Bud was fearful and wanted to flee but I encouraged her to accept a flat. Bud was able to move into her flat after two and a half years of trauma and tribulation in temporary accommodation. Even though she lacked the resources, she renovated her reinforced concrete cell-like flat. She explained that she could not face the neighbours if she did not improve her new home.

A year later Bud's mother died. Bud seemed shattered and continued to shrink both mentally and physically. By 1987 she too was dead. Her fourteen year old daughter, pregnant and unmarried, was left to fend for herself.

When I first met Bud her life seemed better than that of her neighbours. In the end, it seemed more tragic. However, I soon discovered that each member of the community had similar tragedies of their own. Bud's story put into stark relief what was happening to the lives of other members of the community. They too were experiencing a boom and bust in their small-scale income-earning occupations, a loosening of social ties, a growing insecurity about their place of residence and a sense that government was penetrating more and more into their lives. They too had rapidly rising aspirations which were being torn apart.

The same key characters—Bud, Santo, Ateng, Wira, Samilah, Agus, Udin, Mus, the Sanis, Lukman, Ibu Minah and Imah—emerge again and again throughout the pages of this book. Some play a more prominent role in the history of Kebun Kacang because they were older and could remember what the area was like. Others feature more in the chapter on social networks because they had long established kinship ties or battled to maintain social connections in an increasingly competitive and individualistic world. Most of my kampung friends feature in the chapter on income-earning. With the threat of demolition hanging over the community in 1981, the story broadens and deepens to include all members of the community.

1. Jellinek, L. "The Life of a Jakarta Street Trader" in Abu-Lughod, J. et al. (eds.) *Third World Urbanization*, (Chicago, 1977), 244–56; *The Life of a Jakarta Street Trader–Two Years Later*, (Melbourne, 1977); "Circular Migration and the Pondok Dwelling System: A Case Study of Ice-Cream Traders in Jakarta" in Rimmer, P. J. et al. (eds.) *Food, Shelter and Transport in South-east Asia and the Pacific*, (Canberra, 1978), 135–54; "The Changing Fortunes of a Jakarta Street Trader" in Gugler, J. (ed.) *The Urbanization of the Third World*, (New York, 1988).

Glossary and Abbreviations

Agraria	Department of Lands
Air Mancur	the Water Fountain
alang alang	tall grass/weed
arisan	rotating credit or savings society
bajaj	small motorized 3-wheeled vehicle which provides door-to-door service.
bakso	meat ball in noodle soup
Balai Agung	main meeting hall
batako	a hollow brick
Batavia	capital of the Netherland East Indies renamed Jakarta
batik	wax-dyed fabric
becak	trishaw, pedicab, ricksaw
bemo	small 3-wheeled jitney/van which carries 6 passengers
BPS	Central Bureau of Statistics (Abbreviation of *Biro Pusat Statistik*)
bubur	rice porridge
Canda Kulak	Small Traders' Credit Scheme

Darul Islam	a group of rebels in West Java demanding a State based on Islam
DKI	the Jakarta City Government (abbreviation for *Daerah Khusus Ibukota*), formally DCI
DPU	Department of Public Works (abbreviation for *Department Pekerjaan Umum*)
DPRD	Legislative Assembly (Abbreviation for *Dewan PerwakilanRakyat Daerah*)
dukun	traditional healer
favela	Brazilian slums or shanty town
gado-gado	boiled vegetables with peanut sauce
Haji	one who has made the pilgrimage to Mecca
Haj	Islamic pilgrimage to Mecca
Hansip/Hanra	local security system
helicak	form of motorized becak introduced in 1972 to replace the becak. Carries 1 or 2 passengers.
Ibu	mother (abbreviation—Bu)
Idul Adha	a one-day festival celebrating the departure of the pilgrimage to Mecca by the sacrifice of goats
IGGI	Inter-Governmental Group on Indonesia
Imam	Muslim leader
jago/jagoan	tough, strongman, gang leader
jajan	tit-bits/snacks sold by traders
Jalan	road/street (abbreviation—Jl.)
jambu	fruit
jamu	herbal medicine
kampung	section of a village or city

quarter/urban compound

Kartu Keluarga	Family Card (abbreviation—KK)
Kartu Tanda Penduduk	Identity Card (abbreviation—KTP)
Kebun Kacang	peanut garden and the location of this study.
Kelurahan	lowest official administrative subdivision
kenek	unskilled worker/apprentice labourer
kepala	head
Kepala Rumah Tangga	household head
kerja	wage work
Ketua RT	RT chief
KIK	Small-scale Credit Program (abbreviation of *Kredit Investasi Kecil*)
KIP	abbreviation of Kampung Improvement Program
Kota	the city or usually referring to down-town Jakarta formerly Batavia
Kotamadya	District or Municipal Government resided over by a Mayor
langgar	prayer house
Lebaran	religious event celebrated on the day ending the fasting month
Leknas	National Institute for Economic and Social Research
Lurah	local official at the lowest level of the government's administrative hierarchy
mandur	foreman/labour recruiter
Masyumi	*Majelis Syuro Muslimin Indonesia* (Consultative Council of Indonesian Muslims), the largest Indonesian Islamic Party, after

	1952 representing Modernist Islam; banned in 1960.
Mahabharata	a Hindu Epic poem/play
Mesjid	Mosque
Minangkabau	ethnic group from Padang area, West Sumatra
mushollah	prayer house
NU	orthodox Islamic party (abbreviation for *Nahdatul Ulama*)
Opec	abbreviation for Organization of Petroleum Exporting Countries
opelet	4-wheeled minibus, seating 7 to 10 passengers.
Padang	capital city of West Sumatra
Padang Empek-empek	cakes cooked in Padang style
pasar	market
Pasar Induk	the main vegetable and fruit market in Jakarta
pecel	spiced vegetable
pembangunan	development
Pemberantasan Buta Huruf	illiteracy eradication (abbreviation PBH)
peremajaan	urban renewal (literally rejuvenation)
permerataan	equality
Pertamina	National Oil Company
Permesta	abbreviation for *Piagam Perjuangan Semesta Alam* (Universal Struggle Charter). Part of the regional crisis in the Outer Islands in 1957–58 based in Sulawesi
Perum Perumnas	National Housing Corporation
picis	currency under the colonial administration, equivalent to 10 cents

Pitra	obligatory gift at the end of the fasting month
PKI	*Partai Komunis Indonesia* (Indonesian Communist Party)
PNI	*Partai Nasional Indonesia* (Indonesian Nationalist party)
pondok	a communal lodging- or rooming-house
prahu	traditional sailing vessel
Ramadan	Moslem fasting month which takes place in the ninth month of the Arabic calender
Ramayana	great Hindu epic poem
Regeeringsreglement	colonial constitution
Repelita 1	*Rencana Pembangunan Lima Tahun 1* 1968/1969–1973/1974. First Five Year Plan.
Repelita 11	Second Five Year Plan 1973/1974–1978/1979
Repelita 111	Third Five Year Plan 1978/1979–1983/1984
Repelita IV	Fourth Five Year Plan 1983/1984–1988/1989
ronda	defence round/civil security
rukun	harmony, calm, togetherness
Rukun Kampung (RK)	Community Association. Current term for second lowest-level unofficial administrative unit. Equivalent to the *Rukun Warga* (RW) in Jakarta.
Rukun Tetangga (RT)	Neighbourhood Association for sub-unit of *Rukun Kampung*. In Kebun Kacang, one RW was composed of 16 RTs.
Rukun Warga (RW)	Community Association. Current term for second lowest-level unofficial administrative unit.

Rupiah (Rp.)	Indonesian monetary unit (see pp. 190–191 for exchange rates 1968–1981 and in litres of rice 1953–1982).
sarong/sarung	piece of cloth the ends of which have been sewn together. Wrapped around the waist and legs like a skirt.
slametan	festive meal
SMA	*Sekolah Menegah Atas* (Senior High School)
Surabaya	the capital city of East Java
tauke	boss (Chinese)
tukang	skilled artisan/construction worker
warung	small stall or shop
Yogyakarta	Municipality in the Special Region of Yogyakarta, Central Java
Zaman Kurang Ajar	Age Without Moral Code 1970s–1980s
Zaman Merdeka	Independence 1945–1965
Zaman Normal	Normal times 1930s–1942
Zaman Pembangunan	Age of Development 1965–1981
Zaman Perang	War Time 1942–1949

Introduction

This book describes and analyzes the evolution and eventual transformation of one kampung in Jakarta since the 1930s. It is a history of
a community undergoing rapid change. It focuses upon changes in
income-earning, housing and social relationships. The transience of
kampung dwellers' income-earning activities stands out. The appearance and disappearance of these opportunities depended on forces
which were beyond the kampung dwellers' control. As a result the
dominant feature of their lives was vulnerability and insecurity.

In order to understand the process of change within the kampung,
one must address the forces in the surrounding city and hinterland
which brought about the emergence of the kampung in the first place
and led to its ultimate demise. Until the mid-1970s both the kampung
and city were symbiotic, growing together physically and economically. This process culminated in the central-city construction boom
of the late 1960s and early 1970s. The kampung dwellers provided
cheap labour, goods and services for the expanding city, whilst
themselves obtaining better access to employment and a higher
income than if they had remained in the countryside. After the
mid-1970s the forces of change within the rapidly modernizing city
began to undermine the prosperity of the kampung. By 1975 the
small-scale, casual and self-employed jobs which had helped many of
the kampung dwellers raise their standard of living were being
displaced.

By 1980 the existence of the kampung at the centre of Jakarta was
seen by city planners as an unsightly anomaly. The neighbourhood
had already been encroached upon by the modern high-rise city
centre. Planners now viewed the adjacent kampung as a slum, and
determined that its inhabitants would be rehoused in modern multi-

storey flats. A lucky few with regular employment or adequate incomes accepted the government's offer of flats and found regular work in offices or factories. Most of the inhabitants, however, reluctantly chose to leave Kebun Kacang and fled to the periphery of the city, where they tried to re-establish the work and homes they had lost at the city centre.

There was no political or social organization within the community which might have enabled its inhabitants to stand together to resist this onslaught. Even if they had been able to organize, there is no guarantee that they would have been able to prevent demolition. Although city planners ostensibly aimed to reduce poverty and inequality, the resultant breakdown of tenuous community ties, together with other government policies hostile towards petty traders and becak drivers, actually worsened the very problems they were trying to alleviate.

The demolition of the kampung highlighted the opposing views of kampung dwellers and city planners. The former saw the kampung as a bustling hive of activity and a place of hope, a stepping stone to a better standard of living. The latter saw it as a slum whose inhabitants were caught in a vicious circle of poverty.[1] Implicitly, the planners assumed that housing conditions were a good indicator of living standards. If the kampung was an escape route from the poverty and hard work of the countryside then destroying it was a mistake. If, on the other hand, it was a poverty trap, then destroying it may have provided its inhabitants with the opportunity for a better life.

The difference in view between kampung dwellers and city planners in Jakarta is echoed in the literature on the development of other cities. Many scholars argue that slums and small-scale income-earning activities (informal sector) will persist. Others argue that these ways of earning and living will eventually decline as economic development creates new work and housing opportunities,[2] just as in central London after the 1890s petty trade, cottage industry, casual work and the slum eventually disappeared.[3]

Many of the forces which destroyed central-city slums and small-scale income-earning activities in London seem to be evident in Jakarta one hundred years later. In both cities, for example, competition from mass-produced manufactures and more sophisticated retail outlets undermined petty production and petty trade. This was reinforced by changes in consumer taste and the decline of the pedestrian. Jakarta in the 1970s and London in the 1860s reveal growing middle-class hostility towards street-side occupations and government legislation to clear these occupations from the streets and destroy the slum dwellers' homes. In both cities, increasingly expensive central-city land has been taken over by highways, offices, markets and luxury residential areas resulting in central-city depopulation.

Although there are tantalizing similarities in the changing shape of central London and central Jakarta a century apart, there is a risk of over-emphasizing them. Pessimistic writers on the Third World stress that although the external patterns of change may appear similar, the magnitude, speed and causes of changes are strikingly different. The global penetration of capitalism and growing economic inter-dependence between states makes a repetition of Western patterns of more autonomous and self-generated industrialization difficult. The size of cities is now much greater and the rate of labour absorption by modern industry much slower, than in Britain of one hundred years ago.[4]

There is a vast literature on slum communities of Third World cities.[5] The earlier literature highlighted the negative aspects of urban poverty. These included loose family structures, weak kinship ties, the absence of clear values, low and insecure incomes, a paucity of housing, amenities, possessions and a lack of political involve-ment. Later studies emphasized such positive features as tight social networks, individual initiative and community cooperation which helped the poor cope despite the often negative impact of govern-ment on their jobs and homes. These studies have shown people trying to make the best of a difficult situation, though many have also shown people broken and disillusioned by the perpetuation of pov-erty and lack of improvement.

Most of the literature on the urban poor in Indonesia focuses upon employment, incomes and expenditures. The core of this literature arises from a study sponsored by the ILO in Jakarta during the mid-1970s. Based on official statistics, Sethuraman provides an over-view of employment in Jakarta, focusing in particular upon the magnitude of the "informal sector".[6] He estimated that this sector accounted for approximately half of the city's labour force. Flowing from Sethuraman's initial overview, the ILO in conjunction with Leknas surveyed 4367 heads of "informal sector" enterprises in Jakarta to obtain data on the nature and type of these enterprises, their working conditions, employees, modes of operation, income, expenditure, relationship to government and marketing outlets. The survey found that petty trade was the predominant "informal sector" activity, accounting for two-thirds of the surveyed enterprises.[7]

The ILO research coincided with a lively debate amongst observers of Indonesia as to whether the poorer half of the population was benefitting from economic growth. In this debate the key study was the World Bank's Leiserson Report which, along with most ob-servers, argued that economic growth had in fact improved the lot of the poor throughout Indonesia.[8] Although there was argument about the extent and depth of poverty in rural areas most agreed that improvement had occurred for all levels of urban society.[9] In a rigorous study, Sundrum and Booth suggested that the proportion living in poverty declined from 40.4 to 31.3 percent in urban areas; this was however, accompanied by growing inequality and a possible rise in the absolute number of poor people living in rural Java.[10]

In Jakarta, a similar debate occurred over the extent of poverty. Most studies suggested that the incomes of all sections of the population rose from the later half of the 1960s to the mid-1970s. Because of the concentration of wealth in Jakarta, it was suggested that this city's population benefitted disproportionately from development. Over the period 1970 to 1976, real household expenditure in Jakarta increased by more than 50 percent, which was somewhat higher than the average for the rest of urban Java, more than double that of rural Java and more than five times that of the Outer Islands.[11] In Jakarta over the same period, real household expenditure increased significantly for all decile groups. These findings contrasted with those of Evers, based on three micro studies of the poor in Jakarta, which showed a decline in living standards.[12]

These contradictory views were, to some extent, reconciled by a World Bank study which argued that, although the incomes of the urban poor had risen in the early 1970s and their absolute number had declined, they had experienced stagnation or declined towards the end of the decade.[13]

At the other extreme from this literature based on Jakarta-wide surveys, there are a number of studies which focus very narrowly on case histories of individual kampung dwellers. Critchfield provided a vivid portrait of the life of a becak driver in Jakarta.[14] I followed with some life histories of several petty traders.[15] Other vignettes have appeared in magazines and newspapers. More recently I have described how the income-earning activities of kampung dwellers have changed over the past decade.[16] These case studies suggest considerable mobility between "informal sector" income-earning activities.[17]

The gap between city-wide surveys and individual case studies is very wide. Only Sunindyo has studied a community.[18] This is a socio-economic survey of 560 households supplemented by detailed case studies of nine members of the community. She notes that kampung dwellers live in a state of perpetual flux. Loss of their jobs and homes is a frequent occurrence. She does not, however, elaborate upon or analyze this state of insecurity.

Although not dealing with Jakarta, two good studies of urban kampungs are John Sullivan and Patrick Guinness.[19] Sullivan's study of an old kampung at the centre of Yogyakarta argues that the literature on the urban poor over emphasizes their marginal, insecure and transient jobs, homes and social networks. Dealing with a more peripheral and more recently established community in the same city, Guinness also emphasizes harmony and order. It is interesting that both studies of poor kampungs in Yogyakarta emphasize the strength of social ties, in marked contrast with the finding of Sunindyo and my own for Jakarta.

Most studies of the urban poor, whether of the Third World generally or of Indonesia specifically, fail to convey any sense of change or community. The obvious way out of this problem is to try and mesh case studies of individuals with the history of their community and the changes in their work, homes and relationships to one another and to the government. Nevertheless analysis of change within a community is difficult. Change is caused by a wide variety of forces beyond the usual experience and comprehension of kampung dwellers. Their perceptions of the causes of change need to be related to a broader study of the dynamics of change in the city and in the nation at large.

Marxists and neo-Marxists would argue that understanding change in the life of the inhabitants of the kampung requires looking beyond the nation to the relationship between rich and poor countries and the impact they have upon each other. This is the literature of centre-periphery and dependency theories. Obscured as it is by jargon, it undoubtedly contains some important truths. All Third World societies need to be examined within the context of expanding capitalism. Countries such as Indonesia have been kept poor in part because of their unequal relationship with the richer nations of the world, and ultimately this has affected even the kampung dwellers of Kebun Kacang. Nevertheless, neo-Marxists have themselves criticized such theory as being too abstract and mechanistic.[20] Such critics call for theory to be applied to and illustrated by micro studies.

The most useful frame of reference to link the kampung community with the outside world would seem to be the city itself. Here there is an excellent and ambitious approach in the study of nineteenth-century London by Stedman-Jones, who was trying to investigate similar problems of casual (ie. transient) labour and housing conditions.[21] Like the contemporary gatherers of his materials, however, Stedman-Jones provides a many-sided view of the dimensions of poverty, the rich diversity of lower-class trades and occupations and the forces transforming the city, but little understanding of people's lives within the neighbourhoods where they lived or how these communities had evolved.

My approach was to try to understand the dynamics of a small urban neighbourhood and the individuals who lived within it. Looking at the kampung dwellers within the unifying context of their community revealed the many different dimensions of their lives. My task was to try to identify and explain the changes taking place and determine what role the kampung dwellers, their neighbourhood, the city or broader political and economic environment played in determining their fate.

The study of a community naturally lends itself to oral history. I began learning about the community by speaking to individuals about their lives. Because of the near total absence of any written material on the community, there was no alternative source of information. Other scholars who have written on the history of Jakarta have found almost nothing on urban kampungs in Dutch sources.[22] Indonesian government policy towards the kampung was marked until the 1970s by indifference and no official data seems to be available. Without the normal tools of the historian, the author had no choice but to rely almost totally on oral interviews.

Oral history has both strengths and weaknesses. Those involved, better than anyone else, can tell what has happened to their lives and how they have experienced or perceived particular events. Their personal descriptions provide an intimacy and detail that outside observers, let alone survey interviewers, cannot hope to capture. Their views provide an important insight into how poor people think and feel about their lives. Only in this way is it possible to meet the plea that one should try to understand how the shanty-town dweller sees his own society.[23]

At the same time, oral history involves well-known difficulties. Firstly, there is the issue of how informants are selected. My selection was biased towards those who enjoyed speaking about themselves, their neighbours and the world outside. For the first few years I saw the community through the perceptive eyes of my informally adopted mother, Bud. Initially my study focused upon her life and the people most closely associated with her. The study expanded outwards from Bud's home to encompass the neighbours whom she met on a daily basis, knew by name and with whom she frequently exchanged goods and services. Eventually it included all 77 households that made up Bud's neighbourhood. It was only at the time of demolition that both Bud's and my horizons really extended beyond the neighbourhood to encompass other households within the larger kampung. At the end of the study, when it became necessary to obtain the history of the neighbourhood since the 1930s, informants were included from well beyond Bud's neighbourhood, which had too few people who had experienced or could recall Kebun Kacang's more distant past.

Secondly, there are the difficulties of interview technique. According to Bud, the only way to talk to Javanese was gently and indirectly. One never asked a direct question. One never made the listener aware that one wanted to know a particular thing. Direct questioning resulted in shock and fear and inevitably provided a misleading response. There were certain topics about which one simply did not ask, such as debts, incomes, interpersonal relationships and attitudes to government. The only way to get answers to such sensitive questions was to let them slowly emerge by encouraging the informant to speak freely in his or her own way. Interviewing was thus an exceedingly time consuming and cumbersome procedure, often resulting in much aimless conversation.

It was pointless to try and force anyone to speak if they were reluctant or fearful to do so. Any sign of doubt, suspicion or fear automatically made the conversation uncomfortable. If a person was too busy to talk, I politely moved on. Eventually, most of those frightened, shy or busy people wanted to talk and invited me into their homes, but it took visits over ten years to achieve a rapport with most people in the neighbourhood.

When I became frustrated by the collection of so many unrelated scraps of information and tried to switch to formal interviews, the exercise proved artificial, uncomfortable and largely unproductive. By this stage most of my informants were already used to the idea of my sitting around and listening to them talk, but they found the formalized interview a strain. Only Bud and one or two others could sit for hour after hour answering questions and allowing me to jot down notes. These few were even keen to speak into a tape-recorder. But most others were intimidated by the formalized approach. The mere sight of pen or paper frightened them. Consequently I was forced back to a fairly haphazard mode of data collection.

The third major difficulty is the reliability of informants' memories or their reporting of them. Kampung dwellers placed no great store upon truth as such. It was not the truth that counted but rather saving face, avoiding embarrassment, creating a good impression and preserving harmony. Even seemingly simple and inoffensive questions were often answered incorrectly. For example, some people were embarrassed to admit that they did certain jobs such as becak driving or petty trade and instead pretended to be unemployed. Responses to questions about marriage were often misleading, especially if a man wanted to boast about his number of wives or conversely to pretend that he was a bachelor. If a woman had been deserted by her husband she would often pretend that he was dead rather than admit that he had left her, or that she had thrown him out. When sterile women adopted children they were most reluctant to admit they had done so for fear that their sterility would be revealed. There was no shortage of misinterpretations and misunderstandings that could result from interviews. The process of obtaining accurate and meaningful information therefore proved time-consuming and difficult.

Informants' memories were perhaps most unreliable when it came to establishing dates. Many of my informants were illiterate, and even those who could read and write tended to associate events in their lives with what to us might seem a rather unorthodox calender. One of my older informants dated events from the loss of Queen Juliana's virginity. When I asked for the source of his intimate knowledge of the Dutch Royal household, he explained that a Dutch coin in circulation at the time had been reissued with a hole punched through the centre of it and he reasoned that the Dutch would only have gone to so much trouble for an event of such importance. Others referred to unusual climatic events or, more commonly, to the birth of their children. Most of those who remembered the traumatic coup of September 1965 could not recall in which year it had occurred. Older people recalled the Japanese occupation and the Proclamation of Independence but few could recall even those dates. To establish what my informants were doing at any particular time, I had to correlate events with others that they regarded as significant in their own lives.

Bud was the main cross-check for whatever material I collected. Sometimes she told me about certain people of the neighbourhood and I then went out to check with them whether what she had said was correct, without letting them know that she had already told me. At other times, householders told me about themselves and I returned home to Bud to check whether what they had said was correct. If a discrepancy emerged in such information, then both Bud and I consulted the householders again at different times to try to reconcile these differences. Ultimately, I relied on Bud to assess whether such information was plausible from the kampung dwellers' point of view.

Fourthly, there is the almost intractable problem of cause and effect. Although kampung dwellers can, better than anyone else, tell the story of their own lives and that of their community, they have difficulty looking beyond it. Thus, they can tell what has happened to them but not necessarily why. Explanations put forward for events may grossly over-simplify complex factors beyond their immediate comprehension and control. Under these circumstances, the historian may be tempted to discard such "explanations" altogether. To do so, however, may be to throw the baby out with the bath water. Peoples' perceptions of why events have happened, however subjective or ill-informed, may still convey a great deal of insight into their world view. The approach adopted here is to try not to pass judgement on the validity of kampung dwellers' perceptions but to set them in the context of whatever other sources exist.

1. The former viewpoint is best represented by Lloyd, P. *Slums of Hope? Shanty Towns of the Third World*, (Harmondsworth, 1979) pp. 32–33; Mangin, W. "Latin American Squatter Settlements: a Problem and a Solution", *Latin American Research Review*, Vol. 2, No. 3: 1967: 65–98; Mangin, W. "Squatter Settlements", *Scientific American*, Vol. 217, October: 1967: 21–29. Support for the latter view can be derived from Lewis's and de Jesus's descriptions of the urban poor: Lewis, O. *The Children of Sanchez: Autobiography of a Mexican Family*, (Harmondsworth, 1961); Lewis, O. "The Culture of Poverty", *Scientific American*, Vol. 215, No. 4: 1966: 19–25; Lewis, O. *La Vida: A Puerto Rican Family in the Culture of Poverty—San Juan and New York*, (New York, 1966); Lewis, O. *Five Families—Mexican Case Studies in the Culture of Poverty*, (London, 1976); de Jesus, C. M. *Child of the Dark—The Diary of Carolina Maria de Jesus*, (London, 1962). Also see Hollnsteiner, M. R. "The Case of 'The People Versus Mr Urbano Planner Y Administrator'" in Abu-Lughod *Third World Urbanization* 307–320.
2. Armstrong, W. R. and McGee, T. G. "Revolutionary Change and the Third World City: A Theory of Urban Involution", *Civilizations*, Vol. 18, No. 3: 1968: 353–78; McGee, T. G. "The Persistence of the Proto-Proletariat: Occupational Structures and Planning for the Future of Third World Cities" in Abu-Lughod *Third World Urbanization* pp. 259–62.
3. Green, D. R. "Street Trading in London: A Case Study of Casual Labour 1830–1860" in Johnson, J. H. et al. (eds.) *The Structure of Nineteenth Century Cities*, (London, 1982) 129–51; Stedman-Jones, G. *Outcast London: A Study in the Relationship Between Classes in Victorian Society*, (Harmondsworth, 1971) pp. 336, 348–49.
4. Frank, A. G. *Capitalism and Underdevelopment in Latin America: Historical Studies of Chile and Brazil*, (New York, 1967); Amin, S. *Unequal Development: An Essay on the Social Formation of Peripheral Capitalism*, (Sussex, 1976). Reissman compares and contrasts the process of urbanization in East and West: Reissman, L. *The Urban Process: Cities in Industrial Societies*, (Glencoe, 1970) pp. 150–95.
5. Gilbert, A. and Gugler, J. *Cities, Poverty, and Development: Urbanization in the Third World*, (Oxford, 1982); Roberts, B. R. *Cities of Peasants: The Political Economy of Urbanization in the Third World*, (London, 1978); Lloyd *Slums of Hope*.
6. Sethuraman, S. V. *Urbanization and Employment in Jakarta*, (Geneva, 1974).

7. Moir, H. and Wirosardjono, S. *The Jakarta Informal Sector*, (Jakarta, 1977).

8. Leiserson, M. et al. *Employment and Income Distribution In Indonesia*, (Washington D.C., 1978).

9. Sajogyo found that between 1970 and 1976 not only were an increasing absolute number of people falling below the poverty line but their proportion had not changed significantly and the percentage of destitute had increased from 20 to 25 percent in rural Java: Sajogyo "Garis Kemiskinan dan Kebutuhan Minumun Pangan", *Laporan Seminar Nasional HIPIIS periode 1975–1977*, (Menado, 1977). Dapice and Sritua Arief back Sajogyo's view that the position of the poor hardly improved and in some cases, may have become worse: Dapice, D. O. "Trends in Income Distribution and Levels of Living 1970–75" in Papanek, G. (ed.) *The Indonesian Economy*, (New York, 1980) 67–81; Sritua Arief *Indonesia: Growth, Income Disparity and Mass Poverty*, (Jakarta, 1977). Sajogyo used levels of rice consumption rather than levels of cash expenditure to arrive at these calculations which have been criticized in Sundrum, R. and Booth, A. "Income Distribution in Indonesia: Trends and Determinants" in Fox, J. J. et al. (eds.) *Indonesia: Australian Perspectives*, (Canberra, 1980) p. 464.

10. Sundrum and Booth "Income Distribution in Indonesia" pp. 462–64, 479–82.

11. Sundrum, R. "Income Distribution, 1970–76", *Bulletin of Indonesian Economic Studies*, Vol. 15, No. 1: 1979: p. 140.

12. Evers mistakenly compared breadwinners' incomes from the LP3ES survey of 1972 with per capita incomes from the 1978 Jakarta Government survey of poor areas and his own PLPIIS (Social Science Research Training Programme of the University of Indonesia) survey of 1979. See Evers, H. "Urban Subsistence Production in Jakarta", *Seminar Fieldstudies in Southeast Asian Development*, ISEAS, Singapore, 15–19 November 1979, p. 5; DKI, *Hasil Survey Tenaga Kerja Di Kecamatan Miskin DKI-Jakarta*, Kanwil. Dit. Jen. Bina Guna, Jakarta, 1978/1979, pp. 25–26.

13. Steer, A. "Indonesian Urban Services Sector Report", (Washington D.C., 1983) pp. 26–28.

14. Critchfield, R. *Hello Mister! Where are you going?* Part II, (New York, 1970).

15. Jellinek *The Life of a Jakarta Street Trader*; *The Life of a Jakarta Street Trader—Two Years Later*; "Circular Migration and the Pondok Dwelling System".

16. Jellinek, L. "Underview: Memories of Kebun Kacang, 1930s to 1980s" in Abeyasekere, S. (ed.) *From Batavia to Jakarta: Indonesia's Capital 1930–1980*, (Melbourne, 1985); "Three Petty Entrepreneurs—The Wheel of Fortune" in Pinches, M. and Lakha, S. (eds.) *Wage Labour and Social Change*, (Melbourne, 1987); "The Changing Fortunes of a Jakarta Street Trader".

17. Compare the findings of Steele, R. M. *"Origins and Occupational Mobility of Lifetime Migrants to Surabaya, East Java"*, Ph.D Thesis,

xxviii INTRODUCTION

ANU, 1980) to Papanek, G. F. "The Poor Of Jakarta", *Economic Development and Cultural Change*, Vol. 24, No. 1: 1975: p. 15; Sethuraman *Urbanization and Employment in Jakarta* pp. 7, 13 and Moir and Wirosardjono *The Jakarta Informal Sector* p. 35.

18. Sunindyo, Saraswati "Kampung Sawah, Studi Eksploratif Tentang Perkampungan Liar di Jakarta", B.A. Thesis, University of Indonesia, 1981.

19. Sullivan, J. *Back Alley Neighbourhood: Kampung as Urban Community in Yogyakarta*, (Melbourne, 1980); Sullivan, J. "Ruhun Kampung and Kampung: State-Community Relations in Urban Yogyakarta", Ph.D Thesis, Monash University, 1982; Guinness, P. *Harmony and Hierarchy in a Javanese Kampung*, (Singapore, 1986).

20. Palma, G. "Dependency: A Formal Theory of Underdevelopment or a Methodology for the Analysis of Concrete Situations of Underdevelopment?", *World Development*, Nos. 6, 7, 8: 1978: 881–924; McGee "From 'Urban Involution' to Proletarian Transformation"; Pinches, M. D. "Anak-Pawis Children of Sweat: Class and Community in a Manila Shanty Town", Ph.D Thesis, Monash University, 1984.

21. Stedman-Jones *Outcast London*.

22. Personal Communications with Wertheim, W. F. 26 January 1975; Cobban, J. L. 1 December 1975; Abeyasekere, S. February 1984.

23. Lloyd *Slums of Hope?* p. 10.

1

Memories of Kebun Kacang: From Market Garden to Shanty Town

Kebun Kacang is located at the heart of sprawling modern Jakarta. Fifty years ago it was rural land on the fringe of colonial Batavia. The name "Kebun Kacang" (peanut garden) indicates the rural origins of the kampung. Like many other neighbourhoods of Jakarta, it was named after the produce that grew there.[1] By the 1960s the area had been transformed from a market garden to a shanty town. The history of Kebun Kacang begins with what kampung dwellers' referred to as Zaman Normal (the Normal Times). It is followed by Zaman Perang (War Time), Zaman Merdeka (Independence) and Zaman Pembangunan (the Age of Development).[2]

Normal Times (Zaman Normal), 1930s–42

By the late 1970s I could find only three people who could recount what life was like in Kebun Kacang in the 1930s, and even they admitted that their memories were poor. Both Ibu (mother) Minah and Ibu Imah came from families which were viewed as the founders of Kebun Kacang. They had lived there longer than all other surviving kampung dwellers and their families had originally controlled much of the land. Lukman, by contrast, had arrived in Kebun Kacang in the late 1930s and was a temporary migrant, like many who were later to populate the area. By the late 1970s Ibu Minah and Lukman were around 60 years of age and in the 1930s had been teenagers. Ibu Imah, who was over seventy years of age, found it difficult to concentrate and answer my questions.

They all remembered small details about their own lives but little of Batavia more generally. They were preoccupied, as in later years,

1

with obtaining a home and a livelihood. The women's lives largely revolved around the home. They did not have access to newspapers, books or the radio and were ignorant of the major events that dominated the nation and, consequently, Batavia at that time. They were unaffected by nationalist aspirations or the political repression of the 1930s. Kebun Kacang was a backwater and not part of the mainstream of Batavian life.

Ibu Minah's family had been in Kebun Kacang longer than anybody could remember. As far as she knew, her father was a Betawi Asli, a native of the Batavia area. His family had legal title to the land they occupied and had built a substantial village house on higher land towards the northwest, away from the Cideng River, which frequently flooded in the monsoon season. Ibu Imah's family, by contrast, were illegal squatters who had built a flimsy shack amongst the bamboo groves and marshes beside the river, out of view of the dirt road that ran northwest of the area.

Ibu Minah's mother had come to Kebun Kacang from Bogor in West Java in the 1920s and Ibu Minah was born in 1925. The family was the richest in the area. Their 200 square metre house was larger than any other in the area. Like other village houses, it had an earthen floor, woven bamboo walls and a coconut palm roof and was surrounded by vegetable gardens, fruit trees and fish ponds. Chickens and ducks scavenged around the house whilst goats were kept in bamboo pens to prevent them eating the vegetables. Ibu Minah's mother could be seen planting, weeding and harvesting spinach (*kangkung/bayam*), and mustard greens (*sawi*), beets and chillies. Some of these were consumed by the household and their neighbours. The vegetables which were surplus to their own needs were left in bundles by the roadside and traders regularly loaded them onto horse carts or into bamboo crates over their shoulders. These were then sold in nearby Tanah Abang market to the west or Senen market to the east, or distributed door to door in Menteng or China town. Even though Ibu Minah's family was the wealthiest in the area, her mother was always looking for new ways to earn extra income. For example, she made string from banana leaves for sale at the market. Ibu Minah's father, the only one with technical skills in the neighbourhood, worked as an electrician for Dutch households in Kota and Menteng. Sometimes he was sent to do jobs in Bogor, Bandung or even the Outer Islands.

Ibu Minah's immediate neighbours were related and largely made a livelihood from the vegetable patch. Unlike her father, who had been lucky to get an education, her grandfather, who lived next door, was illiterate and earned part of his livelihood from collecting grass to feed to the cart horses which were tethered in the area. Another neighbour drove a horse and cart, an important means of passenger transport around the town. A third looked after the nearby municipal dump and shot the lame and sick horses which were buried there.

Although Ibu Minah lived only 125 metres from the second cluster of houses, there was little contact between the two. The intervening land was not crossed by paths. Tall grass, coconut palms, banana trees, bamboo groves, fish ponds and swamp separated the two and caused one cluster of houses to be obscured from the other. Though my two informants were aware of one another's existence, neither had ever been to the other's house.

Imah and her husband, Harjo, were landless peasants from a village near Bogor who had come to Batavia in the 1920s. After being forced off land which they had illegally cultivated in Matraman, southeast of the expanding suburb of Menteng, they heard of unused land in Kebun Kacang, covered by swamps and tall grass,where vegetables could be grown.

According to Ibu Imah, the municipal government allowed them to cultivate vegetables and erect a small tool shed, but not a house. Consequently, Imah's growing family was forced to squeeze into the tool shed to sleep. Each night, her husband and their seven children crept into the tool shed and went to sleep hoping that they would not be caught and evicted. When the family could stand the cramped conditions no longer, Harjo illegally built a more substantial house. On several occasions a Dutch official who regularly patrolled the area made Harjo dismantle the house, but through persistence, Harjo and his family eventually established themselves in the area.

As Harjo expanded the area under cultivation towards the present-day location of Hotel Indonesia, Jalan Thamrin and Sarinah, he invited relatives or friends from Bogor to assist with the agricultural work. By the late 1930s he had at least four workers to help plant, weed, water and harvest the crops. Later some of these workers were to marry Imah and Harjo's children. They came to view Harjo as their patron and well-to-do landlord, even though, like themselves, he had come from Bogor only 15 years earlier, impoverished and landless. Furthermore, he did not legally own the land but only rented it from the municipal government. Both Ibu Minah and Ibu Imah's families paid taxes to the colonial administration for being allowed to cultivate the land. In time, Imah's house, like Ibu Minah's, was surrounded by four or five other shanties housing relatives who worked their land.

For villagers the journey to Batavia in the 1930s was still fraught with difficulties. Some kampung dwellers like Lukman, who came from Tiga Rasa, a village beyond Tangerang, were still travelling by horse and cart or more often by foot. Lukman, who arrived in Kebun

Kacang in 1938, told of his first journey to Batavia some years earlier
when he was only thirteen. He and his uncle, who had worked in
Batavia, set off from their home village and walked throughout the
day and night till they reached Batavia. They walked along dark unlit
roads and through large fearsome forests. Such journeys were regarded as a major adventure. Villagers feared attacks by tigers,
robbers, evil spirits and Dutch soldiers who, it was rumoured, kidnapped Indonesians and put them in the foundations of bridges.

The move to the city by Ibu Minah's mother, Imah and Lukman
was part of a more general movement of peasants from Bogor and
Tangerang, the main source of migrants to Jakarta.[3] Population
pressure on land and a decline of employment opportunities in rural
areas, especially from the 1920s, forced peasants to move to the city.
Batavia became a magnet because of its growing European and
Chinese population and expansion of offices, banks and infrastructure facilities. These created labouring and service jobs for the village
poor. Between 1905 and 1941 Batavia's population(including the
suburb further south of Meester Cornelis) nearly tripled, from
196,000 to 544,000.[4] Over the decade of the 1920s the city's population grew very rapidly by about 75 percent but slowed down during
the following decade to only 2 percent.

Lukman and his uncle, like those from Bogor who joined Harjo,
came in search of work. *Kerja* was the term used by villagers to refer
to wage labour. Lukman claimed no *kerja* was available in his village.
Labourers were paid in kind. Most villagers had to travel to Batavia if
they wished to obtain money. But without prior contacts it was
virtually impossible to go to Batavia. Invariably, those few who went
had a job and accommodation arranged for them by a relative or
village friend such as Harjo or Lukman's uncle.

Chain migration and occupational clustering were common in
other parts of Jakarta. Like Ibu Imah, Harjo and Ibu Minah's
mother, other villagers from Bogor came to work as market gardeners. Like Lukman, other villagers from areas near Banten and
Tangerang came to work at the city's docks and/or as domestic
servants for Batavia's elite. Domestic servants came from both Bogor
and Tangerang, whilst bread, vegetable sellers and laundrymen came
predominantly from certain villages near Bogor and meat vendors
from Pandeglang (Banten).[5]

No educational qualifications, money or identity cards were
required.[6] After having been introduced to a job and a place to stay,
other work then became easy to find and villagers like Lukman
changed employment and accommodation frequently, often staying
in one job for less than one or two years. Lukman worked on the

Tanjung Priok docks, joined the crew of a boat between Indonesia and Singapore, and did odd jobs like gardening and cleaning toilets for Dutch households in Menteng, at which time he first came to live in Kebun Kacang.

Lukman did not live permanently in Batavia, but moved back and forth between his home village and Kebun Kacang.[7] After working a couple of years Lukman returned to his home village of Tiga Rasa. Within this time he had been able to save up for his marriage and a new house in the village.[8] "We had grand festivals with pageants, clowns, food and parades going on day and night from one village to the next". With Lukman's income of 3 *picis* (30 cents) a day, in addition to a month's supply of rice, sugar, coffee and tea, he could have readily obtained land and accommodation in Kebun Kacang, but neither were thought to be of value. He had free accommodation with his uncle and felt he did not need another house, as he already had one in the village.

In Kebun Kacang, as in the village, most of the kampung dwellers' basic needs were obtained from their immediate surroundings. They washed and obtained drinking and cooking water from the river. Fuel was available from the garden and surrounding undergrowth. Bamboo groves and coconut palms provided house building materials. One's immediate neighbours, usually relatives, helped with home construction. Fresh fish caught in the river or ponds and the surplus fruit and vegetables grown nearby were often shared with neighbouring households.

Because of the low density of settlement and the poor access, few traders came into the kampung. If kampung dwellers wanted to buy rice, salt, sugar or tea they either went to Tanah Abang market— only fifteen minutes' walk away—or shopped at the two Chinese stores on the dirt road that ran west of the community. In Tanah Abang merchandizing was monopolized by the Arabs, Indians and especially Chinese who lived on higher ground and in more substantial houses. A few Chinese or Arab trader came to Kebun Kacang selling cloth, kitchen utensils or sweets.

With the increasing importance of cash in the kampung economy towards the end of the decade, Ibu Minah's mother tried to earn a little extra by renting out small units for accommodation to newcomers who slowly started to come into the area. In 1937 she applied to the municipal administration to build extra units. Ibu Minah remembered a row of huts, the size of chicken coops, with roofs made out of squashed tin cans which her mother began to rent out. It was at about this time that the Dutch government compensated Ibu Minah's mother and her neighbour Haji Tejo for some land which it

compulsorily acquired for the building of what was later to become
Jalan Thamrin. As the city drew closer to Kebun Kacang, the land
became more valuable and began to be subdivided.

Western observers who compared the urban kampung of the 1920s
and 1930s to their own part of town noticed the overcrowding, lack of
amenities, poor living conditions and widespread nature of disease.[9]
They described kampungs as "autonomous enclaves or native settlements that stood out in their general air of backwardness from the air
of light and propriety which prevailed in the European section of
cities".[10] This may have been a valid description of more established
kampungs in Batavia. Kebun Kacang, however, was only on the
periphery, and in fact could hardly yet be classified as an urban
kampung. Ibu Minah and Ibu Imah did not compare their lives with
that of the Dutch elite in the European part of Batavia. Rather, they
compared what they saw as the spaciousness, simplicity and ease of
life in the 1930s with the overcrowding and greater struggle for
existence later on.

The number of people in Kebun Kacang was small, and this had its
advantages. Pollution, for example, was not a problem even though
there was no sewerage system. It was claimed that the colonial
government did at one stage build a public water faucet and privies
on higher land, west of the community, but years later these fell into
disrepair and were not used again.[11] There was space for children to
play and people to meet. Trees were plentiful and provided welcome
shade. Social and religious life was conducted largely within the
privacy of one's own home. The prayer house, a run-down shanty
tucked behind the village homes, was rarely used. People's religious
beliefs were a private matter. Government intruded little into their
lives.

Kampung dwellers felt themselves to be part of a privileged group
with easy access to Batavia rather than part of the vast urban mass
that they were later to become. Being the richest, Ibu Minah had a
large house, bicycle, bed, mattress, Singer sewing machine and even
electricity. Most of the children attended government-run Indonesian
language primary schools (Sekolah Desa or Desascholen) and some,
such as Ibu Minah, had gone to a Dutch (language) Native school
(Hollandsch-Inlandsche School-HIS). Ibu Imah's daughter recalled
occasionally playing ball as a child with Dutch children on the streets
of Menteng. She had travelled by horse and cart and even taxi to
Gambir to watch a film. Members of the community felt that they had
access by foot, bicycle or tram to most parts of the town. Menteng,
Cikini, Senen, Gambir, Kota, Tanah Abang were all within their
reach. In later years they would not feel so entitled to go to these
areas. They automatically accepted that they could never live like the

Dutch and felt that most of the things they wanted or needed were available.

Ibu Minah, Imah and Lukman were still young, without the cares of middle and old age, and perhaps it was an idyllic or romanticized world which they remembered. Nevertheless, their view of the "golden age" was confirmed by other kampung dwellers interviewed by Cohen.[12] Kampung dwellers generally seem to have looked back on the 1930s as a time of tranquility (*ketenteraman*), order (*ketertiban*) and calm (*ketenangan*). There was stability and security. Money still had value. There was greater respect for law and order and more trust amongst people. Fruit had a chance to ripen on the trees without being stolen and vegetables or sacks of rice could safely be left by the roadside. Neighbours were prepared to help one another. There was genuine help without the expectation of financial returns.[13] It perhaps seemed all the more appealing in contrast to the Japanese occupation which ensued. For whatever reason, kampung dwellers did feel that life under the Dutch compared very favourably with the years that followed.

War Time (Zaman Perang), 1942–1949

With the coming of the Japanese in March 1942, the tranquillity, ease and stability of "Zaman Normal" was shattered. Most kampung dwellers, especially those who initially fled from Kebun Kacang in fear of the Japanese but also those who had not yet arrived from the village, remembered the period as the worst in their lives.[14] Family members were separated, sometimes for years, as they sought to elude the Japanese and avoid being associated with the Dutch for whom they had worked.

When the Japanese occupied the city, Ibu Imah and her seven children fled in fear to their home village near Bogor, leaving Harjo and his four assistants to tend the crops and look after their home in Kebun Kacang. In the village Ibu Imah found chaos rather than comfort and security. Food and clothing were difficult to come by. Most people were reduced to eating boiled roots and leaves and wearing hessian bags. Land could not be cultivated because the irrigation works had fallen into disrepair. Seeds were not available because transport networks had broken down. Villagers did not dare go out to cultivate their fields for fear of being caught by the Japanese. Every so often the Japanese raided the village in search of young men for their labour gangs and young women for sexual or domestic services. They requisitioned crops and took metal beds, livestock, food and furniture. Within approximately six months, as

far as Ibu Imah could remember, she and her children came back to
Kebun Kacang.[15]

In contrast to the countryside, Kebun Kacang, like the rest of
Jakarta, remained remarkably calm. The invading Japanese virtually
ignored the kampung. Ibu Minah's family had stayed there because
they had nowhere else to go. Ibu Minah's father had died of natural
causes, and Ibu Minah's husband's main concern was to disassociate
himself from the Dutch for whom he had worked. Association, he
felt, meant certain death. Other relatives of the family also pretended
to have had nothing to do with the Dutch and started to work for the
Japanese, who were short of manpower and only too eager to accept
willing hands. Ibu Minah's husband started to work in the Department of Textiles while other relatives of Ibu Minah's who had
cleaned, cooked and cared for the gardens and houses of the Dutch,
simply carried on with their work and served the Japanese.

With the Dutch interned and the Chinese obstructed by the Japanese, more and more Indonesians began to move into jobs in government and business. It was easier for a Javanese peasant to smuggle a
small sack of rice or a few pieces of fruit or vegetables into the city
than a prominent trader who was likely to have his more conspicuous
wares confiscated.[16] Although kampung dwellers were not aware of
the full details, they had seen the Dutch being hauled away to prison
and all their goods confiscated. They had witnessed Chinese storekeepers being harassed by the Japanese. Japanese rule became
progressively worse, as food, clothing and medical supplies were
depleted. Imports virtually came to a halt and most vehicles were
taken over by the Japanese for their war effort. In and around the
kampung and along the streets of Jakarta, bicycle repair workshops,
becak drivers, prostitutes and pedlars selling empty bottles and old
clothes became more evident.[17] Abeyasekere notes an increase in
local production and sale as people made soap, candles, cigarettes
and other small items that had become unavailable.[18]

Some kampung dwellers felt they were treated reasonably by the
Japanese as long as they responded immediately to demands and
worked hard, but most felt deeply resentful. Lukman, who had
worked for the Dutch in Menteng, changed to driving becaks. He
claimed that the Japanese made him pedal beyond exhaustion: "I was
tired, I could not go on, but the Japanese shouted 'bakaro Indonesia'
(stupid Indonesian) and forced me on. Had I stopped and refused to
go on, I would have been hit and probably killed." During the day
kampung dwellers worked for the Japanese whilst at night they tried
to kill them. They joined conspiratorial groups who ambushed Japanese vehicles by laying trees across the road and killing their occupants with any weapons, spears, axes, knives or guns that were on
hand.[19]

After a year or two, increasing numbers of people began to make their way to Batavia to escape the agony and starvation of the villages.[20] From 1942 to 1944, the city's population increased by an estimated 100,000. This rapid growth was followed by a downturn in the following three years. Not all succeeded in making the transition from the countryside to life and work in the city. One of Ibu Imah's relatives described how he stumbled over dead and dying bodies as he hawked vegetables along the streets of Batavia. Statistics suggest that the death rate jumped quite markedly. In 1942, 14,832 deaths were registered in the city, whereas two years later, 40,845 were registered.[21] Those who were lucky and had personal contacts with people in kampungs like Kebun Kacang made their way there.

Sometime between 1945 and 1949, Haji Tejo, who occupied a house close to Ibu Minah's, cunningly claimed much of the surrounding swamp and marsh land which had been owned by the municipal government. Before the Japanese occupation the colonial administration had bought this land from Ibu Minah's and Haji Tejo's families for the proposed construction of a major road, now Jalan Thamrin. When the Dutch lost power, nobody had clear rights to the land and Ibu Minah's mother hesitated to start using it again. But Haji Tejo had no such qualms and astutely pegged out the land for himself. The Japanese authorities encouraged the cultivation of vacant urban land to help overcome the dire food shortages.[22] During the struggle for independence, the Republicans also encouraged the takeover of land in Jakarta, as a sign of opposition to the Dutch.

With the arrival of newcomers, Haji Tejo built rows of barrack-type units for rent. Belatedly, Ibu Minah's and Ibu Imah's families followed his example. Some relatives who came to the area were simply given parcels of land on which to build or to cultivate. Others exchanged food for the land they used. Land was allocated in plots rather than precisely measured in metres or feet. There did not seem to be any single pattern of land transfer. In Ibu Minah's eyes, however, much of the land was simply taken over by "orang luar" (strangers) once the Dutch lost control.

It remains unclear what Ibu Minah's, Ibu Imah's and Lukman's families did during the struggle for independence between 1945 and 1949. They were so busy trying to survive from one day to the next that in their memories, the Japanese occupation merged with the four years that followed as a period of chaos, uncertainty and confusion. Most kampung dwellers simply assumed that the Dutch had returned and were unaware that the British were part of the occupying force. Udin, who left Cirebon for Jakarta, claimed that trains did not run regularly and he was forced to go by foot. He travelled from village to village and danger lurked everywhere. In the villages of West Java gangs of bandits who had fought against the Japanese and then the

Dutch, now turned against their own people. They raided poor villages, stole their food and livestock, and kidnapped or killed their menfolk. Udin carried no money so he would not be identified with either the Nationalist or the Dutch. Different types of currency were in use in the Dutch and Republican controlled areas and a person caught carrying the wrong currency was accused of being a spy for the other side and killed.[23]

It was difficult to know who was fighting against whom for there were so many rival groups and murder and death had become a way of life. Even members of the same family suspected each other of being spies. Throughout the Japanese occupation and for a number of years afterwards, Udin and his father feared one of them would kill the other. Udin's father had been a soldier in the Royal Netherland East Indies Army whilst Udin had worked for the Japanese. To protect themselves, kampung dwellers lied, kept their distance from those they feared and learned to change sides rapidly. When the Japanese came, they severed all ties with the Dutch. When the Dutch returned in 1945, they pretended to have had nothing to do with the Japanese. Over the next four years as the Dutch struggled from their base in Batavia to regain control over the Indonesian nationalists who controlled much of the countryside, the kampung dwellers swapped allegiances depending upon where they were. In the city they pretended to be pro-Dutch whilst in the village they pretended to be Indonesian nationalists.

Independence (Zaman Merdeka), 1949–1965

Kampung dwellers took advantage of the economic chaos and administrative incompetence that surrounded the Sukarno era. During the early 1950s, they were attracted to the city by the income-earning opportunities created during the boom of the Korean war. Unlike the economists and middle class, they did not appear to be troubled by the hyper-inflation, breakdown in infrastructure and food shortages which occurred after 1957.

During the 1950s kampung dwellers felt a sense of euphoria and freedom. They felt nothing could be as bad as the previous decade. Travel was easy by comparison. Though the buses, roads and railways were in poor condition, they were at least functioning. Documents of identity, though officially required, were not scrutinized.[24] Udin claimed he could travel free of charge. He told railway inspectors, on those rare occasions when he was asked, that he was looking for his parents whom he had lost during the war.

Most of my informants had arrived in Kebun Kacang between 1950 and 1968. Many had started their journey to the city during the late 1940s and early 1950s because of the dislocation caused by the war, violence and economic hardship in the village. This corresponded with a dramatic rise in Jakarta's population after 1948. In a study of 11,500 kampung dwellers in Jakarta, Heeren found that one-third had arrived since 1949.[25]

Most kampung dwellers did not come directly to Kebun Kacang from their original homes. Bud's husband, Santo, had been recruited into the Japanese auxilliary army (Heiho), then joined the Allies against the Japanese and then the Nationalists against the Dutch. He travelled through Java, Borneo and Sumatra. Bud, who had trained with the Red Cross during the war, joined her husband in their search for a new life, as they travelled from relative to relative from Semarang to Solo and Jakarta and back to Solo and Semarang again between 1948 and 1952. Another future inhabitant of Kebun Kacang, Mus, who came from Klaten, traded eggs, chilli and other agricultural produce on trains between Yogyakarta, Semarang and Surabaya. During the early 1950s, Samilah at 11 years of age, fled to Menteng to join her elder sister as a domestic servant. Her parents had died during the war and revolution and she disliked living with her relatives in Depok, 30 kilometres south of Jakarta. Her future husband, Agus also came from the south of Jakarta near Parung where during the war he had lost his parents, their land and many ducks.

The first newcomers to Kebun Kacang were, like Ibu Imah's and Lukman's family, from West Java, near the towns of Bogor and Tangerang. In 1954 Ibu Putro was the first Central Javanese to rent accommodation in Imah's neighbourhood. She then invited her relatives and friends into the area and in doing so, served as a broker for Ibu Imah who wished to lease more shanties. Ibu Imah was in the midst of marrying off her seven children and needed money to pay for the celebrations. Upon marriage, each of her children was allocated a piece of land, close to Imah's home, on which to build a house of their own. Ibu Imah's vegetable garden was progressively whittled away and her livelihood started to depend on rent and trade rather than market gardening.

By 1957, when Ibu Putro introduced Bud to the area, the former vegetable garden had become a slum. Only one mango, one jambu and one coconut tree remained. All other signs of greenery had disappeared. Flimsy houses built of all shapes and sizes and assorted scavenged materials gradually consumed the available land. Bud's own house had been built out of blackened bamboo crates for carrying charcoal. The roof was partly of squashed metal cans and coconut leaf thatching. There were no windows but gaping holes appeared in the roof and walls. The floor was of pressed earth which frequently turned to mud in the monsoon season. By the standards of the 1970s, the shack was large, 60 square metres, but nobody wanted to occupy it and Bud could rent it for only Rp.25 a month (5 litres of rice).[26]

Ibu Minah's family had prudently chosen to build their house on elevated land in the northwest of Kebun Kacang. But the population now spilled out in every direction and built on every available piece of land irrespective of its height above the Cideng River. The latest and poorest newcomers occupied land closest to the river. The river swelled with each monsoon season and almost always overran its banks, sometimes repeatedly. The turgid, pungent waters, often up to a metre in depth, took over the kampung. Each household attempted to move whatever it could out of the reach of the rising waters. Families moved themselves and their few possessions onto their roofs or into the houses of friends if they were lucky enough to escape the deluge. It was difficult to work. They waited for the waters to subside and then set about re-establishing their lives. But the smell of the receding waters, the watermarks on the walls and the outbreaks of gastro-enteritis or other water-borne diseases had first to be patiently endured.[27]

After the floods, the earthen pathways turned to a quagmire so that one had to wade knee-deep in mud. Pedlars came door to door selling sawdust, which was poured over the muddy floors of the homes to soak up the damp. In an attempt to raise the area above the annual floods, planks of wood and boulders retrieved from construction sites along Jalan Thamrin were laid from end to end along the pathways and into the houses.

Kampung dwellers who had been forced away from the land needed for the construction of Jalan Thamrin, Hotel Indonesia, Sarinah or the Senayan Sports Complex moved to Kebun Kacang and added to the growing density. They brought more building materials from their demolished kampung sites. According to official estimates an area like Kebun Kacang of 1.8 hectares contained from 400 to 500 people.[28]

In contrast to their deteriorating environment, kampung dwellers seem not to have suffered from the increasingly chaotic economic conditions after 1957. They were not inconvenienced by the breakdown in the telephone and postal services, which they seldom, if ever, used. They did not complain of the scarcity of buses and taxis, for they walked to most places and otherwise becaks satisfied their transport needs. Becak drivers found themselves in great demand. Curiously, the kampung dwellers did not seem troubled by rationing either. They did not worry as much as the middle class about the time spent standing in queues. Indeed they turned the rationing system to their own advantage, by standing in queues on behalf of people who lacked the time to do so. Sometimes they were able to obtain two or three times their quota, by having more than one member of their family in the queue. Sud described how she and a number of her neighbours obtained rice and textiles at heavily subsidized prices and then resold them on the black market.

The kampung dwellers turned the shortages, rationing and lack of imported goods to their own advantage in other ways as well. They repaired bicycles and radios, carried goods, conveyed messages and redistributed stolen merchandise. They recycled glass, paper, card-board, metal, aluminium and car parts. They sold water, sawdust, firewood, kerosene, charcoal and banana leaves which were in great demand for wrapping food. They traded anything for which they could find a demand. With their simple lifestyle, their flexibility and their easy-going attitude to time, the kampung dwellers seemed indifferent to the increasing chaos in the economy and government.[29]

Kampung dwellers insisted that jobs and incomes were easy to find. Many vacancies were available. In the 1950s Bud applied for one job in a hospital where, she said, there were "eighty vacancies and only ten applicants". This was not atypical even for unskilled jobs. Kampung dwellers referred to it as "a time when jobs sought men rather than the other way around". Officials or employees from the docks, banks and the Municipal Rubbish Department came into the community in the early 1960s to recruit labour.

Because of the availability of work, Bud's husband, Santo, readily changed from one job to another in the hope of finding something better. He tried at least eight different occupations—repairing bicycles, becaks, sewing machines and radios, making and selling crushed ice, working on a building site, buying and selling old radios and other items. This high rate of job turnover was typical of kampung dwellers (especially men) as they sought to improve their lot and find a job they liked.

In the late 1950s, kampung dwellers began to move into petty trade. With the decline in vegetable growing, Harjo and his relatives had turned to vegetable trade, carrying vegetables by foot between Tanah Abang market, Senen and the suburb of Menteng. The arrival of newcomers brought other types of trades to the area.

The rise of petty trade as a major occupation corresponded closely to the transformation of Jalan Thamrin to a major thoroughfare. Kampung dwellers observed that Sukarno's construction boom had moved the hub of the city progressively southwards, towards Kebun Kacang. At first, kampung women were embarrassed to be seen trading. They cooked snacks in their homes and recruited kampung children to hawk them along the new highway. By the early 1960s, however, most of the women took their own wares across a foot-bridge over the Cideng River and hawked them around the new building sites. Construction workers were always hungry and within an hour their snacks were sold and they returned home to cook some more. There were also increasing numbers of becak drivers and pedestrians to feed. Udin recalled working on the construction of Hotel Indonesia and Sarinah department store and having more money than he could spend.

Those who had arrived in Kebun Kacang since the 1950s displayed far greater initiative and enterprise than the long-term settlers. The newcomers were not prepared to take up fixed employment as guards, messengers or peons in government or private offices. The pay was too low. It was the established families like Ibu Minah's and Ibu Imah's whose husbands had accepted secure but lowly paid jobs in government offices that found their earnings eroded by inflation between 1963 and 1967.[30] The self-employed labourers, becak drivers and traders simply raised their prices when their costs went up.[31]

Between 1962 and 1968 most of the newcomers were able to earn enough income to buy their own homes in Kebun Kacang. Though the founding families retained their status and their larger homes, they were short of cash and wanted to sell off the unit they had previously rented. In 1962, a home of 30 to 60 square metres cost between Rp.3000 and Rp.6000 (100 to 200 litres of rice). Prices varied with the size, susceptibility of the land to flooding, supposed legality of the title and the personal relationship between buyer and seller. Those who had rented for long periods were able to buy the land and the shanty that stood on it at concessional rates. Samilah, who worked as a domestic, was one of them. Her husband, Agus, worked as a becak driver. Within five years of their arrival in Kebun Kacang they had saved up enough to buy a 21 square metre shanty. Then Samilah helped her elder sister pay off the house she rented next door. Bud bought the 60 square metre home from Ibu Imah with the proceeds of her cooked-food sales and her husband's becak repair business. By 1968, Ibu Imah had sold off most of her land and rented units not inherited by her children. The same process occurred in Ibu Minah's neighbourhood with clusters of 15 to 20 related families living side by side and newcomers from Java moving in to occupy the interstices, first to rent and then to buy whatever units were available.

Most land sales were not officially registered. Only the founding families in Ibu Minah's area and one or two others who understood the formal government procedures acquired legal title to their land.

Most kampung dwellers had their land or house transactions "re-corded" in adhoc documents. Although these were witnessed by the local headman and stamped and signed by the *lurah*, the city admin-istration would have regarded them as having no legal status.

The incompetence of government during the 1950s and early 1960s benefitted those who lived in central-city kampungs like Kebun Kacang. Petty traders and becak drivers, though criticized, were not cleared away.[32] Kampungs which were demolished to make way for one of Sukarno's dreams were soon resurrected elsewhere. Kampung dwellers did not find it difficult to re-establish themselves in another area near the city centre. Trader clearance or demolition did not pose such a burden as ten years later, when there was nowhere else to move.

Most kampung dwellers were too busy making a living to worry about politics. They were confused by the multitude of parties during the 1950s.[33] Each one tried to gain their support by enticements of one sort or another. Money, food, vocational training and jobs were offered. Having very little, kampung dwellers found these offers difficult to resist. But usually they supported one group or another because they had been advised to do so by a friend, employer or headman. It was difficult determining what the groups stood for or what their differences were. One astute kampung dweller, Udin, pretended to support the three main parties (Masyumi, PKI and PNI) to protect himself against being accused of supporting one and not another. He had learnt only too well during the Dutch period, Japanese occupation and struggle for independence that it was dangerous to take sides. Many kampung dwellers knew from practi-cal experience that whilst elites fought for power at the top, little people were squeezed in between through no fault of their own.

Nevertheless, the kampung dwellers loved Sukarno. From the mid-fifties many had walked from their homes to Merdeka Square each Independence Day, to hear him speak. Some claimed that for such occasions, free transport was provided from many parts of Java. Voices from loudhailers announced the meeting and Jalan Thamrin was full of pedestrians making their way to Merdeka Square. Once there, the masses sat on logs laid out on the ground, whilst Sukarno stood and spoke without notes for hour after hour. He spoke of the country's greatness and their human worth. He spoke personally, as a father to children. They were thrilled and proud that such a worldly and intelligent man was prepared to speak to them. Even if the kampung dwellers lived austerely and did menial work, he made them feel important members of a new society. He walked amongst them and travelled in open and accessible cavalcades not hedged in by military escorts and bomb-proof cars. Prior to the independence day speeches of the 1950s, most kampung dwellers had been unaware of Sukarno or even what the term "President" meant.

The coup of 1965 marked a dramatic change in national politics. The delicate balance which Sukarno had tried to maintain, with the Army on the right and Indonesian Communist Party (PKI) on the left, was shattered. Though to this day, no accurate account of the people and motives behind this horrific event exists, six generals were murdered and hundreds of thousands of PKI members arbitrarily slaughtered over the following six months. The military-dominated government which subsequently gained power blamed the PKI for the coup, whereas some scholars and surviving Communist Party members suggested that the revolt was instigated by a section of the army to justify the elimination of the PKI.[34]

Despite the fact that troops had massed in Merdeka Square, the inhabitants of nearby Kebun Kacang claimed that at the time they had no idea what was going on. In order to protect themselves against arrest they may, to this day, pretend to have known nothing. They claim to have continued as usual with their daily chores of becak driving, domestic service, trade or construction. Only when martial law was declared and kampung dwellers were warned by headmen not to attend meetings or go out on the street, were they aware that something serious had occurred. Then they huddled in their homes, frightened of talking to neighbours or of going out.

In contrast to the countryside, Kebun Kacang remained remarkably calm. At the time nobody was arrested in the area and it was said that the headman protected the community against outside interference. When asked by the authorities he insisted that there were no communists in the area. Two years later, however, two or three kampung members were taken away for interrogation and later imprisoned. It was rumoured that they were innocent, but that the bosses in the offices where they worked had been arrested.

To the kampung dwellers the arrests were the arbitrary acts of those in authority and were without rhyme or reason. Later, after the impact of government propaganda, the kampung dwellers themselves talked derogatively about the "PKI" or "orang merah" (red person or communist). Anyone who criticized the government instantly became "PKI", dangerous and to be avoided. And yet, as I discovered years later, most members of the community knew someone, a husband, close relative, friend or village neighbour who had been arrested or killed, though this was a carefully guarded secret. Some women confided eight or ten years later that their husbands had disappeared at the time of the coup. Others admitted to having been in prison. But as they spoke, they remained guarded and suspicious lest anyone from the kampung should overhear our discussion. It was a dangerous matter to discuss and write about and thus their true feelings would have to remain a secret. But the coup once again confirmed their belief that it was dangerous to take sides.

By 1966, the kampung had become densely populated. Because of population pressure, the quality of life had clearly deteriorated. There was an ever-increasing amount of refuse, but no proper system of rubbish collection. It accumulated in the pathways and progressively choked the Cideng canal. It was left to rot in the heat and humidity. The disposal of human waste created even bigger problems. The community built toilets out over the Cideng canal. They were at least tolerably efficient when the river flowed but not in the dry season or when the river was in flood. The river water had long been too polluted to drink. A number of wells were dug but their water became too contaminated for consumption. It could still be used for washing though one had to queue for a considerable time to obtain a supply. Drinking water became a precious commodity.

Nevertheless, kampung dwellers did not seem to be unduly concerned with the deterioration of their environment. Their basic needs for work, a home, food and clothing were satisfied and their other needs were modest. Consumer goods like a good pair of scissors, table, bed or mattress were few and far between. Kampung dwellers said they often had money, but nothing to spend it on. There were few thoughts of buying prestigious items such as motorcycles, refrigerators, gas stoves or clothes washing machines. Even a radio was a rarity. Kampung dwellers did not recall being aware of substantial economic differences between themselves and felt that even the rich of Jakarta did not have much greater privileges.[35]

The Age of Development (Zaman Pembangunan), 1965–1981

In economic terms, Suharto's "New Order" marked a dramatic change from Sukarno's period of Guided Democracy. After eighteen months of political uncertainty following the coup of September 1965, Suharto formally took over from Sukarno as President and established an administration composed mainly of military men and technocrats. Economic development was to be the prime goal. Politics and political parties were not to play a role. Foreign investment was welcomed. The earliest phase of economic stabilization reduced inflation from over 600 percent in 1966 to 10 percent in 1969.[36] At the beginning of the First Five Year Development Plan (Repelita I) in 1969, economic growth reached a remarkable 10.9 percent and then continued at an average of 7–8 percent per annum throughout the decade.[37] This growth was largely caused by the oil price increases between 1973 and 1975 and again between 1980 and 1982.

Jakarta was the prime beneficiary of these developments. A disproportionate share of foreign, domestic and local revenues was invested in the city. The skeletons of several unfinished buildings scattered along Jalan Thamrin became towering structures of glass and concrete. As far as the eye could see, multi-storey office blocks, hotels and embassies took the place of kampungs and roadside workshops which had formerly lined the highway. For the first ten years, among the direct beneficiaries of these developments were the members of Kebun Kacang, who found themselves in the midst of this building boom.

Kampung dwellers were too frightened to talk about politics and were confused whether Sukarno had given power to Suharto or whether power had been taken from him. Suharto indeed adopted a cautious approach to give the impression that Sukarno was voluntarily handing over power. In any case, the kampung people viewed the time between 1968 and 1975 as a period of unprecedented economic prosperity. Many of the small enterprises that had started during the Sukarno period came to fruition. Construction workers, petty traders and becak drivers gathered around the construction sites that lined Jalan Thamrin. Cottage industries and communal lodging-houses, run by kampung dwellers rather than Chinese, emerged in the neighbourhood. They produced ice-cream, ice-cones, cloth caps, and recycled car batteries.

Petty trade was by far the most important income-earning activity. By 1981, when petty trade had passed its peak, over half the households in Kebun Kacang derived all or part of their livelihood from it.[38] In Ibu Imah's neighbourhood of 77 households, there were 89 petty traders, most of whom sold cooked food. On average, there was a stall in every fifth house. In addition, there were many mobile and semi-mobile traders who plied their wares within and beyond the community.

One small enterprise generated work for others. Construction workers, petty traders and becak drivers bought and sold goods and services from one another. There was a profusion of services within the kampung and whatever goods or service were required could be obtained within minutes. Dressmakers, healers, washerwomen, radio and watch repairers proliferated. Whereas previously Bud had done all her trade and housework alone, she now recruited others to assist with cooking, house cleaning, water carrying and shopping. Other small enterprises recruited more manpower as they found that they had more income and could not cope with the workload.

Initially, the self-employed traders and entrepreneurs seemed to benefit most. In 1972, a few very successful traders were earning over Rp.90,000 (2195 litres of rice) a month. The average trader, however, earned only one-tenth to one-quarter of this. Those in fixed employment, such as cleaners or office messengers were lucky to earn Rp.10,000 (244 litres of rice) a month. They longed for the freedom, independence and hope of petty trade and some turned to these activities.

From 1973 Kampung dwellers started to renovate their houses. By 1980 Kebun Kacang had changed beyond recognition. About half of the houses now had a second storey. Their thatched roofs were replaced by tiles. The corrugated iron and other odds and ends bought or stolen from building sites became less obvious. Houses were rebuilt in brick and timber. Windows that had once been secured by wire mesh were glazed. Solid lockable doors replaced open doorways. Many houses sunk a well of their own so that their occupants could wash in the comfort and privacy of their own homes. By the late 1970s, forty percent of the households acquired electric lighting. In 1974, pressure lamps had still been a luxury. Here and there, the odd shanty remained much as it had been ten or even twenty years before. But for most of the inhabitants of Kebun Kacang, the early 1970s were a period of affluence and well-being.[39]

Consumer goods started to appear, first in a trickle, then in a flood. In the early 1970s kampung dwellers bought crockery, pressure lamps, mattresses and basic furniture. Then the first television set appeared in the community and aroused tremendous interest. By 1980 almost every second house had one. Portable radios, cassette recorders, sewing machines, fans, refrigerators and motorcycles were acquired in ever-growing numbers. Every household had at least one of these items by 1980.[40]

Despite the growing material prosperity, the basic problems of water supply, sanitation and rubbish collection remained. They were aggravated by population growth. By the 1970s, Kebun Kacang was saturated. There were less than five square metres of space for every man, woman and child.[41] Between 1930 and 1980 the population had grown seventy-fold, from less than fifty to more than 3500.[42] In the same time, Jakarta's population had grown thirteen-fold from 500,000 to 6,500,000. Despite this population growth, the kampung was unsewered and lacked a piped water supply. Its houses remained small and as tightly packed as ever. But the inhabitants of Kebun Kacang took a pride in their newly renovated homes and recently acquired possessions. They did not regard their neighbourhood as a slum.

Just as kampung dwellers' aspirations were rising, however, they began to feel the negative impact of government policies. From the mid-1970s, petty traders and becak drivers found themselves increasingly excluded from the streets of central Jakarta. Jalan Thamrin, which had provided the kampung dwellers with their main access to the city's wealth, was no longer open to them. Vacant lots which had served as pedestrian thoroughfares, trade locations or places for storing carts, were taken over by multi-storey buildings and highways.

These trends were reinforced by economic pressures. There was more competition among traders and becak drivers for the limited space available. Modern retail and transport outlets, which had emerged as a consequence of the economic boom, increasingly cut into their trade. With the emergence of a substantial middle class, consumer tastes began to change from petty commodity items to modern mass-produced goods. Central-city depopulation brought about by new buildings replacing densely populated kampungs, rising land prices and environmental decay further reduced their clientele. The prime central-city location of Kebun Kacang had suddenly become a liability as petty producers, traders and becak drivers struggled to find a niche.

By 1978, many kampung dwellers, especially those employed in small-scale activities, were beginning to feel the pinch. Boom and bankruptcy had been the fate of many small entrepreneurs in the past, but the sudden unprecedented prosperity followed by sudden steep decline of the 1970s, seemed to be more dramatic. It differed from the more gentle continuing rises and falls of their fortunes in the past.

As a consequence of their changing fate, families lost their homes and possession. Neighbours benefitted from each other's misfortunes. They could snap up bargains at the enforced sale of a television set or wardrobe. No one could be sure what the next day would bring. Most people in the neighbourhood were heavily indebted to moneylenders who had become widespread since the early 1970s. They went from door to door and charged high rates of interest. Once one was in their clutches it was hard to escape.

With the tide turning against them, petty entrepreneurs tried to obtain salaried work. But they encountered many new obstacles. Competition was great for the few available positions. Personal contacts were no longer sufficient. Educational qualifications, certificates proving non-involvement in the coup of 1965, letters of good conduct and bribes were required. It was a far cry from the 1960s when jobs were easy to find. A minority of the young, more educated, kampung dwellers found secure and prestigious jobs in multinational factories or government offices. Most, however, who were lucky enough to obtain a job in 1979, were forced to accept long hours of work at low pay (Rp.20,000–Rp.30,000) with no hope of improvement.

The Age Without Moral Code (Zaman Kurang Ajar)

After 1978, Kampung dwellers referred to the age as one of disorder and decadence (Zaman Kurang Ajar). It was not entirely clear what they meant but they seemed to be referring to frustration caused by their inability to satisfy rising aspirations, a general lack of concern for one's fellow man and increasing inequality. The sense of mutual care and community that had characterized the neighbourhoods of Kebun Kacang was being undermined.

As more people and money entered the area, life began to change and not always for the better. Strangers moved in and they kept to themselves. A sense of separateness emerged. New occupations appeared. There were wage labourers, landlords, many traders, household servants and so on. Disparities in wealth increased as some did well and others fell behind. Whilst the original inhabitants of Kebun Kacang experienced a decline in land ownership and social status, some of the newcomers from West and Central Java prospered. They spent large sums of money on their houses and consumer goods. One could find a small dark, dingy shack without water or electricity next door to a two storey brick dwelling with a refrigerator, electric fan, television set, well and motorcycle. By 1981, monthly household incomes in Kebun Kacang ranged from Rp.30,000 to Rp. 300,000.

The accumulation of wealth seemed to drive a wedge between people. Most of the renovated homes had doors and windows that could be secured to protect the growing number of possessions within. It was no longer so easy to wander into a neighbour's home. People became secretive about their acquisitions, fearing that relatives would demand a share in their good fortune. Families began to distance themselves from one another. As they accumulated more possessions they became more acquisitive. Once they had seemed content with very little. Now they strove for sewing machines, television sets, electric fans and anything else they could buy. By 1978 a few of the most affluent in the community began to move out of Kebun Kacang into less crowded parts of Jakarta. The loosening of ties between households that had once shared so much was one factor that led kampung dwellers to question the moral basis of their society.

With increased economic insecurity and lack of moral direction, Islam grew in importance. From the late 1960s some evangelizing

Muslims had operated in Ibu Minah and Ibu Imah's neighbourhoods. They had organized mosque improvements and Islamic lectures. But it was not till the late 1970s that revivalist Islam began to gain a foothold. Although most kampung dwellers still practised their religion within the privacy of their own homes, Islam was a growing force and provided the only focus for organizational activity within the kampung.

In the kampung dwellers' eyes, the austerity and moral order of the past had given way to wealth, rising aspirations and moral decay. The Normal Times of the Dutch period had given way to an age of greed and chaos. Kampung dwellers appreciated the new opportunities, possessions, comforts and conveniences of the 1970s, but regretted the weakening of social ties.

1. For example, Kebun Jeruk (lime garden), Kebun Sirih (betelnut garden), Kampung Sawah (rice paddy), Kota Bamboo (city of bamboo).
2. Zaman Pembangunan also incorporates what kampung dwellers referred to as Zaman Kurang Ajar (The Age Without Moral Code).
3. Hugo "Population Mobility in West Java" p. 127 (Fig.3).
4. Hugo "Population Mobility in West Java" pp. 100, 674; Cohen, D. J. "Poverty and Development in Jakarta", Ph.D Thesis, University of Wisconsin, 1975, p. 19.

1905	196.000
1920	306.000
1930	533.000
1941	544.000

5. Hugo "Population Mobility in West Java" p. 130 (Fig.3).
6. Indonesians in Jakarta were required to have identity cards as early as the 1860s [Abeyasekere, S. *Jakarta: A History*, (Singapore, 1987) p. 67]. Since then this requirement has been supervised with varying strictness.
7. For more evidence of temporary or circular migration at this time see Hugo "Population Mobility in West Java" pp. 111–14.
8. For evidence that living standards in Indonesia in 1937 were as high or higher than at any time since, see Papanek, G. F. "The Effect of Economic Growth and Inflation on Workers' Income" in Papanek, G. F. (ed.) *The Indonesian Economy*, (New York, 1980) pp. 83–84; Sunuharyo, B. S. "Analisa Biaya Hidup di Jakarta" in Sumardi, M. and Evers, H. (eds.) *Golongan Miskin di Jakarta*, (Jakarta, 1980) pp. 82–83; Castles, L. *Religion, Politics and Economic Behaviour in Java: The Kudus Cigarette Industry*, (New Haven, 1967) pp. 17, 74–79;

Mears, L. A. "Economic Development in Indonesia through 1958", *Ekonomi dan Keuangan Indonesia*, Vol. 14, Nos. 1 and 2: 1961: pp. 27–28.

9. Tesch, J. W. "The Hygiene Study Ward Centre at Batavia: Planning and Preliminary Results 1937–1941", Dissertatie, Leiden, 1948; Tesch, J. W. "Living Conditions of Municipally Employed Coolies in Batavia 1937" in Wertheim, W. F. (ed.) *The Indonesian Town: Studies in Urban Sociology* (The Hague, 1958) 85–224; Abeyasekere *Jakarta* pp. 93–94.

10. Cobban "The City on Java" p. 228.

11. This may be part of the very limited Kampung Improvement Programme carried out by the colonial government referred to by Cobban, J. L. "The City on Java: An Essay in Historical Geography", Ph.D Thesis, University of California, Berkely, 1970, pp. 161–66; Krausse, G. "The Kampungs of Jakarta, Indonesia: A Study of Spatial Patterns in Urban Poverty", Ph.D Thesis, University of Pittsburgh, 1975, p. 36.

12. Cohen "Poverty and Development in Jakarta" pp. 276–77.

13. Writing more generally, Dick suggests that despite exploitation and oppression, Dutch rule between 1901 and 1942 was "enlightened" and upheld "people's basic rights of peace, justice and an adequate subsistence. . . . peace and order (rust en orde) was undoubtedly the main benefit which the people of Java received from the final century of colonial rule." See Dick, H. W. "The Rise of a Middle Class and the Changing Concept of Equity in Indonesia: An Interpretation", *Indonesia*, No. 39, April: 1985: p. 83.

14. Intense hardship was not suffered by Jakartans throughout the occupation. Probably little changed in the first few months and it was only at the end of 1943 that life really became desperate [Abeyasekere *Jakarta* pp. 138–142].

15. Many Jakartans initially fled from the city but several months later began to return. Hearing of the better conditions in the city, desperate villagers followed [Abeyasekere *Jakarta* pp. 140–141; Hugo "Population Mobility in West Java" p. 243; Kroef, J. M. van der "The City, its Culture and Evolution" in Kroef, J. M. van der *Indonesia in the Modern World*, (Bandung, 1954) pp. 157–58; Heeren.

16. Contradictions as to what happened to medium and small-scale trade abound. Some writers suggest that during the Japanese occupation most Chinese merchants, small Indonesian traders and warung keepers suffered due to restrictions, limited mobility and consumer spending capacity: Swasono, Wir Edi (ed.) *Entrepreneurship in Indonesia*, (Jakarta, 1976) p. 62; Sutter, J. O. *Indonesianisasi: Politics in a Changing Economy, 1940–1955*, (Ithaca, 1959) pp. 268, 269.

17. Becaks or Trishaws, the three wheeled pedicab (sanrinsha) had appeared in Jakarta before the war but became more numerous under the Japanese to overcome the dire shortage of vehicles [see also Sutter *Indonesianisani* p. 164].

18. Abeyasekere *Jakarta* p. 141.

19. Other reports, however, suggest that the time of "bersiap" referred to

the violent actions taken by the Indonesian Pemuda (Indonesian Youth) against the Allies (British and Dutch) in the last two months of 1945. [Smail, J. W. R. *A Study in the Social History of the Indonesian Revolution*, (Ithaca, 1964); Abeyasekere *Jakarta* p. 151].

20. Hugo "Population Mobility in West Java" p. 243.
21. Kementerian Penerangan *Kota Pradja Djakarta Raya* pp. 401, 404.
22. Kementerian Penerangan *Kota Pradja Djakarta Raya* pp. 109, 110, 303; Abeyasekere *Jakarta* p. 141.
23. NICA (from the initials of the Netherlands Indies Civil Administration) money or guilders was the Dutch currency whereas Japanese guilders and after 1946, Indonesian Rupiahs were the Republican currency. Both types of currency were to be found in the city but Dutch currency in the village was taken as a sign of collusion with the Dutch. For more details on currency see Cribb, R. "Political Dimensions of the Currency Question 1945–1947", *Indonesia*, No. 31, April: 1981: pp. 113–35; Cribb, R. "The Nationalist World of Occupied Jakarta, 1946–1949" in Abeyasekere *From Batavia to Jakarta* pp. 99–101.
24. See note 6.
25. Heeren "The Urbanization of Djakarta" p. 704.
26. Given currency instability, Rupiahs are best understood in terms of equivalent amounts of rice. See Appendix pp. 190–2 for rice prices per litre from 1953 to 1981. An average family of 5 members needed 2½ to 3 litres per day.
27. For a similar picture of life near Senen market at this time, see Abeyasekere *Jakarta*, p. 174.
28. Watts, K et al. *Rentjana Pendahuluan/Outline Plan*, (Jakarta, 1957) pp. 13 and 14.
29. For another account of how kampung dwellers survived at this time see Cohen "Poverty and Development in Jakarta" pp. 20–1.
30. Mackie, J. *Problems of the Indonesian Inflation*, (Ithaca, 1967) pp. 81–83 (Appendix 1).
31. Cohen "Poverty and Development in Jakarta" pp. 20–1.
32. Attempts were made by the city administration to clear traders, becak drivers, vagrants and illegal shanties from the city's public areas but met with little success [DKI, Karya Jaya, (Jakarta, 1977) pp. 39, 73, 91, 142; Abeyasekere *Jakarta* pp. 196–99.
33. For the number of parties see Kementerian Penerangan *Kota Pradja Djakarta Raya*, (Jakarta, 1952) pp. 115–16; Ricklefs, M. C. *A History of Modern Indonesia*, (London, 1981) p. 238.
34. Crouch, H. *The Army and Politics in Indonesia* (Ithaca, 1978) pp. 97–157.
35. By contrast, Papanek argues that inequality increased substantially during this period and the city's lower classes suffered most. See Papanek, G. F. "The Effect of Economic Growth and Inflation on Workers' Income" in Papanek, G. F. (ed.) *The Indonesian Economy*, (New York, 1980) pp. 97–100, 109–10.
36. Grenville, S. "Monetary Policy and the Formal Financial Sector" in Booth and McCawley *The Indonesian Economy* p. 108.

37. Sundrum, R. and Booth, A. *Rapid Economic Growth in Indonesia: 1968–81.*
38. DKI, data collected by the Kelurahan of Kebun Kacang (unpublished), (Jakarta, 1981).
39. Other kampungs experienced similar improvements [Sunindyo "Kampung Sawah" pp. 119–22]. Between 1970 and 1980 electricity was extended from 23 percent to 50 percent of Jakarta's urban households. See: Steer "Indonesian Urban Services" Annex 1. Table 5.4.
40. By 1980, 66.4 percent of Jakarta's urban populace had a radio or cassette recorder and 47.3 percent had a television [Steer "Indonesian Urban Services" Annex 1 table 4.9]. Prior to 1975 many of these items had been rare in most parts of the city [Krausse "The Kampungs of Jakarta", p. 84].
41. In Jakarta as a whole there were 120 square metres per person. Even the most densely populated areas were said to have 16.5 square metres per person [Bianpoen "The Pattern of Settlement in Densely Populated Areas of Jakarta" (Jakarta, 1976)].
42. DKI, data collected by the Kelurahan of Kebun Kacang (Jakarta, 1981).
43. For increasing inequality in urban areas see Sundrum "Income Distribution, 1970–76" pp. 139, 141; Sundrum, R. "Change in Consumption Patterns in Urban Java 1970–1976", *Bulletin of Indonesian Economic Studies*, Vol. 13, No. 2: 1977: 115–116; Sundrum and Booth "Income Distribution in Indonesia" pp. 456, 479, 482; Evers "Urban Subsistence Production" p. 5; Papanek *The Poor of Jakarta* p. 14.

2

The Social Mesh: Human Relationships in a Neighbourhood Community, 1971–1981

Kebun Kacang could appear cooperative or individualistic depending upon which level of social organization one chooses to focus. While ties within families, especially between husbands and wives, seemed weak, networks between households, especially neighbouring women, were important. Broader community cooperation was rare. Social ties were certainly important and helped to ameliorate the poverty and insecurity of kampung dweller's lives, but they were not fundamental to the economic survival of individual households in the city.

Kebun Kacang: The Neighbourhood

The whole kampung of 3500 people was too large for any formal organization or sense of unity. The inhabitants identified less with the kampung than with clusters of houses along the several paths. Along each pathway, neighbours knew one another by sight, origin and occupation. Most knew each other's names. Every day they passed each other in the narrow pathways, shared the same market place, patronized the same stall keepers, used the same sanitary facilities and, on special occasions, attended the same prayer house. A number of parallel and intersecting pathways and the houses to either side delineated a neighbourhood.

The focus here is on the neighbourhood community of some 77 households which surrounded Ibu Imah's house. The houses all fronted onto the same intersecting pathways. At first sight there were no obvious physical boundaries separating this neighbourhood of 77 households from the rest of the kampung. Houses merged and

abutted upon one another as far as the eye could see. Social relationships also extended beyond the boundaries of the neighbourhood.

The entire neighbourhood came together only in times of crisis and
festivity. Nevertheless, households were bound together in a mesh of
complex, intersecting and ever-changing relationships which together
defined the community. These relationships were typically based
upon ties of proximity reinforced by kinship and/or common origin.
The essence of all these relationships was the reciprocal exchange of
information, goods and services between individual members of
different households. The strength or weakness of these relationships
was indicated by the frequency and continuity of these exchanges.
Many of these relationships were highly unstable, which reflected the
unpredictable fluctuations in economic fortunes. If one person gave
and the other did not reciprocate, conflict ensued and the relationship broke down. While social relationships helped to protect kampung dwellers against the vagaries of the outside world—in particular
the lack of secure employment, housing and basic amenities—the
degree of protection was often inadequate.

Households

The tension between stability and disorder, togetherness and disintegration, was evident at the level of the smallest units of organization within the kampung, namely the family and the household. The
family was the basic unit whilst the household was the residential
unit. Although there was a wide variety of households in Ibu Imah's
neighbourhood, four basic categories could be identified. There were
those with only mother and children or brother and sister, one
nuclear family (mother, father and children), an extended family
(mother, father and their married children and offspring), or many
breadwinners living together without their families communal lodging-
houses. Within the 77 households there were approximately 140
families or heads of families.[1] In 1979 about 44 percent of the
households consisted of just one nuclear family whilst the remainder
was divided between truncated families—living alone without male
breadwinners—(17 percent) extended families (27 percent) and
communal lodging-houses (12 percent).

The four household categories were extremely fluid and changed as
families were created and dissolved or relationships split apart.
Household composition changed so fast that it was extremely difficult
for even neighbouring households to keep track of the members who
came and went and their relationships to one another.

Even in the household where I lived, I found it impossible to keep
a count. One became used to meeting new faces and accepting that

overnight new people had been adopted whilst others suddenly
departed. The new people were rarely blood relatives. In 1972–73
Bud introduced me to her trade partner, Nanti, who turned out to be
a second wife married to the same man as Bud herself. Their husband
was frequently away, living with his third wife, Ade, in her village.
Bud in fact adopted the first child born of the third wife. Bud's aging
mother, who had rented a small cubicle next door, moved into the
house to help look after the new child. Bud's neighbour, Mimi, was
deserted by her husband and was invited to stay with Bud. To
contribute she diced vegetables and washed dishes, clothes and
floors. As Bud's mobile foodstall flourished, she recruited able-
bodied men from the third wife's village. Having nowhere to stay,
they lived in Bud's house. They came, worked for a month, six
months or year and then left. Others came to take their place. Two
formerly adopted children also turned up and then just as suddenly
disappeared. Altogether, between 1975 and 1978, at least nine people
became members of Bud's household and then left. By 1978 Bud's
trade was in decline and her house was occupied by Bud, her mother
and her adopted child. Because of the rapidity of change in household membership it was difficult to categorize, for within a matter of
years it was transformed from an extended to a truncated household.

In another case, a household which had been a nuclear and then
truncated family became overnight a communal lodging-house. A
group of related breadwinners from a village came to stay and work
on a construction site nearby. Six months later, when their work was
completed, they departed and the household reverted to its truncated
status again. Then, an unrelated friend stayed for months at a time
and it was unclear how the household was to be classified.

Relationships

Ties between husbands and wives revealed the looseness of family
relationships. Most women had married at least three times while
some men had married more often. Men and women who had
married only once were an exception. Such findings, however, are
neither new nor unique to the urban kampung. Jay noted the lack of
intimacy and looseness of marital ties in East Java in the 1950s.[2] Even
though his sample of twenty couples showed little evidence of divorce
(which he suspected they were carefully screening from him), the
registered divorce rate for rural Java was one in every two marriages
in 1953.

Although kampung women placed a high value on having a loyal
and loving husband and living together for a long time, in at least half

the cases the reality was very different. Ibu Wira, for example, had had three husbands, and in each case she felt deceived. The men married her without telling her they had other wives or took other wives whilst still married to her. She was left alone to care for her children who, except for one, she believed to have died of negligence. It was difficult to determine how typical this was, but numerous other life stories repeated this example.

Deception and distrust between husbands and wives was common. One husband deserted his wife and without consulting her sold their shanty to provide for his new wife. Another husband took money from a new wife's foodstall to feed a former wife and children without telling her. Had I been as close to men I may have heard of similar stories of deceit and deception by wives.

Because of the recognized instability of marital ties, husbands and wives often kept their earnings separate. If one gave the other a loan, a careful account was kept. The maintenance of separate earnings and possessions was a rational strategy for a couple who were never sure how long they would be together.

There were a substantial number of single-parent families. Twelve women lived alone with their children whilst another fourteen lived in extended households. It was unusual, however, to find men living alone. Two men lived with their elder sisters and only one lived alone after having divorced several times. The remainder were bachelors or only temporarily away from their wives and lived in communal lodging-houses. Thus, as in other lower-income urban communities, single-parent households were centered around mothers.[3] But this was not only true for urban areas or single-parent families. In East Java in the 1950s, Jay noted that even when families were intact they were dominated by women.

In Ibu Imah's neighbourhood, it was not always easy to determine whether a woman had been widowed, deserted or divorced or whether her husband simply came and went. Timah's husband visited every few weeks, sometimes to give her money but mainly to accept meals and borrow money from her to spend on his other wife. Siti's husband, who had not given anything to his wife or six children for over five years, suddenly started to provide a regular monthly income, even though he lived elsewhere with another wife and their six young children. On one occasion, a man took a younger wife and she then regularly contributed money to the older wife who lived in the neighbourhood.

Men hedged themselves against disaster by having numerous loose marital ties on which they could depend in times of need, even if it destabilized these nuclear families. Women's social security, by contrast, mainly rested with their children. Mothers dedicated their lives

to providing their children with sufficient food, clothing and education. Mothers indulged their children and were most reluctant to
demand income from them when they started to work. They felt their
children, and especially their sons, had a right to a good time before
they married and gained new responsibilities. Daughters, by contrast, were expected to help from an early age. If a teenage son
wished to contribute to the household's daily consumer needs, well
and good. If he did not, then one day he would gain awareness
(*insaf*). This attitude was not entirely unselfish, for most mothers
knew that their future lay with their children rather than husbands. In
old age, mothers often lived with their children, whereas their husbands had either died or obtained younger wives to support them.

Frequent adoptions within the neighbourhood added to household
fluidity, but also provided a means of social security for childless
mothers in old age. It was also of benefit to the adopted child and his
biological mother who could not support him. If a single mother had
more than four young children, one or more was often adopted by a
neighbour, usually a relative. For example, two of Menik's six
children were housed, fed and educated by her sister who lived next
door. Ijah's fifth child was brought up and educated by Omi, a cousin
who lived six doors away. This pattern of adoption was common
throughout both rural and urban Java.

Stable households could also be found. In Ibu Imah's neighbourhood there were at least 20 couples who pooled resources and
worked together as a team. Some had married only once. Most,
however, had previous experience of marriage and divorce but had
eventually settled down with someone who suited them. These couples
worked hard together for the sake of their children and had a warm,
intimate relationship. As was more typical of villagers from East
Java, the husband gave all his earnings to his wife.

Fluid household membership and loose marital ties nevertheless
seemed to be very common. This could only be detected by continu-
ous and detailed observation. What initially appeared to be a conven-
tional nuclear family often revealed a long history of marriages,
divorces and adoptions. If one delved into the lives of individual
women, whether they lived in extended, nuclear households or
alone, one usually found a series of husbands, live, dead and adopted
children and numerous relationships which briefly flourished and
then declined. At one point in time their lives looked very stable and
ordinary, but over time their stories revealed a never-ending saga of
relationships gained and lost.

Extended Households

Extended households seemed to emerge as a consequence of weak marital ties, lack of alternative accommodation and lack of resources. As was the tradition in Java, most married couples wanted to set up a home of their own, but with the growing shortage of housing in the city, this proved increasingly difficult. Thirty years earlier, Ibu Imah had been able to provide each of her married children with separate accommodation. Now most newly married couples had to move into their parents'homes.

The extended family provided support for daughters who suddenly found themselves pregnant before marriage. The majority of first marriages took place after the bride became pregnant. Contraception was not widely used in the kampung and never before marriage. Girls became pregnant as early as fourteen years of age, and their marriages were hastily arranged. The husbands were usually in their late teens to early twenties and the marriages generally broke down within the first year. The young men were irresponsible and immature, but some felt genuinely embarrassed about not being able to provide adequately for their new brides. The young women nagged their husbands for their inability to support them. Consequently, the men ran away. Whatever the state of the marriage, the young husbands seldom had a regular source of income and the burden of supporting the wives and their young children fell upon parents. The extra mouths to feed and the demands on already cramped living quarters often led to bitterness and argument.

Married offspring who lived cramped together with their parents and younger brothers and sisters often tried to move away. They moved to other in-laws and remained there until the situation became unbearable. Then they moved back again. Thus there was a frequent oscillation of poor young married couples with offspring into their parents' households and out again. The "better-off" were better able to buy or rent additional accommodation. It was the poorest who tended to remain trapped in extended families.

One somewhat better-off extended family was the Mandroppi household. In 1972 the Mandroppis lived in a small shanty which barely housed two adults and their seven children. During the mid-seventies three of the teenage daughters were forced to marry due to pregnancies and they brought their spouses to live in their parents' home. With the addition of husbands and new-born children the household expanded from one to four families to give a total of fifteen people. In 1977 a second storey was added to accommodate this influx. For the first few years the young husbands did not look after their wives and the parents were left to do so. Two of the young men disappeared for days at a time and a third vanished altogether. The burden of supporting the extended household became too much for the parents and eventually they requested their married daughters to satisfy their childrens' own food needs. To do this the daughters cooked and sold tit-bits along the kampung pathways. In 1980 the daughters found work in a factory. Their mother looked after the children during the day. Eventually two of the husbands found regular work after having tried numerous temporary jobs and started to support their wives and children.

Some poor households had no choice but to keep dividing up what little space they had. The Sani household, for example, consisted of thirteen people and had a family to each of its three wooden bunks. Those who could not fit simply slept on the floor. Because of their poverty, the Sanis were not able to expand the house they owned or rent extra accommodation for their recently married daughters. As with the Mandroppis, the daughters had married husbands who only intermittently looked after them. Having no other means of survival, they were forced to stay with their parents.

Extended households usually shared space and amenities but not income or food. The sharing of food was tolerated only for a short period of time. Married offspring, even those without husbands, were encouraged to look after themselves. Cooking was mainly done separately, even when a number of families shared the same small space and scant cooking facilities. This separation avoided disputes over how much cash each family had to contribute or how much food they were allowed to eat. Only in extended households where a married daughter had been deserted and was not yet able to earn or where a grandmother supervised the pooling of her married children's resources was shopping and cooking done together. In Omi's household, for example, three families, each with separate incomes, lived and cooked together. The grandmother who still had two young unmarried children, pooled the resources of her two married children from two earlier marriages. Eight people lived and cooked together in a space of less than ten square metres. This level of cooperation, however, seemed rare, especially for households from West Java who had lived in the neighbourhood for a long time.

Communal lodging-houses (pondok)

Although the membership of communal lodging-houses was very fluid, with individual breadwinners coming to stay and then going after a couple of months, they provided an ideal means by which villagers could temporarily survive in the city.[4] The lodging-houses (pondok) were usually based upon ties of common village origin. They were as much enterprises as households. Lone breadwinners were invited by friends or relatives to live and work in the city whilst leaving their wives and children to tend the crops and look after their home in the countryside. Every so often, depending on how far away they lived and how much they had earned, they returned to the village to remit their earnings and see their families.[5] Many of these breadwinners would not have had the courage, know-how or resources to go to the city without the communal lodging-houses or the contacts they had there. In Ibu Imah's neighbourhood the number of communal lodging-houses varied over the decade from five to nine. Each housed from two to fifteen people.[6]

Kampung dwellers noted the solidarity and mutual support offered to kinsfolk who lived in Mus's pondok. The extent of their cooperation and togetherness far exceeded any other ties in the community. Not only did these breadwinners from different families live, sleep and eat together but they often performed similar work. Even though they worked independently as traders and each had to pay separately for many of the items they obtained, they also shared scarce working space, trade utensils, raw materials and amenities. They advised each other on good trade routes, current prices and how to avoid trader-clearance campaigns. They lent each other money and any member of the pondok who returned to the village usually carried money, goods and messages for the families of those who remained in the town. The village-cum-pondok dweller who returned to the city, brought food, news and messages from the families in the countryside, and informed those who had remained in the city if anyone in the village was ill, or if crops were to be ploughed or harvested, or a festivity was to be held. A person who fell ill in the city was taken back to the village to convalesce by two or three pondok colleagues. On those occasions when most of the circular migrants returned to the village, they took part in joint celebrations marking a circumcision, wedding or death. Once a year, they cleaned the graves of their common ancestors.

In the 1970s, Mus's communal lodging-house was the only building in Ibu Imah's neighbourhood, apart for the prayer house, to be rebuilt by *gotong royong* (mutual aid). All Mus's lodgers and others from the village voluntarily gathered in the city to rebuild Mus's house. She provided the building materials and special food for the occasion, but did not have to pay any wages. The house was rebuilt in a matter of days and cost half the price of other houses in the area which had all been rebuilt by paid labour. Many kampung dwellers praised and marvelled at the pondok dwellers' cooperative spirit, for it was unusual in the neighbourhood.

Mus's pondok supports the view that ties between kin or people from the same village could be strengthened by migration to the city. Whereas in the village they lived in separate nuclear households and cultivated separate fields, in the city, they lived, ate, slept and worked in close proximity to each other, constantly sharing each other's joys and sorrows.

As in every household, there was friction between individuals over the sharing of work and costs. Some felt Mus overcharged for the trade ingredients she provided. Others found the communal duties in the lodging-house such as food preparation, carting water or cleaning too onerous. Disagreements resulted in people leaving the household to seek accommodation elsewhere. To survive together, there had to be plenty of give and take, especially when Mus's pondok was full and there was only three square metres of space per person.

The west Javanese communal lodging-houses were more loosely organized than Mus's. This may have been due to the stronger central Javanese tradition of mutual solidarity and support or to Mus's more distant place of origin (Klaten) and her lodgers common village and kinship ties.[7] Unlike Mus's pondok, Bang Ateng's and Burhanuddin's lodgers were neither related to their bosses nor independent entrepreneurs. They had been recruited to come to the city to work and were paid piece rates for the cloth caps or ice-cones they produced. Bang Ateng provided his live-in workers with accommodation but they had to buy their own food and water from the household stalls nearby. Burhanuddin provided his lodgers with all their basic needs and they hardly ventured outside the steaming kitchen where they worked sixteen hours a day-every day-until it was time to return to their village.

The pondok dwellers' hard work in the city and their sense of togetherness militated against their mixing socially with other members of the neighbourhood. The owners of these enterprises had some ties with their neighbours but apart from Burhanuddin, whose family lived in the area, their major preoccupation was to earn enough income to send back to the village. Mus had a mother and daughter to support in the village plus another house to rebuild. Apart from infrequent visits to the town, Bang Ateng kept his family in the village and invested much of his money there. The pondok dwellers' social orientation and ties were to the village from where they came and not to the urban neighbourhood.

Social Ties

A basic tenet of kampung life was to be on good terms with one's immediate neighbours. If a new household moved into the neighbourhood it was customary to deliver a plate of food to each of the adjoining households to establish a good rapport. If immediate neighbours were not actually kinsmen, they soon felt as if they were, for the sheer density of housing meant that scarce space, amenities, possessions, food, problems and gossip were continually shared. With one household directly abutting upon another, each alleyway was like a long, narrow, communal lounge room. Often the work performed in one's home spilled out onto the pathway. Mothers washed and ironed clothes or cleaned kitchen utensils whilst chatting to neighbours. Even if a woman stayed within her home, a neighbour would poke her head through the open doorway and say, "that smells good, what are you cooking?". If the neighbour just walked past, a voice from within invariably called, "come in, sit down and have some food before you go on". Although this invitation was not necessarily to be taken literally, it was a sign of welcome and mutual concern.

Sharing was evident in many forms. As neighbours had long standing credit relationships and were reluctant to walk for any distance to obtain their basic needs, they bought and sold goods and services from each other. During the heat of the mid-afternoon and evening they lounged on their doorsteps and talked. In the early 1970s, when only a few houses had a second storey to retreat to, those without clustered into their neighbours' homes to avoid the monsoon rains that flooded their homes. They remained there, sharing what little food was available until the waters subsided. If a neighbour lacked space for village guests or had a fight with her husband, she could be provided with temporary accommodation next door. Before private wells were dug in each household, neighbours shared the same washing facilities. They chatted together and exchanged problems as they queued to use the toilet over the canal. Before the 1970s neighbours gathered around the few available radios to listen to the Mahabarata or Ramayana legends. Later they gathered around the few available television sets. When there was a celebration, they borrowed cups, plates and chairs from each other. If a neighbour returned from her home village loaded down with food, she was obliged to share her goods with her neighbours. It was considered rude to keep such windfalls for oneself. Likewise, if a neighbour struck hard times and was without food, then each adjoining household was expected to help out with a plate of rice and vegetables. Because of the regularity and intensity of contacts most neighbours found it difficult to keep their problems to themselves and often advised each other on how to trade or cope with disobedient children or unfaithful husbands.[8]

In the kampung, ties of residential proximity seemed to be of greater importance than ties of kin.[9] Some years after entering the community, I still did not realise that many households were in fact related. Kinship groupings were not easily recognizable because households operated as independent units. They lived, earned and ate separately from one another and outwardly had a relationship based on proximity of residence and the sale of goods and services. When occasionally they helped one another and shared amenities, windfalls and tragedies, it was easy to assume that these were ties of proximity rather than kinship. Another reason for the difficulty in establishing kinship ties was that in Indonesia it is rude to exclude any neighbour or friend from a family-style relationship. Older women were usually referred to as Bu or Ibu (mother), older men as Pak or Bapak (father), elder acquaintances of the same generation as Kak or Kakak (elder sibling), younger members of one's generation as Dik or Adik (younger sibling), classificatory uncles as Oom (Dutch for uncles) or Paman, classificatory aunts as Tante (Dutch for aunt) and very old women as Bah or Mbah (grandmother). This contrasts with the more impersonal Western style of address (Mr, Mrs) and can sometimes create the false impression that all neighbours or acquaintances are related.

Who really had ties of blood or marriage to whom became obvious only when the neighbourhood was demolished in 1981. People openly reaffirmed their ties when they felt threatened. Although people came from many different areas of west and central Java and a few came from East Java, Padang and Madura, at least twelve kinship clusters were evident, four of which had more than two related households.

The main kinship cluster revolved around Ibu Imah whose family was one of the first to settle in the area. By the 1970s Imah's relatives accounted for twenty-three households in the neighbourhood and others that extended into the surrounding area. As Ibu Imah's family expanded, she and her husband divided up more and more of their vegetable plot to provide room for their married offspring. They in turn divided up their homes to provide space for the next generation. The same process of subdivision and redivision occurred for other kinship groups in the area.

Between the 1930s and 1960s, Imah and Harjo's kin invited one another to the area. They helped one another with accommodation and jobs. When vegetable growing was no longer feasible, Harjo's kinsfolk followed one another into vegetable trade and then some went into jobs as rubbish collectors for the Jakarta city government. By the 1970s, when I first came into the community, most were living in separate houses and working in their own spheres of activity and it was difficult to trace the common routes by which they had come.

After fifty years, Ibu Imah's group had become too large and amorphous to function effectively as a kinship group. Through years of intermarriage and natural increase they had merged with the surrounding households. They still knew who belonged to their kin group, but unlike other kin groups in the area they did not feel the need to reaffirm these ties or to draw my attention to them until they were threatened by demolition. In contrast to Imah's kin group, other smaller kin groups consisting of only two to three households which had come more recently from further afield, formed more cohesive groups. These small clusters still maintained contact with their village of origin. By contrast, members of Imah's clan had lost contact with their home village and viewed Kebun Kacang as their only home.

On rare occasions Ibu Imah's group functioned as a united bloc. Because of their greater numbers, they ensured that local leadership remained in their hands, passing through three generations from father to son. They controlled the prayer house, which Imah's relatives felt obliged to attend. Within the more private sphere, they adopted children from one another. There was hardly a household in the kin group where one child had not been given or received by another. Because of the way their land and houses had been subdivided they tended to live next to one another. In day-to-day activities, Imah's large kin group broke down into smaller clusters of more intense interaction between households that were immediate neighbours.

Like Imah's, Kuntil's house was surrounded by more than twelve related households, ten of which fell within my neighbourhood. By the early 1970s, they appeared to be independent households, each seeking their own livelihood. Although I frequently saw Kuntil's relatives visiting her house, I assumed they were just being neighbourly. Only when invited to return to their home village near Bogor did I start to understand the kinship connections.

Kuntil's husband, Gani, had come to the area in the 1940s and rented some land from Ibu Imah. He built a house and invited his wife from Bogor to join him. Both invited their brothers to the area and Gani introduced them to car parts trade. After helping Gani with this trade, they set up stalls of their own or turned to other work such as taxi driving.

Gani's house was progressively subdivided to provide more and more room for these newcomers. At first they shared accommodation. Then, when they had become financially independent, they rented from Gani and eventually bought the units they used. When Gani became ill, Kuntil progressively sold off parts of the house to these relatives to help pay for his medical expenses. These relatives who had initially been helped by Gani, then helped Kuntil by occasionally paying for food or medical expenses.

After Gani's death, Kuntil's two brothers who lived next door gave
Kuntil an allowance in return for washing their clothes and providing
them with food. Kuntil's two married offspring and their families also
partook in these meals, for they lived with Kuntil and pooled resources even though each family kept part of their incomes for
themselves.

It was only during emergencies such as sickness, death or bankruptcy that ties between the different households became apparent.
When Gani's younger brother died, for example, his married children, who lived nearby in separate households, came to their step-
mother's assistance. But Suli (Gani's brother's wife) could not rely
for any length of time on gifts from her married step-children for they
had their own families to support. She set up a cooked-food stall and
her four children did odd jobs such as shoeshining and water selling.
Although kinship ties ameliorated hardship, ultimately each family
had to support itself and not rely on relatives who were also strug-
gling to make ends meet.

Samilah's family appeared not to have any other relatives in the
area. Some years later I discovered that Samilah's husband was
actually related through marriage to Gani's brother's daughter (Suli).
I had initially assumed that Samilah had been adopted by Gani whom
she used to massage and from whom she first rented and then bought
her house. I also discovered that Samilah had a sister (Ani) living
almost next door whom she had helped to rent and then buy a house
from Gani. Ani had helped look after Samilah's eight children whilst
Samilah worked as a servant in Menteng. Later when Ani worked as
a servant, the mutual assistance between the two sisters declined.
Samilah felt that by helping each other the two families would be
better equipped to face the difficulties of life. She believed her
children would help Ani and Aswan (Ani's husband) in old age.
Aswan, however, felt too poor to be burdened with Samilah's children and did not like his wife helping Samilah.

The two households drifted apart so that by the time I came to the
community their kinship tie was no longer visible. The only evidence
that they were related was the constant visiting of Samilah's children
to Ani's home. Possibly they hoped to receive a tasty morsel from
their aunt whilst their mother was away. There may have been other
exchanges of food and money which I failed to detect, but by the
1970s each of the households viewed each other as separate units.
Over time, relatives who had once been close, drifted apart. The
expansion of families and the inclusion of newcomers through marriage caused formerly common kinship interests to diverge. Poor related
families such as Samilah's and Ani's were placed in a dilemma. To
survive they needed to help one another and yet their very sharing

dissipated what little they had. The growing scarcity of goods and constant struggle to survive in an increasingly commercialized world caused the former values of sharing to become obsolete.

Households such as Bud's which lacked kinship ties in the area created new ties with immediate neighbours. Bud had originally been introduced to the area by Putro. She lived next-door to Putro's daughter (Sundari) whom she invited to watch television. When Bud originally moved into the area, Mus, also from Central Java, was her closest friend and confidente. They were both food traders and gave each other food and marital advice. Both had husbands who took other wives. Mus had first rented half of Bud's house. Later she bought the part she rented and rebuilt it into a separate house. Ten years later, Bud's mother rented a room from Mus. Bud's mother had a special relationship with Menik who lived on the opposite side of the pathway. Menik had many small children and Bud's mother helped look after them when Menik was busy with her cooked-food stall. In return, Menik frequently gave Bud's mother tasty morsels of food. Sugi, who was Menik's step-son, provided Bud with electricity for which she regularly paid him each month. Sugi's relatives wanted electricity but he preferred to sell it to non-kin like Bud who were more likely to pay a regular fee.

During Bud's trading heyday, she employed both Mimi and Tukirah to clean and dice vegetables and generally help with her stall. Mimi was deserted by her husband and eventually moved into Bud's house. Tukirah's husband neglected her and her young children, so Bud, like the other neighbours tried to support Tukirah by asking her to do odd jobs like carting water, cleaning their homes and taking their possessions to the pawnbroker.

As Bud prospered, she seemed to distance herself from her neighbours. Some called her arrogant. When her trade stall went bankrupt and she fell upon hard times, however, her earlier ties of reciprocity reemerged. Sundari delivered greenbean porridge, cloths for wiping the floor and mosquito repellant which she obtained free of charge from the hospital where she worked. Mus gave her the chipped ice-cones and pieces of ice left over from the ice-cream sales. Menik delivered cooked food left over from her stall. Giving Bud these things when she was doing well might have created offense, but in her poverty she accepted them with gratitude. Although these provisions were not nearly enough to keep her family going, they made their plight more bearable. Some neighbours bought Bud's possessions—sideboard, radio, television set, crockery and trading stall—or helped find other people who wanted to buy them. Bud then had to view Sundari's new television set instead of her own.

Bud stressed that neighbours, not more distant relatives, came to

one's assistance in times of need. Bud and her mother saw their
better-off kinsfolk only once or twice a year, during Lebaran or Idul
Adha. They were ashamed of their poverty and feared their relatives
would think that they had come to beg. Furthermore, they found it
too much of a burden travelling across the city to see them. Other
women in the neighbourhood confirmed these feelings. One relied on
close neighbours for support and not richer relatives who lived
further afield. The durability and effectiveness of these ties was very
much dependent upon the close physical proximity of households.
Their ties were based on daily interaction and daily needs. Such ties
took time to develop and the longer neighbours lived together the
closer they became.

Because of the flux of household membership, ties between unrelated neighbours, especially women, sometimes seemed more durable than ties between members of the one household. Because of
the growing clash in values between reciprocity and market exchange
amongst related households, relationships between unrelated households often seemed smoother. As becomes evident in the next
sections, however, those who belonged to "better-off" households
kept more to themselves and did not mix much with other households
in the neighbourhood.

Outsiders

Not all households located in the neighbourhood had close ties with
other members of the community. Although close proximity was a
necessary condition, it did not ensure that social ties would be
mutually acknowledged. Within the neighbourhood there were
usually about half a dozen households which could be identified as
outsiders. Their relationships with neighbouring households were
almost entirely economic. Socially they mixed little with their neighbours and scarcely participated in the affairs of the community.
Insider or outsider status seemed to be mainly determined by women's
active involvement in the community.

John Sullivan has looked at how kampung dwellers perceived the
requirements of community membership in his kampung in Yogyakarta. He concluded " . . . that membership was not just a matter of
self-identification or the holding of certain values and attitudes" but
required active "participation" (ie. "sharing" and "practical cooperation within the community").[10] He struggled to identify the characteristics of the "non-kampung" group. He found significant correlations
with wealth, extreme poverty, residential location on the fringe
facing main streets, cultural differences, middle-class or outcast social

status and brief or transient residence in the area. Yet in each case he also found exceptions. He did not conceal his frustration with this analytical fuzziness.

In Kebun Kacang the households which appeared to be outsiders seemed to fit categories similar to those of John Sullivan. The five most relevant categories were (1) the better-off (ie. "middle class"), (2) the very poor, (3) the transient, (4) the culturally distinct and (5) the ostracized. Of these, the fifth category applied not to households but to individual household members, specifically several prostitutes.[11] The categories of the "very poor", "the transient" and "culturally distinct" tended to overlap.

The "better-off" regarded themselves and were regarded by the rest of the neighbourhood as outsiders. As described above, even Bud in the heyday of her prosperity distanced herself from her neighbours. More typical of the better-off households in Kebun Kacang was Nano. She kept the doors of her solid, two-storey house closed and her children inside, away from the temptations, dangers and snacks of the kampung pathways. Even though the house fronted directly onto the kampung pathway, once inside it was as if the sights, sounds and smells of the kampung world no longer existed. The house's porous bamboo walls had been replaced by sold brick and glass.

By the end of the 1970s, the family did not rely on their kampung neighbours for any services. They had their own water, electricity and gas connection and did not use the local water or kerosene vendor. They had their own washing facilities and toilet and thus did not need to tread the pathways in common with their neighbours to the communal well or toilet. They did not need to utilize the services of the local clothes washers for they had their own clothes washing machine. For reasons of privacy, economy and trust, they preferred to use a young servant from their home village in central Java rather than recruit a girl from the urban neighbourhood where they lived. They bought most of their food in bulk at discount rates from outside the kampung rather than more expensively from stalls in their immediate neighbourhood.

Their economic independence from the surrounding society reinforced their social independence. The household's children obtained all their cooked food needs from within the home rather than along the kampung pathways. They attended a distant school instead of one nearby which was used by most of the local children. The children were taken to school on their father's motorcycle and did not use the local becak or walk in common with other kampung children. They tended to associate more with people beyond the kampung from their place of work, school or village of origin and were not inhibited by the cost of transport which limited their neighbours' mobility and access to the outside world.

When they first bought a house in the area in the early 1970s, they wanted to gain some acceptance by the community. Reluctantly they let their neighbours view their television set. By the late 1970s, when many others in the area had a television of their own, they moved it out of sight so that they would no longer be troubled by neighbours peering through their windows. For entertainment and a little additional income, Nano's grandmother, who came to live in the household, cooked snacks which she occasionally delivered to Badrun's stall for sale to neighbours. In the 1980s they bought a video recorder and charged a fee for any kampung children who wanted to view it. On two occasions each year, the family felt obliged to make substantial financial contributions to the prayer house. So, although they were not totally isolated from the neighbourhood, their relationships were limited, intermittent and largely economic. After two years, Nano's sister, who had come to live in the household, was still unfamiliar with the faces or the names of the people who lived only a few doors away. She lived in an insulated, closed, middle-class household rather than a more gregarious open kampung home where within days people gained familiarity with those who lived to either side.

As they prospered, other households began to follow a similar pattern of distancing themselves from the rest of the community. In the mid-1970s Itin built a two-storey brick and timber house and his children were rarely to be seen playing outside. When in 1980 a relative lost his job and asked to borrow money, Itin refused. The relative was forced to turn to a much poorer unrelated neighbour for assistance. Prosperity forced Itin to distance himself from relatives and neighbours for fear that they would dissipate his new-found wealth. Towards the end of the decade, one or two families like Itin's even left the community for richer and more salubrious suburbs. Both their neighbours and they themselves admitted that one of the main reasons for their move was to avoid the pressures of having to share.

Over time it became evident that increasing numbers of households which had formerly been part of the community distanced themselves as they tried to accumulate more wealth. Burhanuddin's household had once been very much part of the community. In the 1960s and early 1970s the household had adopted some less fortunate members of Imah's clan. Burhanuddin had given Badrun land for his trade stall. He had lent Mandroppi's son money to set up swimming classes. The money was never repaid and Burhanuddin felt deceived.

Although Burhanuddin and his wife still regularly conducted

Islamic classes for all members of the neighbourhood, by the late 1970s they had erected a high fence around their front door. This was clearly aimed against the prying eyes of neighbours and begging arms of relatives. Few kampung dwellers, even those who were related, dared enter uninvited. Thus, the increasing wealth of some members within the community over the 1970s meant that they consciously distanced themselves from other members, even if they were related.

Most poor households had both social and economic ties with "better-off" households in the neighbourhood. The wives and daughters of the poorest families washed and ironed clothes, carted water, set up stalls, rented out rooms or performed other domestic chores for some of their "better-off" neighbours. These income-earning activities provided an entree into neighbouring households which gave rise to social as well as economic ties.

Only one household could be identified as "outsider" solely on the grounds of acute poverty. The Sani's had only one breadwinner who worked as a guard and sweeper outside the community. His wife and daughters were busy caring for young offspring and did not work in the neighbourhood. They bought their daily needs on credit from local stalls and on one occasion used a neighbour's well when their's broke down. But that was the extent of their ties to neighbouring households. Being barely able to feed themselves, they were too poor to take part in reciprocal exchange. Neighbours felt them to be a liability and one stall eventually withdrew its credit facilities because their debts became too large. When the neighbour who had initially let them use her well received nothing in return, she told them to repair their own.

The Sani's felt intensely ashamed of their poverty and were reluctant to become indebted to anyone for fear they could not repay. They had no relatives in the area or ties with people of common origin. They never invited anyone to their home which was too small to accommodate guests and lacked adequate sitting facilities. Furthermore, they rarely had acceptable food or drinks to offer or plates and cups to serve it on. In turn they were neither invited to nor visited neighbouring households. At most, mother and married daughter sat on the pathway in front of their home, washing clothes or suckling their babies whilst chatting to passers-by. That seemed to be the extent of their relationships.

Because of their poverty and lack of religious belief, the Sani's failed to make any contributions to the local prayer house, even during Lebaran (religious event held at the end of the fasting month). Consequently, apart for a few tiny pieces of goats meat during Idul Adha (religious event which coincides with the sacrifice performed by pilgrims at Mina near Mecca), they received nothing from the prayer

house. Their lack of good clothing and sufficient resources for presents (kado) or financial donations, prevented them from attending
festivities in the neighbourhood.

Several other outsider households were both "very poor" and
"transient". They differed from the Sani's in that they were only
temporarily resident in the community. Social relationships took time
to develop and required a certain amount of residential stability.
Though some transient households came to the community through
kinship or village connections, these appeared to be limited. Neighbours were most reluctant to assist those who were not likely to be
around to repay their kindness when they in turn needed help. Both
parties may have felt it was not worth while investing time, money
and effort in a relationship that would not last. Because of their
footloose existence, the behaviour of transient households was not
subject to the same amount of control as that of their more permanent counterparts who could not get away from the neighbourhood's
gossip and ostracism. Temporary residents were more likely than
permanent ones to abscond without paying their social or economic
dues, which reduced their neighbours' willingness to involve them in
reciprocal exchange.

In Kebun Kacang transient households were either squeezed out of
their cheap accommodation or were pressured by poverty, lack of
secure employment or a desire to move on. A poor widow in sudden
need of cash may have willingly subdivided part of her house for a
transient household to rent. When her fortunes changed, she may
have wanted the full use of her house and asked her tenants to move
on. The transient households were thus forced to move on because
they could not find any other cheap accommodation in the area. They
may have only seen the neighbourhood as a temporary refuge till
they established themselves elsewhere or their stay may have been
just another stop in their perpetual drift from place to place.

The two Padang households in the neighbourhood were separated
from the rest of the community by their refusal to participate.
Although "poor" and "transient," these households bore an air of
disdain towards other members of the neighbourhood and refused to
mix, share or partake in reciprocal exchange. When their children
obtained new toys they did not share them with neighbouring children. This behaviour caused disputes in which mothers also became
embroiled. They never shared their Padang food with neighbours
who consequently viewed them as anti-social: arrogant, snobbish and
stingy. According to kampung dwellers, they lacked the Javanese
quality of *ramah* (friendliness and intimacy).

Unlike many families in the area, the Padang households had no ties of kinship or common village of origin with others in the neighbourhood and had simply come to the area in search of cheap accommodation. Prior to their arrival in the kampung they had fallen on hard times and were fleeing from bankruptcy or debt. They looked upon Kebun Kacang as a temporary refuge where they could live cheaply, save and regain what they had lost and then move on. They were not interested in mixing with the community. Their ties to neighbours were purely economic, based around the rent of rooms and amenities.

Although not strictly households but single members of households, several prostitutes were also regarded and regarded themselves as "outsiders". Although two rented accommodation in the neighbourhood and another two lived with families who were part of the community, they mixed little with their neighbours. They stayed inside their homes all day and hardly ventured out. They felt members of the community did not understand them. In return, they had feelings of disdain towards the kampung rather similar to the culturally distinct and better-off. Through their work and numerous contacts, they had absorbed the aspirations and dreams of the middle class who were their clientele. They felt it was not worth bothering with kampung dwellers whom they believed lived in a closed, isolated, backward world, unaware of the rapid changes and opportunities that existed outside. Their circle of friends were largely drawn from others who worked in bars, restaurants or cafes. Even though they earned well and were the envy of other young kampung girls, they felt shunned by most members of the community. The perpetual gossip and scrutiny annoyed them, so they kept to themselves.

Religious Ties

Islam provided the main focus for more formal social organization in Kebun Kacang. The first prayer house (*mushollah*) in the neighbourhood was built in the late 1960s. In 1964 a Kyai (religious teacher) from Bogor had moved into Ibu Minah's vicinity and tried to promote Islam. The trauma of the coup in the following year led people to become more consciously Islamic. During the 1970s, Islamic activities in the kampung were increasingly well organized. This culminated in the rebuilding of all three prayer houses in the kampung, including that in my neighbourhood. This was the first and only evidence of the entire neighbourhood coming together in some productive venture. All members of the neighbourhood felt com-

pelled to give either cash for building materials, their free labour or
prepared food. A list was drawn up of all those who contributed, so
that those who did not would be embarrassed into doing so. On
Sunday, most kampung dwellers' day off, many members of the
community turned up to help. Some carted bricks and timber while
others mixed the cement. The elder men, mainly from Ibu Imah's
clan, directed what the poorer, younger labourers were to do. Wives
came forth with tasty dishes.

Each evening fifteen to twenty men, mainly from Ibu Imah's West
Javanese clan, regularly gathered for prayer.[12] Mustapha, the chairman of the mosque, called them to prayer through a loudspeaker.
Often he sat in the doorway of the prayer house, eyes half closed and
seemingly in meditation but actually looking out at those who failed
to attend. Scrubbed clean, in loose sarongs, crisp shirts and barefeet
the men relaxed in the prayer house, casually sitting on mats on the
floor with their heads covered by black velvet caps. In groups of twos
or threes they spoke of the day's events or simply sat alone, meditat-
ing. Eventually they all stood up in a row to pray, rising and falling to
the ritual movements of the Islamic prayers. Then, their relationship
was to God and no other man. Women, of course, were not welcome
when the men were at prayer.

After the mid-1970s Ibu Sum, the daughter of the chairman of the
prayer house, organized a gathering of women each Wednesday
afternoon. Mainly the middle-aged or elderly women from Ibu Imah's
clan attended. But elder ladies from Central Java like Bud's mother,
Ibu Darmo and Ibu Putro also came. Most younger women of
child-bearing age did not seem interested. The women came to the
prayer house dressed in their best clothes with coloured shawls over
their heads. They gathered around outside or inside waiting for the
guest speaker to arrive. Then for an hour the women listened to a
charismatic woman with a mellifluous voice tell them how to behave
towards their husbands, neighbours and children. She placed greatest
emphasis on their cleanliness and relationship to God. At the end of
each session a request for money was made. On such occasions, Ibu
Sum openly conducted a trade in shawls and *kebaya* (blouses) with
her relatives and neighbours. Each time the women met some of
them paid Ibu Sum for the items they had bought from her on credit.
There was no sense of embarrassment in combining commerce with
Islam.

In the late 1970s Ibu Sum organized a smaller women's group of
five to ten people who met once a week at alternate members' houses
to recite the Koran. Elegantly dressed women sat in a circle on mats
on the floor. In between the Koran reading they discussed personal
problems. The Koran reading circle was very important for people

like Wira, who was on non-speaking terms to at least eight people in the neighbourhood. It was only there that she found people to talk to. Otherwise she felt very much alone.

Islam, however, was mainly practised alone, within the privacy of one's home. For the kampung dwellers it was primarily concerned with each person's own relationship to God. Bud, who never prayed when I first came into the community in the early 1970s, increasingly adhered to ritual prayer after her small enterprise went bankrupt. Five times a day she laid out her prayer mat and covered her body in white cloth whilst murmuring prayers. Then she rose and fell to her knees, with her head almost touching the mat, a set number of times. It was a personal, very private experience between herself and God. Her concentration was complete and no other individual could intrude. Most people in the neighbourhood, especially women, experienced Islam in this very individual, personal and private way. A kampung woman in prayer was alone, seemingly in another world and not to be disturbed.

A few women in the neighbourhood such as Mus, who came from Central Java, and Sani, who had never been taught about Islam, did not pray. Although other kampung women felt it was a matter of personal choice, they referred to them derogatively as "orang merah" (red person—meaning communist), "abangan",[13] "PKI" (communist) or "orang bodoh yang tidak punya adat" (a stupid person who has no culture). In contrast to the West Javanese, the Central Javanese seemed to take Islam more lightly, though this was not always the case. Wira for example, was poor, illiterate and central Javanese, but took her prayers very seriously. Islam for her, as for Bud after she went bankrupt, provided the only hope and security in this ever-changing world. By contrast, those who traded busily every day such as Mus, or Bud when she was successful, had no time for prayer.

Islamic Festivities

Cooperation and good neighbourliness was most evident during the two Islamic festivals of Lebaran and Idul Adha. According to local convention each household was supposed to contribute three and a half litres of rice to the prayer house during Lebaran, the festival at the end of the fasting month (Ramadan). Ibu Sum, the prayer house chairwoman, collected money throughout the year which she then used to buy new clothes for the neighbourhood widows and poorer families during Lebaran. The ostensible purpose of the exercise, however, was for the kampung rich to share their wealth with the kampung poor at least once a year in accordance with the Muslim's obligation to provide alms (*zakat*).

Members of Ibu Imah's family, who were both the religious and secular heads of the neighbourhood, determined how the mounds of rice were to be distributed. Many kampung dwellers suspected that a disproportionate amount went to the poorest, and perhaps even not so poor, members of Ibu Imah's clan. Menik, the wife of the deceased headman Tole, always received a lot of rice, even though she ran a flourishing cooked-food stall. Ibu Imah received much rice, perhaps because she was the oldest and most respected woman in the neighbourhood, the founder of the community and a widow—but she was by no means one of the poorest. Those with the largest and/or poorest families outside Ibu Imah's clan such as Samilah, Aswan, Siti, Bani or Wira received little or nothing.

Lebaran was a time when neighbours, friends, employers and employees, patrons and clients reaffirmed their ties to one another. Each household felt obliged to prepare elaborate food. In the mid-1970s Bud put aside a week's income to buy the necessary ingredients of chicken, beef, sticky rice, banana leaves, coconuts and spices. Then she and the others in her household toiled away preparing food for two days. By 1980 such food preparation seemed to be in decline and kampung dwellers just bought a tin of biscuits.

New clothes and shoes were supposed to be bought for all members of the family. Some families went into debt for this purpose so that their children would not feel out of place. On the first day of Lebaran these new clothes were paraded along the pathways and as neighbours, friends and old acquaintances met each other, they shook hands, lowered their heads, asked forgiveness for any sins committed during the year and wished each other a good new year. Kampung dwellers went door to door, visiting those with whom they had a special relationship. Inside each house a table was covered with the delicacies cooked over the preceding days. Guests were invited to eat and drink. Small parcels of food were carried to the homes of those with whom one had a particular relationship or debt.

During each Lebaran, Bud carried food to Enji, telling me that she was a special friend from Semarang. It was only much later that I discovered Bud owed her a lot of money. To my surprise, this young attractive female who frequently visited the community, but did not live in it, was the local Chinese moneylender. During Chinese New Year she gave Bud cloth and cakes. Bud also distributed food to Menik, Mus and Sundari and various other people with whom she had a special relationship. A similar pattern of giving to select friends and receiving took place between other households in the neighbourhood.

In a lesser way, Idul Adha drew the community together through the sacrifice of goats and distribution of their meat. Like Lebaran it emphasized giving by the rich to the poor. Usually a number of the wealthier households of the neighbourhood contributed money with which the live goats were bought. Kampung dwellers claimed one could judge the prosperity of the community or state of the kampung economy by the number of goats tethered by the prayer house a day or two before their slaughter. Some of the poorer households who had particular religious requests to make also contributed money for this purpose. A year or two after Bud's trade had collapsed she contributed enough to buy a goat's hindquarter.

Masses of screaming children and adults gathered around as the goats were to be killed. As they beat drums by the prayer house, children chanted and sang. Four or five men mainly from Ibu Imah's clan were the organizers and slaughterers. A religious leader (*imam*) sharpened the knife and prayed as he slit the goat's throat. The crowd roared, united, writhing with the goat. Islamic chants came across the loudspeaker. All over Jakarta, all over Java, the same process was taking place. The goats were hung upside down, skinned and their meat carried into the prayer house, where it was subdivided into many small bundles. These were placed into plastic bags and by the end of the day distributed from house to house. Bud and her mother were dismayed that they only received one small plastic bag, like everybody else, and not the hindquarter they had paid for. It seemed surprising that, after so many years, they still did not understand the way this meat was distributed. They suspected foul play, claiming that somebody from Imah's clan had pocketed the money or a larger share of the goat. Meat was, of course, a luxury for the poorer families, who all busied themselves that evening, cooking goats stew or *sate*.

Rotating Credit Society (Arisan)

A new form of organization which became popular in the kampung during the 1970s was the rotating credit society. Kampung dwellers claimed that this activity, which combined social and economic features, had been copied from the middle class.[14] Credit societies usually involved from ten to twenty-five individuals who contributed a constant amount each day, week or month to a common fund administered by a kampung woman. The organizer initially went from person to person asking whether they would join her society. Usually she selected people who lived nearby, were friends and had money to spare. The amounts contributed depended on the means of the participants and the frequency of contribution. The smallest were Rp.50 (0.5 litres of rice in 1977) and the largest Rp.10,000 (100 litres of rice). The amount people got back depended upon the number of people involved. Lots were drawn to determine in which order each member would collect their money. Once a week or once a month when a person drew the money, coffee and biscuits were provided which added a social dimension to the association. A number of people mentioned that they had to be careful when their turn came to collect the pooled resources, for needy relatives or neighbours often asked for a loan. Each participant in the society used the resources as she pleased. Apart from the coffee and biscuits, there was never any combined use of the pooled resources. For her administrative services the organizer of the society usually received a small fee each time the money was drawn. She had to ensure that every person paid at a set time and place and, if one person failed to do so, she was obliged to make up the difference and settle the debt with the defaulter later on.

Like other ties in the kampung, the membership of rotating credit societies was highly fluid. The societies dissolved after each member had received their share of the cash. The societies were then re-started, often with the same organizer but with different members. Because the kampung dwellers' economic fortunes fluctuated so much, they felt able to contribute one year and not the next. For example, when Bud's trade was going well in the early 1970s she joined both Maryati's and Dini's rotating credit societies. In Maryati's she contributed Rp.5000 (100 litres of rice in 1973) a month whilst in Dini's she contributed Rp.1000 a week. When her turn came to draw within ten months, she obtained Rp.50,000 minus Maryati's administrative fee. From Dini's she obtained nearly Rp.10,000 within two and a half months.

When Bud's trade went badly she decided not to join any of the societies for fear she would not be able to pay the required amount each week or month. Other members of the community such as A'on joined rotating credit societies with colleagues at their place of work or with members from their home village who lived elsewhere. Kampung dwellers could, at the same time, join as many rotating credit societies in or outside the community as they wished. At any one time there were at least four or five societies operating within the neighbourhood.

Community Cooperation

Apart from the Islamic festivals of Lebaran and Idul Adha, only in times of natural crisis, sickness or death, did the entire neighbourhood mobilize. As in most societies, crisis brought out a sense of unity amongst kampung dwellers. At no time was cooperation so marked as at somebody's death. People were never left alone in times of dire need and when a person died neighbours helped wash, wrap and bury the body. When Bani's child died at birth, all the women in the neighbourhood filed past the dead body, offering money and condolences. A bucket of sand was put beside the dead child into which money was placed. Chairs were gathered from neighbouring houses and placed along the pathway in front of the home. Men from nearby sat talking deep into the night. Previously, I had rarely seen neighbours show much sympathy to Bani's family, which consisted of three young brothers, one of whom had a wife. Their father had left them to marry another woman and their mother had died. The youths made a living from becak driving, shoeshining and fresh iced-fruit sales. On occasion, neighbours said they were also thieves. They stole small items, like chickens, from other areas, not their own neighbourhood, so the kampung dwellers tolerated it. With the death of their first child, however, all was excused and kampung dwellers rallied to their support.

Although I was unable to keep a record of all the deaths in the neighbourhood during the decade, at least one adult and one child died each year. This meant that at least twice a year the entire neighbourhood pooled resources and sympathy to help overcome another family's grief. Because of tradition, the narrow pathways, limited space and time, people came in small numbers to the house of the bereaved as it suited them throughout the day and night. There was no formal ceremony where all members of the community gathered together at one place and time.

In addition to the spontaneous contributions of kampung neighbours, a more formalized rotating fund for funerals existed in the community for those willing to contribute. Each month a fee (Rp.200) was collected by the headman or his assistant for the dana kematian (burial fund). This fund helped pay for the white cloth in which the body was wrapped and the numerous religious ceremonies which had to be held to ensure the deceased safe passage to the next world.

In times of jubilation and festivity, neighbours helped to cook and provided extra space, mats or chairs and crockery. During circumcisions and marriages, twenty to thirty people would sit together with their legs neatly crossed on mats on the floor of a room often no larger than 10 or 15 square metres. Elaborate food–half moon shaped mounds of yellow rice, fried chicken, spicy vegetables, prawn crackers and numerous little multicoloured rice cakes wrapped in banana leaves—were served. Sometimes neighbouring women or relatives helped to prepare the food, but often it was bought or a cook was employed.

Marriage festivals brought the community together in the same haphazard spontaneous manner as funerals, except that the occasion was merry, with plenty of food. There were at least one or two marriages each year. Some were performed in style, over two days with many dishes of food and numerous changes of clothing for both the bride and bridegroom. Formal printed invitations were taken to every household in the neighbourhood. As with deaths, all neighbours did not go to the celebration at the same time. At their own time and choosing they put on their festive clothes and filed into the celebrants' home during the wedding day or night. They paid their respects, unobtrusively placing an envelope containing some money into the bride's mother's palm, and then sat down to taste the variety of food laid out in front of them. People met along the pathways heading to or from the celebration. The community was abuzz with comments about the wedding, how much it cost, whether the food was good, and whether the bride was already pregnant.

Towards the end of the decade, kampung dwellers were horrified to find newspaper instead of cash tucked inside the envelopes given to the bride's mother. This deception was viewed by all as a sign of moral decay. They claimed it had never occurred in the past. It was unclear how frequently this practice occurred but kampung dwellers believed that it was increasing. The pressures of the cash economy were too much for many people. They felt unable to pay for housing, food, clothing, schooling let alone giving presents to neighbours. They felt embarrassed if they did not make an offering and tried to cover up by making false contributions. The increased density of the community and the fact that many neighbours did not really know one another, increased the temptation to deceive. When Ibu Sum (Burhanuddin's wife) celebrated her daughter's wedding in 1981, she immediately opened the envelopes to make sure that they contained money. She also made a list of how much each person contributed.

For a relationship to continue, a balance of giving and receiving had to be maintained. Bud explained that people had traditionally kept an account of what they gave to their kampung neighbours on festive occasions (circumcisions, children's birthday parties, marriages) and in future expected to receive an equivalent amount in return. Some people even felt compelled to celebrate in order to retrieve all the contributions they had made to their neighbours over the years.

Cooperation and Competition

Social relationships in Ibu Imah's neighbourhood were neither purely cooperative nor purely individualistic. They could best be character-ized as ordered anarchy. There was little formal social organization yet individuals spontaneously related to and helped one another. At the lowest level, relationships between members of the same house-hold or family seemed loose. This related to the insecurity of ties between household members especially between husbands and wives, and to the high turnover of household membership. As if to compensate for the looseness of family and household ties, relation-ships between neighbours helped to cushion the kampung dwellers against the insecurities of daily life. Individual neighbours helped one another with work, housing, food and during crises like illness or death. Although neighbours were often related by ties of marriage or blood, close residential proximity rather than kinship seemed to be the main organizing principle. Apart from the rebuilding of the prayer house and the occasional festivities surrounding Lebaran, Idul Adha, marriages and deaths, community-wide cooperation, how-ever, was almost non-existent. The absence of community-wide cooperation may have been due to the instability of the society, pressures of daily survival, lack of shared values and leadership. It seemed the more effort kampung dwellers put into making their immediate environment more secure by developing personal ties, the less time and energy was left for joint activities on a broader basis.

Ironically the very insecurity which gave rise to social networks, also helped to undermine them. They emerged mainly because individuals lacked resources and needed to help one another in the struggle for daily survival. The networks were a defence against the harshness of urban life. At the same time, however, these networks were highly vulnerable and threatened by the very economic and social insecurity which had brought them into existence. Kampung dwellers were well aware that these ties were fragile and that a balance had to be maintained between giving and receiving. Such ties were reciprocal rather than redistributive. Ultimately each family had to support itself.

Although kampung dwellers placed a high value on social har-mony, in Ibu Imah's neighbourhood they were convinced that social ties were breaking down with the passage of time, penetration of wealth and rapidity of change. They argued that twenty years earlier, when the society was less populous and more egalitarian, there was more mutual assistance and concern for one's fellow man. Good neighbourliness made up for the lack of resources. The sudden and dramatic accumulation of wealth by some households meant that they tried to distance themselves from the rest to avoid dissipation of their wealth. There was a constant tension between the need to accumulate wealth for oneself and one's own family and the tradition of sharing and exchanging with neighbours and kinsfolk.

1. N. Sullivan ("Masters and Managers" pp. 152, 207a, 208) also found there was an average of two or more households (hearthholds) per house. In a survey in Jakarta, Noormohamed found that about half the households consisted of nuclear families while the remainder were extended: Noormohamed, S. "Alternative Approaches to Low-Income Housing: A Case Study of Jakarta", Ph.D Thesis, ANU, 1981, pp. 16–17.
2. Jay *Javanese Villagers* pp. 62, 96–97.
3. N. Sullivan found that 30 percent of her sampled households were headed by females: Sullivan "Masters and Managers" pp. 212–19, 228. See also Lewis "The Culture of Poverty" pp. 19–25; Lewis *Five Families*; Lomnitz *Networks and Marginality* pp. 93–94.
4. Although different types of communal living arrangements for urban migrants exist in most parts of the world, there is a paucity of information. Wilson and Mafeje, Mayer, and Reader refer to barrack-like accommodation amongst mine workers in South Africa: Wilson, M. and Mafeje, A. *Langa: A Study of Social Groups in an African Township*, (Cape Town, 1963) pp. 39, 47–55, 72–3; Mayer, P. *Townsmen or Tribesmen*, (Cape Town, 1961) pp. 79–80, 124–91, 209–10; Reader, D. R. *The Black Man's Portion. History, Demography and Living Conditions in the Native Locations of East London Cape Province*, (Cape Town, 1961) p. 124. The kongsi houses of single immigrant Chinese in Singapore are far more formally organized than pondok. See Tan Kim Swee "A Study of Kongsi Houses Housing Immigrant Men", (Singapore, 1963). The nearest thing to the Indonesian pondok are the chummeries of India described by Bulsara but these too are mainly for migrant labourers rather than self-employed petty traders: Bulsara, J. F. *Patterns of Social Life in Metropolitan Areas—with particular reference to Greater Bombay*, (Bombay, 1970) pp. 283–92. All of these lodging-houses mainly provided accommodation and none

precisely resembles the togetherness of the rooming-house-cum-enterprise of the Indonesian pondok [Jellinek "The Pondok System and Circular Migration" pp. 9–10, 15]. Forbes identified pondok amongst becak drivers in Ujung Pandang only they lacked the tightly knit social organization of Mus's pondok [Forbes D. "Development and the 'Informal' Sector: A Study of Pedlars and Trishaw Riders in Ujung Pandang, Indonesia", Ph.D Thesis, Monash University, 1979, pp. 230–32].

5. In the literature this phenomenon is known as circular migration. See, for example, Hugo "Population Mobility in West Java"; Jellinek "The Pondok System and Circular Migration" pp. 10–16.

6. In other parts of the city the writer found communal lodging-houses consisting of forty to fifty people. Although not in Kebun Kacang, there were also communal lodging-houses consisting of women who had left their husbands and children in the villages of central Java.

7. The community spirit found in Mus's pondok was similar to the type of cooperation described for Yogyakarta by J. Sullivan "Rukun Kampung and Kampung"; N. Sullivan "Masters and Managers"; Guinness *Harmony and Hierarchy*.

8. N. Sullivan ("Masters and Managers" pp. 234–42) paints a very similar picture of the daily interaction between small clusters of female neighbours. There was, however, much more non-monetary exchange and sharing of every aspect of life (i.e. shopping, food distribution, washing, ironing, childminding, massage, gossip) than in Kebun Kacang.

9. N. Sullivan ("Masters and Managers" pp. 227, 258) also suggests that residential proximity rather than kinship is a more important principle of organization in Yogyakarta. See also Jay (*Javanese Villagers* pp. 188–239) for East Java and Sunindyo ("Kampung Sawah" pp. 150, 173, 182, 233) for Jakarta. For similar findings in other Third World cities see Lomnitz *Networks and Marginality* pp. 133–39; Lloyd *Slums of Hope* p. 167; Roberts *Organizing Strangers*.

10. Sullivan "Back Alley Neighbourhood" pp. 13–4.

11. By contrast the few thieves seemed to be tolerated as long as their activities were carried on elsewhere. See also Guinness *Harmony and Hierarchy* pp. 93–5.

12. The Central Javanese men in Ibu Imah's neighbourhood seemed to observe these practices less faithfully. Although most of them claimed to be Islamic, they rarely set foot in the mushollah. Abangan and Kebatinan beliefs were widespread but people largely kept these to themselves. See Geertz (*The Religion of Java* pp. 11–112, 309–34) for the nature of these beliefs and rituals.

13. In Javanese abangan means "red". It is thus the same as orang merah in Indonesian, implying that one is not a devout Muslim (who in Javanese is called putihan, a "white" one).

14. For the widespread nature of arisan elsewhere in Indonesia see Geertz, C. "The Rotating Credit Association: A 'Middle Rung' in Development", *Economic Development and Cultural Change*, Vol. 10, No. 3:

1962: 241–63; Dewey, A. *Peasant Marketing in Java*, (New York, 1962) p. 100; Jay *Javanese Villagers* pp. 203, 416–19; N. Sullivan "Masters and Managers" pp. 314–5; Guinness *Harmony and Hierarchy* pp. 147–53, 161–4; Forbes "Development and the 'Informal' Sector" pp. 203–6.

3

The Transience of Income Earning Activities

The fluidity of kampung dwellers' social ties corresponded with the transience of their income-earning activities. The literature about the urban poor has emphasized their lack of material possessions and given scant attention to the variability of their incomes. This chapter describes and analyses the rapid transformation in ways of making a living at the centre of the city between 1971 and 1981. Within less than twenty years kampung dwellers experienced first a boom and then decline in many of their small-scale income-earning activities, most notably becak driving, cottage industry, petty trade, construction work and small-scale kampung services. When these small-scale jobs became less viable, in the late 1970s, kampung dwellers found it difficult to get into the less transient formal sector occupations in offices and factories.

Kebun Kacang was typical of most Third World urban communities in that most people earned an income from the small-scale sector. This did not necessarily mean that they earned low incomes. In the early to mid-1970s, for example, those in petty trade were prospering beyond their wildest dreams. They could afford to rebuild their houses and furnish them with modern consumer durables such as television sets and lounge suites. By the end of the decade, however, they could earn barely enough to feed themselves and many of their possessions had been sold, leaving their houses bare. The fundamental problem of their lives was not so much poverty as the instability of their incomes. This was not just a matter of the normal rise and fall of small enterprises due to personal capacities and force of circumstance. The rise and fall of individual enterprises such as Agus' becak driving, Mus's ice-cream enterprise and Bud's cooked-food trade was part of a more general rise and fall of those income-earning activities in response to changing economic conditions.

It is impossible to obtain an accurate estimate of the size of the small-scale sector in Jakarta. It has been estimated that from 45 percent to 65 percent of the city's work force operated within this sector.[1] In 1971, however, Jakarta's total work force estimate of 1.4 million was an extremely low participation rate for a population of 4.5 million.[2] Many of the people working in small-scale occupations were not included in the official labour force estimate. The Census had difficulty identifying all those working from their homes or on the streets. Nevertheless, most scholars agree that about half of Jakarta's work force was engaged in small-scale activities.[3] This was true not only for Jakarta but for other cities of Indonesia and the Third World.[4]

In Ibu Imah's neighbourhood at the end of 1970s, small-scale income-earning activities were much more important than in Jakarta as a whole.[5] In contrast to the city-wide average of about half, in Imah's neighbourhood approximately three-quarters of the bread-winners were engaged part- or full-time in small-scale income-earning activities.[6]

Becak Driving

In Kebun Kacang in 1972 only 4 becak (trishaw) drivers remained in my neighbourhood of 77 households. Although statistics were un-available, it was clear that this had once been a very important occupation. From the 1950s virtually every fit young male in the neighbourhood had tried becak driving at some stage during his working life. By 1972, however, some were too old or sick to drive or felt harassed by government and had turned to other occupations such as construction work or petty trade.

Becak driving better than any other occupation illustrates the transient nature of small-scale income-earning activities at the city centre. It is therefore important to trace the rise and fall of this occupation, even though this involves turning for evidence on the lives of becak drivers to other parts of Jakarta rather than focusing solely upon those four who remained in Kebun Kacang.

The becak was introduced to Jakarta from Singapore or Hong Kong in the 1930s, but there were only 100 of these vehicles in the city prior to the war.[7] It became a popular vehicle of transport during the Japanese occupation, gradually replacing the delman (horse-drawn cart).[8] The latter was regarded as a nuisance and health hazard, dirtying the streets with manure and requiring space and grass on which the horses could graze. By the mid- to late 1950s there were 25,000 to 30,000 becaks operating in the city.[9] While no accurate figures are available, by the early 1970s, there were five times this number (100,000 to 150,000) operating in the city and ten times the number of drivers (250,000 to 350,000).[10] By 1980, however, the number of becaks had dropped to an estimated 55,000.[11]

In the 1950s and 1960s, becak driving was one of the easiest occupations to enter for a young man just arrived in the city. No overhead capital, equipment or skills were required. The technique could be learned in half an hour. The main problem was to find a becak that was temporarily not in use. Usually a village friend or relative who regularly drove a becak allowed the newcomer to practise while he rested. Alternatively, when a regular driver returned to his village he allowed a friend to drive his vehicle until he returned. The newcomer would be introduced to the Tauke (boss-usually Chinese) who owned and hired out becaks and eventually he would obtain the regular use of a vehicle.

Most becak drivers had previously worked as farm labourers. Some had performed urban and rural labouring jobs before turning to becak driving.[12] Few of their fathers had driven becaks, as the occupation was of recent origin. Although strenuous, the attractions of becak driving were its flexible and more lucrative nature compared to casual day labouring. In 1975, Soedarno estimated that becak drivers could earn five times as much as a village labourer.[13] Becak drivers pedalled only for as long as they pleased and then handed over their vehicle to another driver. They could not be forced to drive by the owner of the vehicle. All the becak owner could do was require them to cover their daily rental of Rp.200 (2 litres of rice) in 1975/76. This rental could be paid up to three days late. If it was not paid after a certain period the becak owner could refuse to lease his vehicle.

Most importantly, becak driving allowed a great amount of flexibility, enabling men to work as labourers or farmers in the village as well as becak drivers in the city.[14] During the planting or harvest season most becak drivers returned to their home villages (many of which were located along the northern coast of central Java) where much work was to be done either on their own fields or as paid labourers working the fields of others. When the work was completed and there was no income-earning activity in the village, they returned to Jakarta to pedal becaks again. Droughts, floods or insect pests in the village which damaged crops, stopped agricultural work or resulted in a poor harvest encouraged more becak driving in the city. So the becak drivers moved to and fro according to where the income-earning opportunities were best. As different villagers planted or harvested their crops at different times, the becaks in Jakarta were kept in operation by different sets of drivers.

Although the primary reason for becak drivers operating in the city was the lack of income-earning opportunities in the village, during the 1950s and 1960s there was a great need for their transport services in Jakarta. The city's very limited public transport system could not satisfy the needs of its rapidly growing population. Trams were taken out of operation in the 1950s. The limited number of private vehicles and 300 buses could not cope with the rising demand and frequently fell into disrepair.[15] Old cars from the 1930s were cannibalized and converted to small buses (*opelet*) to play a role in public transport but could not satisfy the rising demand. Lack of spare parts and fuel, especially between 1957 and 1967, made it difficult to keep them on the streets. The locally produced and manually driven becaks had no such problems. They filled the transport vacuum and provided transport for all classes of the city.

The rich used becak drivers to chaperon their children to and from school. Traders used becaks to transport their raw ingredients to and from the market. Housewives used becaks to ferry them to and from the market each day. Office workers used becaks to take them to work. Beds, tables and all types of furniture were taken across the city by these vehicles. Even the ill were carted to and from hospital by them. Often it was the only type of vehicle apart from a bicycle or motorcycle which could enter the narrow pathways of the kampung. Unlike motorized vehicles, becaks were not so handicapped by the ill repair of the roads. They were more readily manoeuvred over or around potholes than a rapidly moving truck or car.

Becak drivers recalled the ease with which they had pedalled around the city in the 1950s and 1960s. They conveyed passengers from Kebayoran Baru in the south to Tanah Abang in the west or from there to Senen in the east. No area was beyond their reach. They were referred to as the "kings of the street".

Becak drivers suggest that becak driving was more organized between the 1940s and 1960s. Some recalled wearing uniforms of long white socks and white shorts. Others remembered having to obtain licences and being tested on road rules. As with other small-scale occupations there was a sliding price scale for the rich and the poor but prices were set for certain distances and there was a code of ethics amongst drivers ensuring that one did not undercut another.[16]

In the city most becak drivers lived in large communal lodging-houses called *pondok*. At least two such lodging-houses, each housing up to 50 drivers, existed near my neighbourhood in Kebun Kacang up to the early 1970s, before the government banned becaks in the central-city area. Although the becak lodging-house near Kebun Kacang no longer existed or were moved to the edges of Jakarta by the mid-1970s, other large clusters of becak drivers remained on the north, south, east and west of the city. A number of studies found over twenty becak drivers living together in communal lodging-houses.[17] The drivers came from the same villages on the north coast of west or central Java and hired their becaks from the same boss. Often food and washing facilities were also provided. In the early days some becak drivers claimed their *taukes* took a paternalistic interest in their welfare, providing loans when they were ill and gifts of clothing and money at Lebaran. They also helped with the repair of vehicles.

As the government became increasingly hostile towards becak drivers during the 1970s, the earlier paternalism gave way to a more commercial relationship. If a becak driver failed to pay his rent for a becak the vehicle was confiscated and given to another driver. Becak ownership increasingly passed out of the hands of the Chinese and into the hands of the newly emerging Indonesian middle class, largely consisting of police, military men, bureaucrats and school-teachers.[18]

No becak driver would have stayed in the occupation if another equally or more productive job had been available. Becak driving was viewed as a lowly, difficult and dead-end job. By the 1970s, many government officials viewed becak drivers as criminals rather than "kings of the street". The four becak drivers who remained in Kebun Kacang continued to pedal because they felt they had no option. Unlike most becak drivers they were permanent residents of Jakarta, not circular migrants who could retreat to the village and try to eke out a livelihood there. They lacked the skills for other jobs in construction or trade. By the mid- to late 1970s these jobs were also experiencing difficulties at the city centre. So they continued to drive becaks despite the ever-growing threat to their livelihood.

Although hostility towards the becak was already evident in the 1960s with the introduction of *bemos*, motorized becaks, the main impetus to eliminate the becak began after 1970 when the *helicaks*, another form of motorized becak, were introduced. Becaks were viewed as an embarrassment and anachronism. They symbolized Indonesia's backwardness. They were blamed for cluttering up the streets and causing traffic jams. Becaks moved at only 15 kilometres an hour, whereas other motorized vehicles moved at two or three times that pace. Many becak drivers did not understand road rules and caused traffic accidents. Many had simply bought their licences from other drivers or becak owners and thus had not passed any road tests. Many remained unregistered.[19]

Between 1970 and 1972 the city government issued a number of decrees which aimed to restrict the operation of becaks in the city. In 1970 the production of new becaks was forbidden. New licences for becak driving were not to be issued and all existing drivers had to have a licence.[20] Becak drivers were forbidden to operate in certain parts of the central city area. Their hours of operation on the main roads of Jakarta were restricted to after 10 pm and before 6 am. If a vehicle was caught, fines of Rp.15,000 (366 litres of rice) had to be paid or it was confiscated.[21] Becaks were divided into those which could operate in the night and those which could operate during the day in order to restrict the numbers using the roads at any one time. In addition, becaks in the north of Jakarta could not cross over to the centre or south of Jakarta, where only becaks of a specific colour were allowed to operate.

These policies plus the influx of many motorized vehicles caused the numbers and incomes of becak drivers to decline between 1970 and 1977.[22] The dramatic increase in the number of motorized vehicles meant that many people who had formerly used the becaks in the 1950s and 1960s now went by car. Meanwhile the kampung poor who would have liked to use the becak still found it more economical to walk or go by bus. Kampung dwellers who could afford to pay for becaks often found these vehicles were not allowed to operate where they wanted to go.

The stated intention of the municipal government was to assist becak drivers to switch to motorized vehicles. About 10,000 motorized minicars (consisting of *bajajs*, *helicaks*, minicars and superhelicaks) were supposed to replace the 150,000 becaks by 1980.[23] These new vehicles were noisy and expensive for the customer and increased the driver's overhead costs for petrol, maintenance and rent. Nevertheless, most becak drivers would have loved to become drivers of such vehicles had they had the opportunity. The government retraining program for becak drivers was not, however, well-conceived. For a start, many drivers were illiterate and, because they could not read the newspapers, were not aware that such a program was available. Even if they were informed and knew where to apply, numerous practical problems stood in their way. Most had families to support and could not afford to stop work long enough to be re-trained as minicar drivers. Few had the Rp.35,000 (280 litres of rice in 1978) needed to pay for the course. They were lucky to have Rp.1000 feed their wives and children each day. If they attended the course for several weeks, who would support their families? How would they pay for the minicar rental or petrol charges? They felt the government had failed to provide a viable alternative to their becak driving.

Despite intense government hostility and competition from

motorized transport, new becak drivers continued to make their way to the city. This was especially true between 1977 and 1981, when Cokropranolo was Governor and relaxed policies towards becak drivers. He realized that becak drivers were having difficulty finding alternative forms of employment and advised a gentler approach towards them. This resulted in an influx of becak drivers to the city centre and relatively good incomes for a brief period of time.[24] The Jakarta middle class which drove its own vehicles was hostile to these developments and looked back to Governor Sadikin's period (1966–77) as a time of disciplined, clean and organized government. Poor kampung dwellers, by contrast, applauded Governor Cokropranolo's more humane approach in giving them more time and space to seek out a livelihood.

Between 1970 and 1977 the price of becaks fell as many becak owners tried to get out of the business, enabling some of the becak drivers who remained to purchase their own vehicles. Unlike the drivers, the former vehicle owners had the information and foresight to see that the days of becak driving were numbered. Astutely, they sold their vehicles cheaply to willing buyers. The kampung dwellers became the proud owners of becaks at just the wrong time. The new Governor of Jakarta, General Suprapto, decreed that becaks would be eliminated from the city by 1985. A ruthless program of clearing them from all parts of the city, not just central Jakarta, was carried out. Many drivers lost their vehicles and became impoverished. Some drivers pedalled their vehicles back to their villages to see if they could gain a living from becak driving there. It was reported that Bogor had suddenly become cluttered with becaks.[25] Most of the drivers who remained in Jakarta progressively moved to the city's periphery. Some new drivers tried to operate at the city centre for a while without realizing what the government would do to them. After they suffered from an anti-becak campaign they also moved to the periphery, another occupation or back to the village.

It is difficult to know what happened to the many becak drivers who lost their jobs. Most presumably moved into other occupations such as construction, labouring or petty trade. But these sectors of employment were already saturated by the mid-1970s. Although it is impossible to prove, the destruction of one small-scale labour-intensive sector of employment such as becak driving seemed to have repercussions throughout the city on many other small-scale labour-intensive activities such as petty trade. Dorodjatun argued that the elimination of 200,000 becak drivers from Jakarta would harm the livelihood of the 400,000 petty traders, many of whom relied on becak drivers as customers.[26]

The four becak drivers who remained in Ibu Imah's neighbour-

hood in the 1970s clustered near a small illegal market on the road
that ran past the community. Every day and often deep into the night
they could be found there sitting in their becaks waiting for customers. Most had regular kampung clients who wanted their children
taken to school or themselves taken to the market, Jalan Thamrin or
the polyclinic. In between serving these customers they slept in their
becaks, sat at the nearby stalls drinking and smoking or talked to
traders or other becak drivers. A regular group of becak drivers met
at this location every day and each knew the other by name. If I was
seeking Bani or Agus, two drivers from my neighbourhood, the other
traders or becak drivers could tell me where they were or get
messages to them.

Occasionally the becak drivers ventured on to the main road if they
desperately needed more income. The main roads and centres of high
population density were most lucrative. The driver, however, had to
be forever on the look-out for Government anti-becak raids. In the
late 1970s, a few of the becak drivers, like Agus, had been able, after
20 years, to buy their own vehicles. Agus had never dreamed that he
would one day own his own vehicle. Nevertheless, in 1979 he and his
wife managed, with much difficulty, to amass the necessary capital.
His elation at owning a becak and not having to pay daily rent was
not to last. In 1982 he was caught in an anti-becak raid and his vehicle
was confiscated.

Until this time Agus had been very careful to avoid the Jakarta
clearance team. After he had earned sufficient money to cover the
daily food needed by his family, he never ventured out to the streets.
He was caught by the Jakarta clearance team when he was not even
driving or seeking passengers but just returning home after having his
vehicle repaired. Had he sufficient money to pay the bribe of
Rp.15,000 (60 litres of rice) when he was caught he would have
avoided his vehicle being confiscated. Once impounded he needed
even more money to get the vehicle out. In the earlier days the
owners of becaks had helped the drivers retrieve the vehicles once
they were impounded, but now Agus was operating on his own.
Bitterly he realized that his one treasured possession, his one means
of survival in this all too difficult world, had been crushed.

Agus knew of only three ways of making a livelihood—farming,
charcoal selling and becak driving. He was illiterate, frightened, aged
and poor. During the war all his father's ducks and property in
Parung were lost and as an orphan, Agus had made his way to
Jakarta. There he found employment with a Chinese trader, distributing charcoal door to door. In 1957 he was introduced to becak
driving and continued in this occupation till his becak was confiscated
in 1982.

During the years that Agus was becak driving, his family experienced some minor improvements. In the early sixties they managed to buy the 21 square metre house they rented from Gani. Agus' wife, Samilah, claimed this was largely due to her own efforts at dressmaking and repairs rather than Agus' becak driving. Agus' daily income of between Rp.1000 and Rp.2000 (6–12 litres of rice in 1979) was barely enough to feed the family whilst Samilah earned the extra they needed to buy their house and educate their eight children.

Agus felt Samilah was wasting money and effort educating their children. He could not envisage them getting better work than himself. Having driven a becak for over 20 years he assumed there were few other ways, apart from labouring, of earning an income. Agus was sullen, silent and difficult to talk to. He had limited experience of the world and expected little from it. His greatest prize had been to buy his own becak after having had to hire one for 20 years. After its confiscation, he was a broken man. His hopes were dashed. His fatalistic view of the world was reconfirmed. While Samilah clung onto the hope of improving her children's lot, Agus felt only despair.

Cottage Industry

As cottage industries typically operate within the home they were particularly difficult to identify and enumerate. Often only one or two family members were involved in the enterprise and they may have had other income-earning activities as well. In Jakarta, the frequent combination of petty production with petty trade meant that these two income-earning activities were hard to separate, especially in the case of cooked food sellers. Many of those employed in cottage industry were circular migrants, living only temporarily and often illegally in the city whilst leaving their families in the countryside.

During the mid-1950s, Heeren's urbanization survey of 11,700 household heads in Jakarta hinted at a boom in cottage industry.[27] Almost half of the informants were employed in what were defined as "industry", but this also included transport workers other than becak drivers.[28] Most of these "industrial" workers were employed in small-scale enterprises.[29] According to the survey, "Jakarta is not a typically industrial town, though in some kampungs nearly everybody works in industry".[30] It described the road between Menteng and Kebayoran as "completely filled up with small industries and repair workshops".[31] No other information on cottage industry seems to be available for Jakarta during the Old Order, but for the nation as a whole small-scale industry seemed to boom in the late 1950s to early 1960s.[32]

Surveys carried out in Jakarta in the early to mid-1970s suggested that cottage industries were not a major employer of labour. From official statistics, it has been estimated that in 1967 only 32,000 people (7 percent of Jakarta's informal sector work force) were employed in small-scale production. Between 1961 and 1971 the numbers employed in manufacturing declined from 147,000 to 110,000, though it was not clear whether this decline involved both large and small-scale enterprises.[33] In 1975, a large ILO informal sector survey found that only 6 percent of its enterprises were involved in petty production.[34] A Jakarta government survey found that of the 1983 small industries registered in 1974 only 21.02 percent or 417 survived in 1979.[35] But other small enterprises which were not registered in the survey may have come into existence during this time.

It is equally hard to identify trends for cottage industry in Kebun Kacang between the late 1960s and 1970s. Kampung dwellers' increased capacity to consume seemed to have given a stimulus to kerosene stove, lamp, mattress, mat, furniture, leather bag and kitchen utensil enterprises. At the same time, however, there was evidence within and beyond Ibu Imah's neighbourhood of a number of workshops having gone out of existence by the early 1970s, most notably car repairs, becak making and radio repairs.[36] They had suffered from imports and increased competition from modern large-scale manufacturing.[37]

Throughout the late 1950s and 1960s a number of households had a lucrative business repairing old cars. Tools still hung inside their houses and some car repair workshops still remained on the road that ran west of the community. The mechanics, however, complained that their work had declined dramatically with the import of many new cars since 1967. A similar story was reported by those who had worked in becak making and repairs. It was estimated that up to 75,000 people in Jakarta as a whole were employed in this activity in the late 1960s, but after the ban on becak production this activity declined.[38]

Some of the people who had been forced out of car repairs, becak making and driving may have moved into battery recycling, which thrived in Ibu Minah's neighbourhood between 1968 and 1978. By the mid-1970s at least 90 men were involved in this activity. Lukman, who introduced battery recycling to the area, had originally been a becak driver. In 1968 while delivering batteries by becak to a place where they were recycled, he noticed it was profitable and set about learning how to recycle batteries himself. Between 1970 and 1978 he ran a thriving business and recruited more and more people to help him. Some of his assistants broke away to set up enterprises of their own. Each recycler sought his own secondhand batteries in different parts of the town and brought them back to the kampung for dismantling. The lead plates were extracted and cleaned and the battery containers repaired if they were still in good condition. The enterprise expanded at such a rate that by the mid-1970s Kebun Kacang was recognized as one of the major centres of battery recycling throughout Indonesia. Truckloads of batteries were sent there from as far afield as Surabaya in east Java and Palembang in south Sumatra.

By 1978 this enterprise was encountering difficulties. Groups of battery recyclers had hived-off and there was competition from many other battery recyclers elsewhere in Jakarta. Large-scale factories had been established by successful Chinese entrepreneurs who produced better quality mass-produced batteries at a competitive price with a three-year warranty. The emerging middle class saw no reason to buy secondhand car batteries when they could get new ones for a similar price. The shortage of lead which had made its retrieval from old car batteries a very lucrative business changed after 1978 when there were large imports of lead from Singapore. By 1980, electricity had reached an estimated 50 percent of Jakarta's urban households so that fewer and fewer batteries were needed to power television sets.[39]

In Ibu Imah's neighbourhood, radio repairs experienced a similar obsolescence. In the 1960s and early 1970s Bud's husband, Santo, had been able to make a livelihood from repairing radios. He was the only one in the community who knew the trade. Kampung dwellers from far and near brought their radios to his home for repairs. Previously he had worked in the bicycle and becak repair business along Jalan Thamrin and in the repair workshops along Jalan Kebun Kacang XI. From the early 1970s he started to complain that competition from cheap imported Japanese transistor radios was undermining his business. Kampung dwellers were no longer using old radios which frequently fell into disrepair but buying new radios from shops which had a warranty and could be readily, cheaply and more reliably repaired at shops.

By the time I came to Ibu Imah's neighbourhood, 4 cottage enterprises provided employment for about 10 percent of the work force. The most common small-scale enterprises were those preparing food. They were often impossible to distinguish from petty trade. Before Mus set up her ice-cream making enterprises in 1968, there were few others in the area. One communal lodging-house in Kebun Kacang and another in Mangga Besar were known for the particular ice-creams they produced. High standards had to be maintained. The ice-creams were made of wine, eggs, coconut milk and lots of fresh fruit and cane-sugar. If an ice-cream maker did not adhere to the correct recipe he was asked to leave to avoid damage to the firm's reputation. Each ice-cream enterprise had specially coloured carrier containers so that it was readily identified. The ice-cream sellers were patronized by all classes of society but mainly the better off. Although set prices were informally recognized, there was a sliding price scale for the rich and the poor.

One ice-cream seller followed another into the city until some communal lodging-houses consisted of up to 40 or 50 people. One villager taught another how to make and sell ice-cream and so the skill was passed on from person to person. As with becak driving, the equipment was rented from the Chinese boss (*Tauke*) who also provided the raw ingredients, shelter and other basic amenities they needed. By the late 1960s some kampung dwellers began to copy the Chinese and set up their own lodging-houses.

Mus observed the operation of the Chinese lodging-house enterprise and decided to set one up of her own. She encouraged male relatives who formerly lived and worked with the Chinese to move to her lodging-house in Ibu Imah's neighbourhood. Between 1975 and 1978 when Mus's enterprise was at its peak, there were up to ten ice-cream sellers as well as other traders staying there.[40]

Each of the ice-cream sellers made and sold their own ice-cream. Although they relied on Mus for accommodation, equipment and raw materials, they were each self-employed. Apart from accommodation which was free, they paid Mus for whatever they received, and worked for as long as they pleased. They were all circular migrants with their home base in Klaten, Central Java, and viewed their stay in the city as a means of improving their income. Every three to four months, when they had earned enough to feed their families for a couple of months, they returned to their village homes. During these times, another relative could occupy their place in Mus's pondok and use their trade equipment. As with becaks, by reutilizing scarce resources—urban living space, personal contacts and trade equipment—two people instead of one could earn a livelihood in the city.

Mus prepared the coconuts, sago, avocados, chocolate, powdered milk, sugar, salt and ice for the ice-cream sellers. She bought some of these ingredients in bulk from the market in the evening or at 4 or 5 am. Her husband helped carry the enormous blocks of ice into her home. Between 6 and 7 am the ice-cream sellers, who slept side-by-side on the hard wooden floor of Mus's attic, clambered down the steep rickety steps, washed and started to prepare their ice-cream. For two to three hours they twisted and turned pails of coconut milk and sugar in larger round metal containers of salt and ice. Each ice-cream seller added his own special flavour of fruit, chocolate or vanilla. When the mixture had set, they washed, changed their clothes, ate their breakfast for which they each paid Mus Rp.100

(1 litre of ice in 1976). Then each man helped the other lift their heavy pails of ice-cream surrounded by ice and salt into brightly painted push-carts. One by one the ice-cream sellers pushed their carts through Mus's narrow doorway and out into the equally narrow kampung path. In the kampung they were forced to sell small serves at low prices. They preferred to push their carts across Jalan Thamrin into the richer suburb of Menteng, where they could sell larger quantities at a higher price to the middle class. Most followed set routes, stopping in front of schools or near parks and fair grounds where children patronized their wares. The sellers usually returned in the evening and only then paid Mus for the materials, meals and equipment she provided. In 1976 these payments amounted to approximately Rp.1000 (10 litres of rice) though varied depending upon the quantity and quality of the ingredients each trader used. They made a daily average profit of Rp.500 to Rp.1500 but this, too, varied according to each trader's luck and skill. One trader earned a daily average of Rp.2000 to Rp.3000 because of his special avocado and chocolate flavoured ice-cream and regular middle-class customers. Seasonal variations also had an impact on ice-cream sales. There were few customers during the monsoons rains and most of the ice-cream sellers returned to the village to plant their crops. A big demand for ice-cream during the dry or festive season meant that all the ice-cream sellers returned to the city again.

The more ice-cream Mus's traders sold the more ice-cream cones they demanded from Burhanuddin's cone-making enterprise which stood five doors away from Mus's lodging house. Unlike Mus's self-employed lodgers, Burhanuddin employed four to eight workers to make ice-cream cones. From 7 am till 10 pm they sweated over hot stoves in Burhanuddin's kitchen. The work was so tiring they could only last two weeks. Then they returned to their village near Bogor and village neighbours came to take their place. They were paid according to the number of cones they produced. In 1979 they could earn from Rp.500 to Rp.1000 (3–6 litres of rice) per day in addition to board and food. Because of their hard work and dependent status, they were hardly ever seen on the pathways of the kampung. It took me some years to realize that Burhanuddin had a cottage industry in his kitchen.

Between 1978 and 1980, the ice-cream sellers began increasingly to complain about competition from mass production, rising prices, a lack of clean water and trading space. Mass-produced ice-creams had become readily available from refrigerators in small stalls and shops throughout the city. This also had negative repercussions for Burhanuddin's ice cone sales. Only four to five years earlier there had been a substantial price difference between the hand made ice-creams and

mass-produced ones. The petty producers sold each serve for between Rp.15 and Rp.25 while the mass-produced ones sold for
between Rp.100 and Rp.200 (1.5 to 3 litres). This difference was
whittled away as petty producers were forced to raise their prices to
between Rp.75 and Rp.150 due to increasing overheads, while the
large firms, due to their economy of scale, were able to maintain their
original prices. The ice-cream sellers complained about the rapidly
rising prices of their raw materials in the later half of the 1970s, and
contrasted it to the remarkable price stability of the four years
between 1969 and 1972. In addition, they were faced with the
growing difficulties of obtaining clean water and trading space. With
the growth in the number of cars along Jalan Thamrin they found it
increasingly difficult crossing that road to get into the lucrative
suburb of Menteng.

The influx of more petty producers into the market caused the
quality of hand made ice-creams to decline and this was reinforced by
hostile advertising and government policies. Petty producers themselves admitted that instead of using fresh fruit, cane sugar and
coconut milk they used artificial flavouring, synthetic sweeteners and
other thickening agents. Their customers were not deceived and
realized that for a little extra they could buy the numerous varieties
of nicely packaged and more prestigious mass-produced ice-creams.
Widespread advertising in favour of these new products and government propaganda advising against the consumption of the hand made
varieties, for health reasons, further undermined their position. The
ice-cream traders found themselves banned from where they had
previously made a thriving business, in the parks, fair grounds, schools
and bus-stations of central Jakarta. Instead of push-carts there were
now refrigerators and kiosks selling international brands.

Cap making, unlike food and drink preparation, seemed less subject
to competition from large local or foreign firms or other small-scale
enterprises. The costly sewing machines, greater skills involved in
sewing the caps and need for contacts in the modern sector prevented
other cottage industries from flooding the market. Large-scale firms
could still not made caps of as good quality or as cheaply as Komar or
Ateng. Unlike the larger firms, Komar and Ateng operated with a
flexible, skilled labour force, in a limited space with low overheads.
Between 1972 and 1981, they were able to link themselves into the
expanding modern economy. The growing middle class—the motor-
cyclists, bureaucrats, schoolchildren, athletics clubs and youth groups—
were all potential customers.

Virtually penniless, Ateng had arrived in Kebun Kacang in 1972
from a village near Bandung. He carried cloth caps by bus from
Bandung and tried to sell them along Jalan Thamrin. In 1973 he

rented a 4 square metre cubicle in Kebun Kacang. He borrowed two sewing machines from a relative and started producing caps. Within one year he had bought the sewing machines and added two more to his enterprise. Together with his workers, he lived austerely. From 7 am in the morning to 11 at night, while his workers sewed, Ateng cut the material for the caps and trimmed, checked and packed the finished ones. Late at night the sewing machines and materials were pushed aside to allow for sleeping space. One or two workers slept on tables while others slept below them on the floor, amongst the caps and materials. The room was cramped and conditions of work extremely difficult.

By the mid-1970s, Ateng's enterprise provided income for at least 20 other people in the neighbourhood. They cooked food, washed clothes, provided accommodation and washing facilities for Ateng's workers. Eight to ten young men from villages near Bandung sold Ateng's caps along the major highways of Jakarta and they too rented units and required food and amenities from Ibu Imah's neighbourhood.

Ateng and his employees were not permanent residents of Jakarta. Every two to three months the cap sewers and sellers returned to their village, for they had earned enough money and could no longer endure the conditions in Ateng's enterprise. Ateng also returned to the village to recruit more cap sewers to replace them. During the first few years he had difficulty recruiting young men to work under such conditions. The demand for caps seemed to be highly seasonal and there were other cap enterprises in Bandung and Jakarta where conditions were not so bad. Between 1977 and 1978 Ateng even tried to transfer his enterprise to the village where there was a constant labour supply, but encountered difficulties with marketing and the supply of raw materials. With numerous changes of fortune, Ateng was eventually able to obtain regular workers who took it in turns working in the city and recuperating in the countryside.

Ateng was one of the few entrepreneurs in Kebun Kacang who adapted his mode of operation to the expanding modern economy and bureaucracy and so survived and even thrived into the 1980s. Unlike most other small entrepreneurs in Kebun Kacang, Ateng was able to overcome the constant harassment by police by transferring his sale of caps from street-side pedlars to direct sales to shops and government offices which required caps for uniforms. He received credit from the Chinese shopkeepers in Tanah Abang and Kebayoran market who gave him bulk orders. He obtained the cloth for the caps on credit from a regular Chinese textile merchant who lived nearby. If in the beginning the demand for his caps had been highly variable, as time went by he often had difficulty satisfying the demand. Bulk orders for his caps came from as far away as Palembang.

Ateng's brother-in-law Komar had set up a similar enterprise producing caps a few doors away. He used 4 sewers and occasionally unpaid family members, and in the 1970s had utilized the services of Ateng's sellers to distribute his caps along the major highways. In the 1980s when Ateng could not satisfy the bulk orders for caps from shops and government department, Komar helped to fill those orders.

Petty Trade

The movement of kampung dwellers into trade was already evident during the Japanese occupation and the Revolution. The difficulty of doing agricultural work and the lack of imported goods meant that more small-scale local production and sale took place. As the larger Dutch and Chinese retailing outlets were most harmed by the Japanese occupation, indigenous petty producers and sellers started to take their place. Most petty traders claimed they originally learned their skill from the Chinese. Like the ice-cream makers and sellers, the noodle soup and *bakso* sellers learned their recipes from the Chinese in the 1940s and 1950s. Either through direct contact with the Chinese or via a village relative they came to live in communal lodging-houses in Jakarta where a particular product was produced and sold. This trend was reinforced after 1957 when the larger, mainly Dutch-owned shops and firms were closed down and the Dutch were forced to leave. The growing demand for goods and services from a rapidly expanding urban population and the lack of industrial jobs to turn to meant that more and more people entered these occupations.[41]

In Jakarta, the number of petty traders increased rapidly from the late 1950s, reaching a peak in the central city area in the late 1960s to mid-1970s. Estimates for the total number of petty traders in Jakarta have varied greatly. Some have counted only 17,500 petty traders[42] while others have suggested a figure of 500,000.[43] Most, however, agreed that there were between 100,000[44] and 400,000[45] petty traders in the city. The ILO informal sector survey found that 65 percent of the surveyed small-scale enterprises were involved in petty trade.[46] Cooked-food selling was the most common, accounting for three-quarters of all trade enterprises.[47]

In Ibu Imah's neighbourhood, by 1970 petty trade was by far the most important means of earning a livelihood. Out of 200 breadwinners, 33 percent were employed part- or full-time in petty trade, selling their wares to people outside the kampung. Another 11 percent who are treated under kampung services sold goods from household stalls within the neighbourhood. An official estimate for Kebun Kacang, after petty trade had past its peak, suggested that 50 percent of the work force was employed in petty trade.[48]

Most of the petty traders in Imah's neighbourhood related the boom in their trade to the multi-storey construction taking place all around them. Pedlars gathered around each building site ready to provide the drinks, snacks, rice, cigarettes and ices needed by tired and hungry construction workers who were often in the city without their families. With the expansion of office space came more office workers, police, guards and military men to patronize the traders' wares.

Kampung dwellers employed in menial or unskilled office jobs, construction, becak driving or domestic work, battled to amass enough capital to move into petty trade. Trade rather than these occupations was viewed as the best way to improve one's lot. But by the late 1970s, the reverse process was taking place, as petty traders battled to get out of their insecure street-side occupations and back into more secure office or domestic jobs.

Like the rest of Jakarta, Ibu Imah's neighbourhood had a great variety of traders. Most were cooked-food sellers who pushed mobile carts through kampungs and along main roads into the richer sub-urbs. Some parked their carts in one particular location throughout the day or night, whilst others continually pushed them or carried their wares from place to place. Usually the smaller the quantity of goods sold, the more mobile the trader. Men with fresh fruit or vegetables carried them from door to door in baskets suspended from poles over their shoulders. Women carried cakes in bamboo trays balanced on their heads or spicey vegetable snacks wrapped in cloth slung over their hips and shoulders. The largest traders operated fixed stalls selling more durable items such as rice, dried salted fish, soap, clothing and mosquito coils etc. along the main road running past the community.

By observing Bud between 1967 and 1980, we see the evolution of her enterprise from a small mobile part-time activity dealing in rice cakes cooked and sold by only one person to a large semi-mobile stall employing up to five people and selling an assorted variety of foods. By 1973, Bud's stall was bigger than most but her experience of sudden prosperity followed by sudden decline was typical of many traders in the city. The rise and fall of her enterprise well demon-strates the transience of petty trade. In a period of only ten years (1968–1978), she went from being one of the most successful cooked-food sellers in Ibu Imah's neighbourhood to bankruptcy.

In 1967, Bud had progressed from hawking rice cakes around building sites along Jalan Thamrin to operating a cooked-food stall.

Bud's husband rebuilt and extended Bud's cart from the parts left over from his becak and bicycle repair business which was in decline. Bud sold her cooked food in front of Sarinah department store, just across the road from Kebun Kacang where she stored her cart on a vacant plot of land. After 1971, however, she was forced to move further north along Jalan Thamrin to Air Mancur (the fountain) to avoid constant harassment by Jakarta's police. To minimize possible encounters with the trader clearance team, she changed from selling cooked food during the day to selling it throughout the night (from 5 pm to 4 am) to police and military men who manned a military depot and guarded the nearby offices and banks. She was lucky to have these clients for not only did they warn her against impending trader clearance campaigns but they protected her if she was caught. As the police and military men belonged to Jakarta's newly emerging middle class they had money to spend and wished to eat well. There were few alternative food outlets and Bud catered to their needs, providing fried fish, chicken, beef, assorted spiced vegetables, eggs, banana fritters, hot lemon juice, beer, fried nuts and numerous other delicacies. Bud's clients were pleased with the cheap, convenient and good quality food she provided. She often had over a hundred clients a night.

Like other small enterprises, Bud's had a multiplier affect as she recruited more and more people to help with the work. By 1974/75 she had up to five people helping with her stall. One helped with the shopping, another two with the food preparations and pushing the cart to its trade location, whilst others helped with the cooking and selling throughout the night.

Bud's prosperity enabled her to have her house rebuilt by two neighbouring construction workers. She had her dresses sewn and drinking water carried to her door. She bought numerous consumer items such as a television and radio and had a well and electricity installed. She employed a woman to keep the house tidy and wash her clothes. Instead of walking, Bud used a becak driver to convey her to the market and back and to her trade location each night. In exchange for this service, she gave the driver money and food.

After 1975/1976, however, Bud's fortunes began to change. The anti-trader campaigns were becoming more ruthless and Bud was often advised by her military protectors to stay at home. In 1974 she had been forced to move off the main road of Jalan Thamrin to a back street, between the banks and military depot to avoid these raids. She was later informed that most of her clients were to move with the military depot to the edges of the city because it stood in the way of a proposed new highway. Although the depot was not demolished, her former clients did move elsewhere and the new personnel who occupied the depot set up an official canteen which competed with Bud's stall. By 1976, Bud had less than half the number of customers she had had two years earlier. The new staff of the depot created problems for Bud and on a number of occasions she was asked to leave the trading site. It was claimed that the area was to be used as a carpark.

Increasingly, Bud had to fight on many fronts. In 1974, the vacant plot of land along Jalan Thamrin which she had used for storing her cart was taken over for the construction of a multi-storey building. The footbridge across the Cideng Canal by which Bud and other traders had gained access to Jalan Thamrin and the central-city area was dismantled. They now had to walk further, along winding back streets and between speeding cars, to get to their trading sites. Transport was made even more difficult and expensive by the banning of the becak from the centre of the city. Petty traders such as Bud had relied on the becak for the transport of their raw ingredients to and from the market and to their trade locations.[49] Now they had either to carry their wares by foot or hire the more expensive minicar.[50] Whilst the shortest ride in a motorized becak (helicak or bajaj) in 1978 cost from Rp.150 to Rp.200 (1.3–1.7 litres of rice), manpowered becak cost Rp.100 (0.9 litres).[51]

In 1977, Bud was eventually forced to move from her trade location at the city centre. The threats against her had become unbearable. With an assistant she pushed her large cart along dusty, sun-scorched roads in search of a new trade site. But none was to be found. All other locations at the city centre were either occupied by other traders or subject to frequent anti-trader campaigns. By this stage, Bud was lucky to find ten customers a day. After a month of searching and sleeping beside her cart to protect it against police raids, she gave up.

Bud became increasingly depressed and felt that whatever decisions she made were wrong. She was caught in a downward spiral from which there was no escape. She lived off the sale of the many possessions she had accumulated during her days of success. Her neighbours advised her to sell her cart because it restricted her mobility and cost her money for storage. She also had to pay, house and feed the assistant who pushed the cart.

After not trading for some time, Bud regained some of her strength through rest and the compassion and sympathy given by her neighbours. She following their advice and became a mobile trader, carting her wares in a sash tied over her hip and shoulder. Finding a safe and lucrative trade location at the city centre, however, proved a major problem. She would stand by the roadside near Hotel Indonesia or Hotel Asoka and be hounded this way and that by one policeman after another. When international dignitaries came to stay, traders like Bud were cleared from the streets. It was difficult for Bud to establish a new clientele when she was perpetually being cleared away. For a time she sold morning snacks to a couple of minicar and helicak drivers, but they were often short of cash and she had to wait till noon, when they had received money from their passengers, to be paid. By this stage, the police had come to clear her away. Consequently, Bud was lucky to earn enough to feed her mother, daughter and herself. In six years her daily income had dropped from Rp.4000 to Rp.1000 (from 100 to 9 litres of rice).

Eventually, Bud decided that it was better to be a domestic servant than a petty trader. She loved the freedom, independence and hope of petty trade but was tired of the insecurity of the streets.[52] She resented the lowly status of a domestic servant, but felt she could earn at least Rp.30,000 (200 litres of rice) a month and not have to endure the fear and paranoia of being caught by police. In 1979, with my assistance, she became a cook for an expatriate household. Many petty traders in Ibu Imah's neighbourhood wanted to follow suit but lacked the necessary contacts to gain such employment.

Bud was not alone in her experiences of boom and bankruptcy. Her neighbour, Wira, had graduated from a small mobile cigarette stall in front of Hotel Indonesia during the mid- to late 1960s to a large immobile cooked-food stall beside the Pertamina building, near Kebun Kacang. Between 1970 and 1973 she made a thriving business selling to construction workers who worked on that building site. She earned Rp.1000 to Rp.2000 (20 to 40 litres of rice) a day. When the building was completed and the construction workers departed her trade started to decline. By 1975, she had returned to mobile trade and sold spicy vegetables along the kampung pathways. She was lucky to earn Rp.500 (6 litres of rice) a day, which was barely enough to feed herself and her daughter. By 1978, she looked in desperation for a secure job. A neighbour who worked as a washerwoman in a maternity hospital nearby knew of a vacancy, and introduced Wira to the job. In 1979, she earned Rp.18,000 a month, or in terms of rice, less than a fifth of what she had earned seven years earlier.

Bud was not alone in feeling harassed by government policies. Daily press reports described the removal of thousands of traders from their central-city sites. They were cleared from the major market places of Tanah Abang and Senen when these were renovated and their access routes widened. Thousands more lost their sites when the central bus station at Lapangan Banteng was transformed into a park.[53] A study of Jakartan street traders in 1976 found that 66 percent felt their major problem was a lack of a secure and strategic trade location which was due primarily to government harassment.[54]

The municipal government aimed to move most traders off the streets of Jakarta and into the new multi-storey market places it was building. But traders such as Bud and Wira were not able to afford the higher cost of these new facilities. Traders paid much less for their street locations than the government expected them to pay in the new official markets. Most traders, such as Bud, paid the occasional bribe or illegal tax to an official who patrolled the area where they traded; in 1978 this ranged from Rp.50 to Rp.200 (0.4–1.7 litres of rice) per day.[55] By contrast, the rent in the official markets was at least five times and possibly as much as thirty times Bud's daily overheads on the street.[56]

Not only were the kiosks too expensive for most petty traders but they were poorly designed. Customers refused to patronize the small, dark, dingy, unventilated cubicles at the centre of markets or go to the upper floors to do their shopping. So even when the government offered these undesirable kiosks at very low rentals of Rp.200 per day, traders refused to use them because there were no customers.

In those few cases where the markets had been designed especially for poor traders there were many more applicants than available stalls. In 1978, at the newly renovated poor man's single-storey market at Senen, there were 6843 applicants and only 1576 kiosks.[57]

Traders encountered numerous bureaucratic obstacles to their entry into official markets. To apply for a stall in the first place required a certain amount of information, literacy and confidence, which most traders lacked. To be allocated a stall one needed contacts within the market administration. Various documents were required proving residence in Jakarta for more than 5 years and a valid Jakarta identity card. It was necessary to become a member of the City Traders Association which entailed an additional fee. Bribes to facilitate one's entry into a strategically placed stall were indispensible. Traders needed time—perhaps months— to wait out the process of market renovation and kiosk allocation. Most petty traders could not stop working because they had no reserves and had to feed their families each day.

As a consequence of financial, bureaucratic and design problems over 40 percent of the kiosks in Jakarta's newly renovated markets remained empty many years after their completion. It was reported that "some 23,600 market stalls in the 148 markets handled by Pasar Jaya, the city's market authority, are standing empty giving some Jakarta markets a ghost-town ambience, ... traders feel (these markets) are about as exciting as a graveyard".[58] Like the ice-cream and cone producers, petty traders complained about the rise in transport, market and food costs from the mid-1970s. The prices of most basic food items rose approximately five-fold between 1972 and 1981.[59] The renovation of most of Jakarta's central city markets during the mid-1970s and the relocation of the main fruit and vegetable market from Tanah Abang and Senen to Pasar Induk on the southern periphery of Jakarta further added to the price rises.[60]

By the mid-1970s most petty traders were becoming caught in a cost-price squeeze. While the prices of their raw materials kept rising the number of customers was contracting or the customers they had were only the poor. The restricted budgets, transport, storage and refrigeration facilities of the poor meant that they continued to buy minute quantities daily from the petty trader, but they could not afford to pay higher prices. Meanwhile, the middle class who had formerly patronized petty traders was more attracted by the new restaurants, shops, cafes and supermarkets. Apart from the greater prestige of buying these new items of food, the goods produced by these new retail outlets were often more hygienic, nicely packaged and of better quality. As noted, there was no longer such a price difference between the food of petty traders and the larger retail outlets. Due to economies of scale, larger firms were able to keep their costs down whilst the costs of space, raw materials, equipment and labour rose for the central city trader.[61]

Government policies reinforced this cost-price squeeze. Increasingly petty traders were being pushed off the streets of central Jakarta, their most lucrative trade location. Once they lost their trade niches it was difficult finding others for there was a growing number of small traders competing for the increasingly limited permissable sites. The Jakarta clearance teams continually roamed the streets looking out for traders' carts and wares they could fine or confiscate.

Faced with such difficulties, petty traders had three options. First, despite great odds, they could try to continue to trade at the city centre. Second, they could continue to trade but move to the edges of city, to a lesser town or to the village. Third, they could try to shift into another occupation. Towards the end of the 1970s, some petty traders such as Bud and Wira managed to move into service sector jobs such as domestic service and laundry work, but the numbers moving out of petty trade and into services were difficult to estimate. Without contacts and letters of recommendation it was much harder to get regular service sector jobs than it had been ten to twenty years early. Furthermore, kampung dwellers who had been petty traders found such service sector activity restrictive and degrading, even if it removed them from the insecurity of the streets. Some young girls whose mothers had been traders, domestics or laundresses preferred prostitution. It was a less arduous and in some ways more glamorous, although frowned upon, way of making a living. At least it linked them to the modern sector and provided them with substantial windfalls.[62]

Construction

Unlike becak driving, cottage industry or petty trade, construction work during the 1960s and 1970s displayed a recurring rise and fall in demand, rather than a single phase of boom and decline. The first construction boom occurred between 1960 and 1965, when Sukarno promoted the building of multi-storey hotels, sports complexes and monuments. The second construction boom occurred during Indonesia's economic recovery between 1968 and 1975, when Jalan Thamrin became lined by many skyscrapers. A third and perhaps more minor upsurge in construction occurred after 1978, when government revenues received a boost from a second rise in oil prices.

Between 1961 and 1967 there appears to have been little change in the total number of construction workers in Jakarta. Of the estimated 80,000 workers, 85 percent were employed within the "informal sector".[63] After 1968, the numbers employed in casual construction work seem to have risen rapidly. According to Census figures, in both 1971 and 1980 construction accounted for not quite 7 percent of the work force or about 130,000 and 190,000 people respectively. But estimates of the numbers employed in construction can be very deceptive. Even during a building boom, the demand for construction workers was very irregular. Most labourers worked for an average of only six months a year.[64] Furthermore, many construction workers who were circular migrants would not have been enumerated.

In Ibu Imah's neighbourhood, there were never more than about ten construction workers during the 1970s. Prior to this, however, many male breadwinners had taken part in the construction or widening of Jalan Thamrin and the multi-storey buildings on either side. There was hardly a man in the neighbourhood who had not tried construction work at some stage during his life. Like becak driving, it was an easy occupation to enter and provided a means of entry to the city. Some who worked as becak drivers and repairman, artisans or petty traders turned to construction during the building boom.

In the 1960s, the main department for recruiting construction labourers was located just opposite Kebun Kacang. At that time, there was a problem recruiting enough men to complete the numerous half-finished buildings that lined Jalan Thamrin. Young men were invited by their relatives or friends to join a labour gang. They started by doing the least skilled chores like carting soil, stone and cement, and then progressed to more skilled work and specialized in joinery, stonemasonary or painting. Anyone with the courage, contacts, organizational skills and initiative to win a contract for a construction job could become a foreman. Udin, for example, managed to move from unskilled construction work to being a foreman in only five years. He then recruited skilled construction workers and unskilled apprentices to do the work and organized their payment. It was accepted that the foreman would receive a substantially higher income than the workers. The others in the group were paid a set rate according to skill. On the next construction project, the person occupying the role of foreman could become a skilled worker if somebody else won the contract. Thus there was both a hierarchical and egalitarian element in the organization of small-scale construction work and a skilled worker could be a supervisor on one job and a labourer on the next. On any major project there were many groups of labourers each working for their own foremen and specializing in carpentry, plumbing, electricity, tiling, painting or other skilled tasks. When the job was finished, the group dissolved and each individual sought new work elsewhere.

Around the mid-1970s, for the builders of Kebun Kacang, the nature of construction work changed. They moved from working mainly on the large multi-storey buildings along Jalan Thamrin to rebuilding kampung houses.[65] For this, they had to be jacks-of-all trades. Whilst kampung dwellers cooked and lived inside, they knocked down the house, redesigned and rebuilt it. They had to be able to work in wood, brick, tiles and glass. As the work lasted three weeks they received a higher daily wage than if they worked for a longer time (2–3 years) on a larger building site. In rice terms, their incomes ranged from 8 to 12 litres per day over the decade, with a slump in the mid-1970s to about half this amount. They also received cigarettes, coffee and food.

During the construction slump of 1975 to 1978, there was a change in the recruitment of construction workers for the larger building sites. Previously, labourers had mainly been recruited from within the city. By the mid- to late 1970s, gangs of labourers from East and Central Java were being recruited by labour contractors to work on the larger constructions. Workers from further afield accepted lower wages, poorer working conditions and were more diligent. The foreman had more control over them and could fire them at will. When labourers were no longer required, they were simply sent home. Their trip to and from Jakarta was paid by the foreman. Improved and cheap transport made this feasible. This system of labour recruitment was not new, having existed in Indonesia for over one hundred years.[66]

Timin had worked in at least six jobs before becoming a construction worker. For nine years, from 1962 to 1971, he had worked as a becak driver. Before and during that time, he had worked as a messenger, day labourer, bicycle and car repairer, cigarette seller and fresh fish vendor. In the early 1970s he apparently developed tubercolosis and was forced to stop working for a year or so. His wife Dini, who had previously worked as a domestic servant, set up a vegetable stall in front of their kampung home and became the family's main breadwinner. On a domestic servant's daily wage (Rp.166/3 litres of rice) she could never have supported the family.

With the growing prosperity of the early 1970s, an increased demand for construction workers emerged within Ibu Imah's neighbourhood and casual labourers such as Timin turned to rebuilding kampung houses instead of working along the major highway. Timin could, for a period, obtain a lot of work. He invited his father from Bogor, who was also a builder and one or two other men from the neighbourhood to help him. They could complete a kampung house within one month.

In the 1970s there were two to three gangs of construction workers in the neighbourhood, each consisting of two to three people. Timin, a West Javanese, was hired to rebuild the houses in his immediate vicinity, which were mainly the houses of the West Javanese. Ibu Putro's son-in-law, Sarwoto, a Central Javanese, was hired to rebuild most of the houses surrounding his home which were mainly owned by central Javanese. This division of labour, however, was not rigid and occasionally Timin and Sarwoto worked on the same building. Members of one gang worked together on one site and then moved into other labour gangs as new opportunities arose. Each builder had to ensure that he had a wide range of contacts, so that when one job was finished he would be asked to do another with the same or a different group of men. Jobs were mainly obtained by word of mouth. Most often, however, there were long breaks without work between each job.

A construction worker's family had to have alternative sources of income to stave off the periods when construction work was not available. For one or two months a construction worker worked hard and earned relatively well. Then, for two to three months he could be out of work. Construction workers in Imah's neighbourhood for example, sold noodle and meat-ball soup, helped with car parts trade, did numerous odd jobs such as repairing bicycles or house painting if construction work was not available.

When Timin lacked construction work he did odd jobs around the community. He raised a little money by giving Islamic tuition to young boys in the neighbourhood. He was paid for helping to complete the local prayer house which had been partly built by voluntary local labour. During Lebaran he helped divide up the Pitra (obligatory contribution of rice) and distributed it from house to house. During Idul Adha he collected the money from neighbouring households with which to buy the goats. Then he bought the goats and looked after them till they were slaughtered. He also helped divide up the meat and distribute it to each house. It was difficult determining what he received for these activities—perhaps a little rice, meat or even money.

Without Dini's trade, the household could not have obtained food each day. The vegetables left over from the day's trade formed the basis of the family's next meal. But Dini was not a successful trader and was often short of capital. Between 1975 and 1981, Dini's vegetable trade went bankrupt several times, but somehow she was able to raise the capital to get going again. She frequently borrowed money from moneylenders who circulated around the community and charged exorbitant interest rates of 28 percent per month. She often had a battle paying the money back and was indebted to a number of people in the neighbourhood. Somehow, the family survived.

From 1978 onwards, Timin and other construction workers from my sample spent more and more time away from Kebun Kacang, seeking construction work on the periphery of the city or even as far away as Bogor. The centre of the construction boom seemed to have moved out of town, to the new housing and industrial estates and the kampung's construction workers were forced to follow if they were to obtain work. Whilst Dini remained with her children in the kampung trading, Timin lived for a couple of weeks at a time at construction sites elsewhere.

Kampung Services

Like kampung construction work, small-scale services expanded as a consequence of the increased prosperity of kampung dwellers who worked outside the kampung. As an office worker or trader prospered he or she hired neighbours to wash clothes, cook and clean the home. Instead of sewing clothes themselves they went to the local seamstress. Instead of carting buckets of water or raw produce from the market, they asked an unemployed neighbour to get it for them.

Many, but not all of these services, were performed by the poorest kampung dwellers. They were usually women whose husband's earned too little income or who were divorced, deserted or widowed. They performed the unskilled chores, such as laundry, domestic work and carrying. They moved from one activity to another depending upon what their neighbours required. Wives of the better-off sometimes did the more skilled service activities such as sewing, healing, brokerage and mid-wifery as a side-line.

In the 1970s, due to the increased prosperity of some members of the kampung and their growing demand for all types of kampung services, there was a trickle down of resources from the wealthier to the poorer. An integration or redistribution of wealth occurred as the better-off asked poorer neighbours to do jobs for them. The former paid for many services which could conveniently be obtained within a minute's walk of their homes.

Although the relative significance of small-scale services was increasing with time, in the early 1970s they were third in importance to petty trade and becak driving as employers of labour in Jakarta. In 1967, approximately 145,000 people were employed in the city's informal sector services.[67] It has been suggested that it was the most important and rapidly growing sector of employment and accounted for 30 percent of Jakarta's informal sector work force.[68] By contrast, the ILO survey found small-scale services came second to petty trade as absorbers of labour and accounted for 18 percent of employment in their sample.[69]

In Ibu Imah's neighbourhood in 1979, approximately 30 people or 15 percent of the labour force were employed in services. An additional 22 household stalls and cooked food producers (11 percent of the labour force) provided basic items such as raw and prepared food, salted fish, soap, matches and mosquito coils needed by the community each day.[70]

The demand for kampung services was even more intermittent than the demand for construction work. Consequently most of these services were occasional, performed only a couple of times each week or month. One day a kampung dweller paid for his clothes to be laundered, food to be cooked or goods carted from the market; the next day, when short of cash, he or she did these chores.

At the lowest level of the kampung economy was the household stall (*warung*). Although better off than the laundresses and domestic servants, these women lacked skills, had limited capital and were tied to their homes by children. From 1975 to 1981, from fifteen to twenty two women or 11 percent of the households, operated household stalls or prepared food for them. Few operated continuously. They came into existence and soon collapsed. Most commonly, however, a woman would trade until she ran out of capital and then start up again when she had borrowed some money from a neighbour, moneylender or her husband or had earned it from some side line activity such as massage, laundry or room rent.

In the 1970s each household stall was patronized by five to ten households that lived to either side. Most households shopped at the stall closest to their home but if a particular item was not available, or too expensive, they went to another stall. The local stalls were mainly used because they were conveniently located and sold items in tiny quantities and on credit. Each stall-owner set a credit limit of approximately a quarter of a poor household's monthly income. If a customer's credit limit was exhausted with one stall he or she went to another. Often social rather than economic factors affected kampung dwellers' decisions as to where they would shop.

Stalls varied greatly in the quantity, kind and quality of food they sold. One stall specialized in noodle soups whilst another sold rice, cooked meat and prawn crackers. One woman sold *gado gado* (boiled vegetables with peanut sauce), another specialized in *bubur* (porridge) whilst Ibu Imah, sold rice cakes. Each particular type of food was eaten at different times of the day. Porridge was sold between 6 and 8 in the morning along with the rice cakes whilst the noodle soup was sold at midday. Ice-cream was popular in the heat of midday and late afternoon to evening.

Children were introduced to snacks at an early age. It was the main way to keep them occupied in an environment full of traders and little playing space. A mother who did not permit her child to snack was called stingy. Traders who sold snacks to small children were most vulnerable. Children were often short of money and it was difficult to deny them food. The traders own children invariably ate into their mother's sales. Some mothers traded mainly to provide snacks for their children. The daily food allowance was first spent on preparing titbits for sale as well as for one's children. This prevented them from being enticed to buy food from neighbouring stalls or crying if they were not allowed. What little was earned from the sale of snacks not eaten by one's children was then used for the family's main meal.

Because most household and stall budgets were combined it was impossible to estimate their capital or earnings. Traders rarely held onto cash. Whatever money came into the enterprise was immediately reinvested in new stock. The faster the turnover the better the trade. A successful household trader managed to feed her family out of her earnings or the food she prepared for trade. The less successful trader managed only to provide her children with snacks and relied on other income for her family's daily food. The main advantage of cooked-food trade was that the family could obtain food from their own stall even if they had little cash.

1 & 2   Village work and home. Most of the inhabitants of Kebun Kacang came from the countryside. In the early days they built houses in Kebun Kacang which looked very much like their village homes. Some of the migrants to Jakarta frequently returned to their villages.

3   Ibu Bud with her husband's second wife, Nanti on her right and
an assistant on her left. Compare this photo of Bud in 1973 to the one
taken eight years later (no. 15).

4   The community of Kebun Kacang across the Cideng canal. The
only storage space for bicycles was on the banks of the canal. To gain
extra space, second storeys were added to the original houses and
wooden ramps were built out over the canal.

5 & 6   Sociability of the kampung pathway. The kampung pathways were like a communal lounge room with each door of every house fronting on to a common area where children played, mothers set up stalls and cooked or chatted to neighbours while fathers smoked, gambled or did woodwork.

7   *Above* Inside a typical kampung house. This was the room in which the author slept, wrote and spoke for hours with Ibu Bud.

8   *Right* Waiting for the flood to subside.

9 & 10   Coming from the market. Mimi, Bud's assistant *above*, carts live chickens and vegetables. Meanwhile, *overleaf, top* Bud travels home by becak with rice, eggs, bananas and numerous other ingredients for trade.

11 *Right* Bud at home, preparing snacks for sale. The sticky rice snacks were wrapped in banana leaves and steamed. The cooking facilities were simple and no cutlery was needed for the food was eaten by hand.

12　*Left* A herbal-medicine seller carting her wares from door to door in the kampung. The bottles contain the answer to aches and pains, infertility or unwanted pregnancies. The herbs from special roots and leaves were crushed and prepared into medicines by each herbal-medicine seller.

13　*Above* A vegetable seller distributing spinach, beans, chillies, cabbage, potatoes and red and white onions by push-cart.

14 *Right* The flats which replaced the community of Kebun Kacang in 1984. These were four-storey, fully serviced, walk-up flats of 21, 42 and 51 sq. metres. Compare with the original community in no. 4.

15 *Below* Bud after the decline of her trade in 1981. Compare her face with no. 3.

In contrast to the middle class, most kampung dwellers did not budget, but spent whatever money came to hand each day. Towards the end of the decade, however, with the rise in cost of living, increased desire for consumer goods and greater education, the emerging middle class from within the kampung became more budget conscious. Being more mobile, they bought their food in bulk further afield or in new cooperative stores at their place of work. It was the poor, who had no access to such stores, needed credit and had little money to spend, who mainly patronized the local stalls.

For the first half of the 1970s, Kunto was the main water seller for the neighbourhood though a number of other kampung dwellers distributed buckets of water as a sideline. Kunto also worked as a rubbish collector for the Jakarta City government in the mornings. Each afternoon he moved through the kampung distributing water in 40 litre containers suspended from a pole over his shoulder. He earned from Rp.15,000 to Rp.30,000 (150 to 300 litres of rice) a month depending upon whether it was the wet or dry season. He mainly delivered water to the houses of the better-off who were too busy, lazy or embarrassed to cart water themselves. They did not want to walk 100 to 200 metres and queue at the water tap for up to half an hour.

Water carrying was viewed as demeaning and as soon as a household had some extra money, they paid a vendor to deliver it. Door-to-door distribution of drinking water seemed to become most important during the early to mid-1970s. Clean drinking water was difficult to obtain as old water taps broke down and wells were increasingly polluted. Canal water had long been too polluted to drink.

Aswan also started to cart water after his vegetable trade declined in the mid-1970s. Aswan's piped water was considered cleaner than Kunto's bore water and thus Aswan gained many of Kunto's customers. The main threat to the livelihood of both water sellers, however, was the expanded installation of piped water to wealthier households just beyond the neighbourhood. These households sold their water directly to kampung dwellers at Rp.1 per litre instead of Rp.2½ and so bypassed Kunto and Aswan's services.

The washing and ironing of clothes was an important, if lowly, occupation. At least seven washerwomen worked within the community at any one time. Three others worked as regular clothes washers for wealthier households or institutions just beyond the area. It was difficult to tell who was a paid laundress and who was not, for most women washed their own family's clothes every second day and it was unclear whether they were washing their own or other people's clothes.

Tukirah's main means of livelihood was laundry and ironing. Her husband hardly ever supported her and their two children. Occasionally he did construction work or helped the local headman, but mostly he sat around the kampung, playing cards, gambling or sleeping. Tukirah washed the clothes of one or two households in the kampung and in 1979 could earn from Rp.8000 to Rp.15,000 (53–100 litres of rice) per month. She was paid Rp.25 (0.16 litres) per item of clothes by one family and a lump sum of Rp.8000 per month by another. Richer families with a monthly income of over Rp.100,000 (666 litres) or bachelors utilized her services. Each laundry woman had a particular family or group of families to work for. As the income was unreliable and inadequate, Tukirah continually looked for other chores. She carted drinking water, carried goods from the market, helped dice food and served as a broker between the kampung dwellers and the pawnshop. She took kampung dwellers' valuables to the pawnshop and redeemed them later on, thus saving her neighbours the embarrassment of being seen pawning their possessions. For each of these chores she received Rp.100 (0.7 litres of rice) bringing her total monthly income to between Rp.11,000 and Rp.18,000 (73–120 litres of rice).

Being a domestic servant was an open admission of poverty. Like clothes washing it was viewed as the lowest paid and least prestigious job. Only three residents of the neighbourhood worked regularly as domestics there, the remaining four servants had been brought in to the neighbourhood from outside. Ani, Aswan the water seller's wife, worked for one of the wealthiest families in the neighbourhood—Warung Kakah. Her employers owned a large dried-food stall along the road near the community. Ani's job was to buy and prepare her bosses' meals and to keep the house tidy. For this she received Rp.8000 (43 litres of rice) per month plus two or three meals a day (equivalent to Rp.6000/40 litres a month). Thus in 1979, her total monthly income was Rp.14,000 (93 litres). Before working in the kampung, she had worked for a number of wealthier middle-class families in Menteng. Apart from domestic work she had no other experience. Nor did she have any capital for a household foodstall.

Although the neighbourhood boasted five dressmakers, only one of these was full-time. The main orders for new clothes came during Lebaran when the dressmakers could not keep up with the demand. At other times of the year, most of the kampung's dressmakers sold cooked food as a sideline. Ibu Siti, for example, prepared small cakes and snacks in the morning and only occasionally sewed in the afternoons. In 1981 she could earn from Rp.1000 to Rp.2000 (4.8 to 9.5 litres of rice) for each garment and had only two to three orders a week. The dressmakers had regular clients who lived just a few doors from their home. The customers delivered the material to the dress-maker and after agreeing on the design, the garment was ready within a matter of days. By 1980, the finished garments sold in the market places and shops were often cheaper than those made-to-order in the kampung, and kampung dwellers started to buy ready made clothes with well known international (often fake) brands.

Other skilled services in the community were midwifery, tra-ditional healing, massage, and the preparation of decorations for marriage celebrations. All of these services were required only on an occasional basis and the women who performed them had other income earning activities. The women employed in these occupations were not necessarily the poorest in the neighbourhood. Ibu Imah with the help of Ibu Tukinem, a neighbour, had delivered almost all the children in the neighbourhood. Even though Imah was nearly eighty years of age, kampung women preferred her to deliver their children, rather than doctors at the local maternity hospital. She provided a personalized and cheaper service. She charged Rp.6000 (40 litres of rice) per delivery which compared with Rp.30,000 (200 litres) in the hospital. Ibu Imah enabled them to have their children in their homes. By 1980, however, as fashions changed and kampung dwellers became informed about modern medicine, more of the younger women went to the local maternity hospital.

Although the community had five traditional healers, none of them viewed this activity as full-time. Their skills were usually inherited and involved the use of massage, potions and incantations. If kam-pung dwellers were unwell, they called a traditional healer to their homes. Payment was indirect and flexible. In 1979, kampung dwellers paid between Rp.300 and Rp.500 (2–3 litres of rice) and, if they lacked money, they could pay in kind or at some later date. If kampung dwellers were not cured they consulted different healers. Only towards the end of the decade did more kampung dwellers turn to government polyclinics or private doctors. Thus healers began to lose part of their clientele.

Each of the healers had other income earning activities. Mbah, for example, also hired out bridal gowns and decorations for kampung marriages. She acted as a broker between the Chinese store-keeper who owned the gowns and the kampung dwellers who wished to hire them. Fatma, Imah's daughter and the most popular masseur in the neighbourhood, ran a household stall selling porridge. She did not restrict her masseur business to the neighbourhood, but had some rich clients in Menteng. She could earn five to ten times more per massage (Rp.5000/33 litres of rice) from her Menteng clients than from the kampung dwellers (between Rp.500 and 1000). In between their petty trading and moneylending activities Mus and Ibu Putro acted as traditional healers.

Towards the end of the 1970s, the increasing wealth of some of the better-off kampung dwellers, their changing consumer tastes and the growing centralization of services and efficiency of government reduced the demand for kampung services. Some households could now afford their own washing machine, water and electricity connections. They started to budget by shopping from the cooperative at their place of work rather than utilizing the local store or vendor. They bought their clothing from the official markets or central city department stores rather than the local seamstress. They increasingly utilized western medicines and modern medical treatment rather than the local healer. Instead of employing women from the neighbourhood as domestic servants, they brought in newcomers from the village over whom they had more control and who, without complaint, would do all their household chores for less pay. The ILO survey similarly found that beyond a certain point, the growing prosperity of the middle class did not benefit the small-scale sector because the rich turned their patronage elsewhere.[71]

The Formal Sector

In contrast to the informal sector, the formal sector has been described as larger scale, capital-intensive, bureaucratically organized, with regular hours of work and fixed salaries. It is officially assisted and enumerated by government and has regular contacts with formal institutions such as banks. It consists of people employed in government or private offices, shops, hospitals, hotels and medium or large scale factories.

Nowhere is there a clear enumeration of Jakarta's formal sector. In 1974, Sethuraman estimated that it accounted for slightly over half of Jakarta's labour force, somewhere between 500,000 and 800,000. Although figures are notoriously unreliable and difficult to obtain, there is evidence that during the economic boom of the 1970s employment opportunities within the formal sector expanded. More work became available in large and medium scale firms, government and private offices and the trade sector. While the number of wage workers increased, the number of self-employed entrepreneurs, family enterprises and unpaid family workers declined as a proportion of the work force.[72] By 1982, at the end of the economic boom, the formal sector was estimated to account for 73 percent of the city's total work force or approximately 1,500,000 jobs.[73] If the Sethuraman and BPS estimates are comparable, then the formal sector increased its share of the work force by about 50 percent. The informal sector, by contrast, was estimated to have halved its share of the work force while remaining constant in absolute terms.

Between 1970 and 1981, the increase in formal sector and decrease in informal sector employment was also evident in Kebun Kacang. Whereas in 1970 there were no factory workers and kampung dwellers had never heard of the term *pabrik* (factory), by 1979 at least 12 people worked in factories. Whereas there had been only 16 salaried employees in the 1960s and early 1970s, by 1980 there were nearly 40. By 1979, a quarter of the kampung's work force had salaried or wage employment.

Under Guided Democracy in the early to mid-1960s, when public sector employment expanded rapidly, approximately fifteen breadwinners in Ibu Imah's neighbourhood worked in office jobs. There were four dock workers, four bank messengers and guards, six municipal rubbish collectors and a man who worked at the Department of Justice. Such jobs were usually obtained through personal contacts rather than skill. Employers often asked their workers to obtain new recruits. People from the one kin group or neighbourhood therefore tended to cluster in the same jobs. Office jobs were accepted mainly because of the regular rice rations, pensions and security.[74] In Ibu Imah's neighbourhood, those who had lived longest in the city, mainly the west Javanese, seemed most likely to take up regular employment, although this was difficult to prove. They may have had more and broader contacts throughout the city or been attracted by the greater security and social status of even menial office jobs compared to work on the streets. Certainly these jobs were less tiring.

In the 1960s and early 1970s, most kampung dwellers were reluctant to take up these positions as the pay was too low. In 1972, a rubbish collector for the Jakarta City government received a cash income of only Rp.7000 (170 litres of rice) a month while petty traders such as Bud or Wira could earn at least four times that amount. Because of the low pay, an office worker needed to have another job to support his family. A rubbish collector for the Jakarta City government, for example, privately cleaned gardens and collected rubbish for wealthier households in Menteng, while his wife washed clothes and cooked snacks in the kampung. Burhanuddin worked as an accountant for the department of Justice and ran an ice-cone making enterprise in his home, while his wife worked as an Islamic teacher and sold kitchenware on credit.

By 1978, however, public sector employment had become more attractive. With the second big Opec oil price rise and the resultant rise in government revenues, the salary and working conditions of government employees improved quite markedly. The menial or unskilled office jobs, which between the early 1960s and mid-1970s had been viewed as unattractive, started to gain appeal. Whilst petty traders, cottage industries and becak drivers were experiencing increasing difficulties, those in office jobs had stable or rising incomes. In 1978 a minimum wage rate was legislated for office jobs. According to Manning "overall government basic salaries had increased ten-fold from 1969".[75] Numerous other benefits were offered: free or cheap medical care and midday meals, uniforms, cheap goods on credit from cooperative stores, maternity leave, double incomes during Lebaran, superannuation, subsidized housing and pensions.[76]

Just as the public sector was becoming more popular, it became more difficult to enter. One rubbish collector in Ibu Imah's neighbourhood wanted his uneducated and unemployed son to take over his position when he retired as had been the tradition but found he had to pay his superiors a bribe of over Rp.150,000, which was more than three times his monthly wage. In the kampung, only five educated young people with a senior high school certificate (SMA) were able to get government jobs in the late 1970s and all claimed this was only possible because, in addition to passing the necessary examinations, they had friends in the departments where they had applied to work, had the required documentation and the time, money and knowledge to make the necessary job applications.

Until the mid-1970s, kampung dwellers seemed to be unfamiliar with the nature of factory work. Four or five years later, when modern multi-national firms had been established on the city's periphery, most kampung dwellers felt that only members of the middle class could gain access to them. A high school certificate, contacts and knowledge of how to apply were required.

Upward mobility into employment in multi-national factories seemed possible only for young people whose parents could pay for their education and then support them whilst they searched and applied for jobs. By 1980, three young high school graduates were privileged to gain employment in a large new foreign-owned textile firm outside Jakarta near Tangerang. Their parents in the kampung belonged to the richest families. One worked in a bank on a salary of over Rp.100,000 (666 litres of rice) whilst the other was a successful fixed-stall roadside trader, whose children had been adopted and educated by a former employer who ran an antique shop in a prestigious street in Menteng. Factory workers' earnings started at Rp.50,000 per month, with the prospects of salary increases each year. They received medical benefits, meals, uniforms, maternity leave plus superannuation.[77] The workers feared the loss of their jobs for they knew that it would be difficult obtaining similar work elsewhere.

Work in medium size factories in downtown Jakarta, by contrast, was poorly paid and insecure. Working conditions were bad, wages did not increase and there were none of the benefits provided by the multi-national firms. In 1979, only Rp.20,000 (133 litres of rice), or little more than a domestic servant's wage, was paid per month and half of this was absorbed on travel to and from the factory. Most kampung dwellers claimed that no serious breadwinner could accept such work. In Ibu Imah's neighbourhood, six unmarried teenage girls, who had dropped out of school, were prepared to accept work in a pen assembly and drink bottling factory because it allowed them to escape from the confines of the kampung where at most they could help their mothers' trade. Their factory earnings provided a little for snacks, make-up, clothes and some occasional money for their parents. The turnover of manpower was high as, after a year or two, these girls left to marry or moved to another factory.

By the late 1970s, children whose parents had arrived in the city in the 1950s and 1960s and found employment in the informal sector did not wish to follow in their parents' footsteps. They had been brought up to believe that their lives would be better than those of their parents. They aspired for secure and better paid jobs in government or private offices or factories rather than the hard, arduous and insecure work on the streets. But the possibilities for employment in industry remained limited.

In Ibu Imah's neighbourhood in the late 1970s, there appeared to be a trend towards formal sector employment. The more educated kampung dwellers were able to get work in offices and factories. Nevertheless, this appeared to be only a passing phase. Most kampung dwellers were able to move only into the medium scale factories which provided low pay and poor working conditions. They provided little more security than jobs in the small-scale sector.[78]

In the 1980s, modern formal sector jobs were becoming limited to the children of the middle class who possessed not only education but also contacts and money. This limited evidence suggests that Jakarta may be replicating the experience of Latin America in the 1960s. There, the growth of the formal sector was to the benefit of a limited, even if expanded, middle class. There was little permanent mobility out of the small scale, labour-intensive sector and into the large scale capital-intensive sectors of the urban economy.[79]

Reasons for the Transience of Income-Earning Activities

The changing relationship between the formal and informal sectors can be seen in three phases. From the late 1950s to the mid-1960s, the modern sector declined whilst the small-scale sector continued to grow, largely because of a vacuum in production, retail and transport. Then, during the initial five to ten years of the New Order government, 1965/68 to 1975/78, both the formal and informal sectors of the economy thrived. After the mid-1970s, however, the very growth of the large-scale economic sector resulted in structural and locational changes, especially at the city centre, which undermined the small-scale sector.

The varying and sometimes divergent rates of growth between the large and small-scale sectors can be explained partly by changes in the demand for the supply of goods and services. During the 1950s and 1960s, and especially between 1957 and 1965, both public utilities and the large-scale private enterprises could not function properly. Government agencies were hampered by too many employees, poorly qualified staff, irrelevant rules and regulations, extremely low salaries and corruption. Private firms were undermined when the Dutch were forced to leave in 1957 and there was discrimination against the Chinese, especially after 1960. As the formal sector did not satisfy most peoples basic needs for food, transport, amenities and housing, an estimated 80 percent continued to patronize the goods and services of vendors, becak drivers, messengers and petty producers. It was during the late 1950s and 1960s that Gani set up his car part selling business. Lukman his battery recycling and Santo his radio repairs. Agus began becak driving and Mus and Bud set up their petty production and trade.

The rehabilitation of government-owned utilities by the late 1970s and the promotion of large-scale private enterprise resulted in more centralized and efficient food distribution, transport, electricity, gas, water, the telephone facilities. These developments supplanted the need for many small-scale sector activities. Lukman's batteries were being replaced by electricity and Agus' manually driven becaks by the motor car. The kampung's water and kerosene vendors found their better-off customers preferred centralized direct piped water, electricity and gas distribution rather than the more expensive daily deliveries.

The rise in incomes during the 1970s caused the expanding middle class to change its patterns of consumption.[80] This middle class could now afford to buy such expensive items as cars, refrigerators and large houses. Between 1970 and 1980, the number of motor vehicles almost trebled from 200,000 to 600,000 in Jakarta.[81] Becak drivers lost the patronage of middle-class customers whose greater mobility enabled them to drive to shops or supermarkets to do their shopping instead of waiting for vendors to bring their daily needs to their door. As people purchased refrigerators and built larger kitchens, additional storage facilities enabled housewives to buy much of their food in bulk more cheaply at cooperatives or supermarkets, rather than shopping daily in small quantities at small street stalls, open-air markets or from mobile vendors. It was more prestigious to buy mass-produced goods with well-known brand names or go to a shop, cafe or restaurant than be seen eating on the streets from a petty trader. Bud's former military clients preferred to patronize and subsidized canteen at their place of work or go to a Madurese, Padang or Chinese restaurant. Mus's ice-cream sellers found many of their former middle-class customers preferred to buy the better quality, more varied, nicely packaged and competitively priced mass-produced ice-creams.

Changes in consumer tastes and technology caused certain products to become obsolete. By the late 1970s, many of the items handled by petty producers and sellers were rapidly replaced by mass-produced ones. Banana leaves, for example, which had been used for wrapping food were replaced by plastic bags. Pottery, coconut husks and tin containers which had served as cooking utensils were replaced by imported porcelain. Mats woven from locally grown reeds were replaced by multicoloured plastic ones. Mattresses made from kapok were replaced by rubber ones. The rattan tables, chairs and furniture rapidly gave way to vinyl coated armchairs and plastic or glass tables. The fresh fruit avocado, pawpaw, mango and pineapple juices were replaced by mass-produced and bottled Teh botol (sweetened bottled tea), Coca Cola, Seven Up and Green Spot. The rice cakes and cassava snacks were replaced by bread, biscuits, hamburgers and hotdogs. Most of these new products were uniformly designed and made from imported rather than local materials. They could be made by larger-scale firms rather than the diversity of small-scale labour-intensive activities of the kampung.

The decline of many informal sector activities after the mid- to late 1970s was nevertheless accompanied by the rise of new opportunities. Traders selling books and magazines, plastic toys, raincoats, kitchen utensils, thongs and mass-produced ice-creams still operated on the streets, near market places and in the kampungs. Others serviced minicars, made vinyl furniture or hired out video cassettes. It was difficult to determine precisely how many people or which segment of kampung society gained access to these new opportunities. The better-off few, like Ateng, Burhanuddin and Nano, could take advantage of the government's new markets, shopping centres, low cost credit programs and introduction of motorized vehicles to replace the becak. In the 1980s, they were able to move out of kampung society and into the middle class. Their children, who had a high school or technical education and failed to gain access to formal sector employment, probably moved into the new informal sector activities which were being created.

Three main factors were responsible for the transience of small-scale income-earning activities in Central Jakarta in particular. First, Jakarta, especially its central business district, was the main beneficiary of national economic growth, receiving a disproportionate amount of foreign and domestic investment and public sector urban spending.[82] At least 50 percent of the nation's money circulated in the city, which had less than 4 percent of the nation's population.[83] Second, physical changes at the city centre initially increased and then reduced the size of its population. And third, government policies reinforced these developments and had their most direct impact on the city centre.

Economic growth resulted in spatial changes, especially at the city centre, near Kebun Kacang. As the heart of Jakarta moved southward towards Kebun Kacang between the 1950s and mid-1970s, its inhabitants found themselves in the midst of a building boom. The demand for construction workers stimulated a demand for the services of food traders. These traders required the transport services provided by becak drivers, who in turn patronized the food traders. Moreover, the growing population of Jakarta and the emerging middle class could not yet obtain all their basic needs from the embryonic modern sector. Those on regular but still low wages in the formal sector were forced to patronize petty traders and becak drivers. All sectors of society utilized the washing, cleaning, healing, sewing and construction services of the kampung dwellers. This chain of buying and selling resulted in a trickle down of wealth from the better-off to the poor.

The initial advantage of being located close to the construction of major hotels and office blocks became a disadvantage when the buildings were completed and the kampung labour force was no longer required. By the late 1970s, most of the hotels and office blocks in the central-city area were almost self-sufficient units as far as the indigenous small-scale sector was concerned. They provided their own capital-intensive transport, food, and laundry facilities and required little from the surrounding society. Fences were erected around most of the new buildings to keep kampung dwellers out. Numerous guards stood at the doors and gateways of these new structures scrutinizing whomever entered. Kampung dwellers felt intimidated and believed these new edifices were only for foreigners and the Jakartan elite, as indeed they were. Thus Jakartans like Bud, Mus and Agus felt like aliens in their own town. The paths over which they had freely travelled or places from which they had traded were suddenly out-of-bounds.

The rapidly rising cost of land meant that only large commercial firms, government offices, embassies and the rich could afford to occupy the city centre. The densely populated kampungs such as Kebun Kacang, which had provided a low-cost haven for the poor who mainly worked in small-scale enterprises, were demolished to make way for new capital-intensive developments. Big firms wanted close access to government. Furthermore, unlike the kampung dwellers, they had the necessary capital, contacts and legal permits to maintain a foothold at the city centre. People like Bud or Mus could not afford to pay for a legal stall or house at the city centre. They lacked the resources, contacts or knowledge of legal requirements. They felt intimidated by rules, documents and legal procedures. An environment dominated by self-contained offices, embassies, hotels and richer households equipped with modern technology and the motor car made their small businesses unviable.

Demolition of densely populated kampungs to make way for office blocks, embassies, road widening schemes, markets and luxury housing estates resulted in population stagnation and further reduced the market for small-scale goods and services. The informal sector required a high pedestrian and population density for survival. Between 1971 and 1980 Jakarta's registered centry-city population declined by 3 percent and many more unregistered people probably left the area. Tanah Abang's registered population, in which Kebun Kacang was located fell by 6 percent. The inner-city poor were forced to the city's periphery or back to the villages from where they had come twenty or thirty years earlier. Four of the better-off households in Ibu Imah's neighbourhood migrated to the greener and more spacious suburbs to escape the congestion, noise, pollution, and constant threat of demolition.[84]

Until 1970, the municipal government's opposition towards the small-scale sector had little impact. During the 1950s and 1960s, the government had enough difficulties coping with the day-to-day problems of administration. It turned a blind eye to the encroachment on inner-city land by more and more people from the countryside. Attempts to restrict the operation of pedlars and becak drivers in the central-city area proved largely futile. Kampung dwellers felt they virtually had a free run of the town. Becak drivers such as Agus and Lukman were viewed as "kings of the street" and traders such as Bud and Mus felt free to sell as they pleased.

After 1970, however, the municipal government began to implement legislation against becak drivers, petty traders and migrants coming to the city. This marked the beginning of a determined effort to get rid of them from the central-city area. The city's planners viewed the small-scale sector as an anachronism which obstructed the transformation of Jakarta into a modern metropolis. Traders were to be forced off the street into modern markets whilst becak drivers were to move from their manually driven vehicles into motorized ones. Neither the petty traders like Bud nor the becak drivers like Agus, however, could afford these new facilities and struggled, against great odds, to maintain their former roles on the central-city streets.

By the late 1970s, most kampung dwellers in Kebun Kacang therefore faced a difficult choice of whether to try and gain access to formal sector employment at the city centre or move out to the periphery and remain in informal sector jobs. By then, however, most had missed their opportunity to move into the formal sector. In the mid-1970s, when they were earning high incomes, they had spent them on immediate consumption. They also lacked education and contacts so that the salaried jobs that were open to them were very poorly paid. Furthermore, many of these jobs would disappear with the recession of 1982. The informal sector, therefore provided their only means of survival, but its very insecurity made it a poverty trap.

1.

Estimates of the Size of the Small-Scale Sector in Jakarta, 1967–1971

Occupations	Minimum number	Maximum number	% of City's (a) labour Force
Becak drivers*	250,000	375,000 a.	18–25
Cottage ind.**	32,000		2
Petty trade***	100,000	500,000 b.	7–35
Construction**	80,000	85,000	5–6
Services**	145,000		10
Total	605,000	960,000	45–65

(a) Total Jakartan Work force was 1.4 million (Population Census 1971)

a. includes all those involved in becak driving, making and repairs

b. this figure may also include cottage industries and services

Source: * DKI *Penghapusan Becak di Jakarta*, (Jakarta, 1977) p. 12; Soedarno "Mobilitas Tenaga Kerja Antara Desa dan Kota Studi Kasus: Pengemudi Becak di Jakarta Timur", (Jakarta, 1976), pp. 5–6; Critchfield *Hello, Mister* p. 47.
** Sethuraman *Urbanization and Employment* pp. 7, 4.
*** McGee, T. G. and Yeung, Y. M. *Hawkers in Southeast Asian Cities: Planning for the Bazaar Economy*, (Ottawa, 1977) p. 33; Hugo "Population Mobility in West Java" p. 521; Dorodjatun Kuntjoro Jakti "Ekonomi Abang Becak", *Tempo*, 29 January 1972.

2. Hugo "Population Mobility in West Java" p. 49.
3. Sethuraman *Urbanization and Employment* pp. 7.5; Moir and Wirosardjono *The Jakarta Informal Sector* p. 125; Mazumdar, D. "The Urban Informal Sector", *World Development*, Vol. 4, No. 8: 1976: pp. 658–9.
4. Forbes "Development and the 'Informal' Sector" p. 188; Hidayat, "Sektor Informal dalam Struktur Ekonomi Indonesia", *Profil Indonesia*, (Jakarta, 1979) pp. 44–6; Herrle, P. "The Informal Sector: Survival Economy in Third World Metropolitan Cities", *Economics*, Vol. 26: 1982: p. 114.

5.

Classification of Work force according to Income-earning Activities in Ibu Imah's Neighbourhood in 1979

Occupations	Number of workers	Percentage
Informal sector (total)	(153)	(76)
Becak drivers	4	2
Cottage industry	20	10
Petty trade*	67	33
Construction	10	5
Kampung services	52	26
(Incl. household stalls*)	(22)	(11)
Formal sector (total)	(49)	(24)
Government/Private office	37	18

| Factory | 12 | 6 |
| Total | 202 | 100 |

* The 2 categories of petty trade and household stalls could be placed together as petty trade making up a total of 44 percent of the neighbourhood's work force.
Source: Field work 1975–1979

6. For a more detailed breakdown of income-earning activities in each of the 77 households see Jellinek, L. unpubl. Thesis Monash U.
7. Ministry of Information, *Short Guide Djakarta-Bogor-Bandung*, (Djakarta, 1956) p. 82.
8. Dick, H. W. "Urban Public Transport: Jakarta, Surabaya and Malang Part I and II", *Bulletin of Indonesian Economic Studies*, Vol. 17, Nos. 1 and 2: 1981: pp. 74–5.
9. Ministry of Information *Short Guide* p. 82.
10. Critchfield *Hello Mister!* p. 47; Soedarno "Mobilitas Tenaga" pp. 5–6; DKI *Penghapusan Becak* p. 12.
11. *Jakarta Post*, 9 September 1983.
12. Soedarno "Mobilitas Tenaga" pp. 45–56; Sartono, K. *The Pedicab in Yogyakarta—A Study in Low Cost Transportation and Poverty Problems*, (Yogyakarta, 1981) p. 51.
13. Soedarno "Mobilitas Tenaga" p. 50.
14. For circular migration amongst becak drivers see Hugo ("Population Mobility in West Java") and Soedarno ("Mobilitas Tenaga" p. 4) for Jakarta, Sartono (*The Pedicab in Yogyakarta* pp. 59–60) for Yogyakarta, and for Ujung Pandang see Forbes, D. "Urban-Rural Interdependence: The Trishaw Riders of Ujung Pandang" in Rimmer *Food, Shelter and Transport* pp. 223–34.
15. Dick "Urban Public Transport" p. 74; Johnson, R. et al. *Business Environment in an Emerging Nation*, (Evanston, 1966) pp. 226–9.
16. These memories are difficult to substantiate for Jakarta, but Frederick describes how the Japanese in 1943 tried to organize Surabaya's becak drivers by requiring them to join a cooperative, have identity cards, licences and determining their dress, fares and training: Frederick, W. H. "Indonesian Urban Society in Transition: Surabaya, 1926–1946", Ph.D Thesis, University of Michigan, 1978, pp. 427–30.
17. Silaban, B. and Djazuli, A. *Kelompok Migran Sirkuler Di DKI Jakarta*, (Jakarta, 1978) pp. 44–8.
18. For evidence of a similar process in Malang and Surabaya see Dick "Urban Public Transport" pp. 76–82.
19. DKI *Penghapusan Becak* p. 13; see also Sartono *The Pedicab in Yogyakarta* pp. 36, 42.
20. Dick "Urban Public Transport" p. 76; Hugo "Population Mobility in West Java" pp. 521–2.
21. *Kompas*, 30 March 1973.
22. Papanek "The Poor of Jakarta" pp. 9–12.
23. Dick "Urban Public Transport" p. 76.
24. *Kompas*, 9 September 1977, 3 December 1977, 2 March 1978.

25. As becak drivers were forced away from Jakarta, other cities such as Bandung, Semarang, Yogyakarta, Solo, Surabaya and Cirebon began to feel the impact of Jakarta's hostile policies. From the early to mid-1970s, these towns followed Jakarta's example, introducing motorized minicars and banning or restricting becaks to certain areas. See *Kompas*, 25 June 1973, 1 October 1973, 26 July 1974, 8 October 1974, 9 November 1977, 26 November 1977, 27 March 1978, 12 May 1978; *Jakarta Post*, 22 July 1983; for Surabaya and Malang see Dick "Urban Public Transport"; for Magelang see Surachman Samiun "Perantau Pengemudi Becak dan Gambaran Masa Depan Mereka: Kasus di Kota Magelang", (Yogyakarta, 1978) pp. 6–10; for Bandung see Hidayat et al. (eds.) *Penelitian Sosial Ekonomi Golongan Usaha Kecil di Sektor Informal Kotamadya Bandung*, (Bandung, 1978) pp. 153, 235; for an overview see Sartono *The Pedicab in Yogyakarta* p. 34.
26. Dorodjatun "Ekonomi Abang Becak" p. 50.
27. Heeren "The Urbanization of Djakarta" pp. 706–8.
28. Heeren "The Urbanization of Djakarta" p. 728.
29. Wertheim, W. "Urban Characteristics in Indonesia" in *East West Parallels: Sociological Approaches to Modern Asia*, (The Hague, 1964) p. 170.
30. Heeren "The Urbanization of Djakarta" p. 707.
31. Heeren "The Urbanization of Djakarta" p. 699.
32. Swianieswicz indicated that the number of small-scale manufacturing enterprises in Indonesia were increasing: Swianieswicz, S. "Tendencies to Development and Stagnation in the Indonesian Economy", *Ekonomi dan Keuangan Indonesia*, Vol. 11, Nos. 1 and 6: 1958: pp. 96, 99. Sadli and Ibrahim implied that under Sukarno there was a "sellers' market" for small-scale manufactures: Sadli, Moh "Indonesia's Experience with the Application of Technology and its Employment Effects", *Ekonomi dan Keuangan Indonesia*, Vol. 21, No. 3: 1973: 147–60; Ibrahim, M. A. "The Growth of Indonesian Industry: A Sectoral View", *Prisma*, No. 6, June: 1977: pp. 30–1. Palmer argued that, due to the absence of competition from large firms and imported products, in rural areas cottage industries reached their peak in the mid-1960s: Palmer, I. *The Indonesian Economy Since 1965: A Case Study of Political Economy*, (London, 1978) pp. 119–20. Sundrum also found a rise in employment in small-scale rural industry between 1961 and 1971: Sundrum, R. "Manufacturing Employment 1961–1971", *Bulletin of Indonesian Economic Studies*, Vol. 9, No. 1: 1975: 58–65.
33. Sethuraman *Urbanization and Employment* 2.9, 2.16.
34. Moir and Wirosardjono *The Jakarta Informal Sector* pp. 7, 74.
35. DKI *Hasil Survey Tenaga Kerja Sub-Sektor Industri Kecil DK-Jakarta 1979–1980*, (Jakarta, 1980) pp. 9, 42.

36.

Approximate Date of Birth and Decline of Cottage Industries in Kebun Kacang

Cottage industry	Birth	Decline
Car repairs	1950s	1968→
Becak making and repair	1950s	1970→
Radio repair	1950s	1972→
Battery recycling	1968	1978→
Ice-cream making	1968	1978→
Ice-cone making	1968	1978→
Kerosene stove	1972	1980→
Cloth cap making	1972	–

Source: Field work 1972–1981

37. Moir & Wirosardjono (*The Jakarta Informal Sector* pp. 84, 109) found that cottage industries more than any other informal sector activity in Jakarta suffered from competition from cheap, higher quality imported or locally made standardized goods from the formal sector. Evidence for Jakarta, however, is scarce. Karamoy, A. and Sablie, A. "The Communication Aspect and Its Impact on the Youth of Poor Kampungs in the City of Jakarta", *Prisma*, No. 1, May: 1975: p. 63, and Ibrahim "The Growth of Indonesian Industry" pp. 31–2. Hidayat (*Penelitian Sosial Ekonomi* pp. 233–4) suggested that competition from large firms producing Coca Cola, Seven-Up, Van Houten's chocolate etc. caused many food and drink cottage industries in Bandung to go out of existence within six years. Hill and Mubyarto found a decline in cottage industries between 1970 to 1976, especially in urban Yogyakarta: Hill, H. and Mubyarto "Economic Change in Yogyakarta", *Bulletin of Indonesian Economic Studies*, Vol. 14, No. 1: 1978: pp. 31–2. Forbes identified a similar phenomenon in Ujung Pandang with hand-made and machine-made ice-creams: Forbes, D. "Development and the 'Informal' Sector" pp. 20, 143–58, 191–2; "Production Reproduction and Underdevelopment: Petty Commodity Producers in Ujung Pandang", p. 11. Sritua Arief (*Indonesia* p. 126) found a decline in small-scale manufacture throughout Indonesia after 1971. McGee suggested that in Hong Kong cottage industries were destroyed by the modern sector at an earlier stage than petty trade: McGee, T. G. *Hawkers in Hong Kong: A Study of Planning and Policy in A Third World City*, (Hong Kong, 1973) p. 27.

38. DKI *Penghapusan Becak* p. 12.

39. Steer "Indonesian Urban Services Sector Report" pp. 34–5.

40. Jellinek "Circular Migration and the Pondok Dwelling System"; "The Pondok System and Circular Migration".

41. See also Swasono *Entrepreneurship in Indonesia* pp. 24, 62–5; McGee *Hawkers in Hong Kong* p. 171.

42. Atma Jaya *Hawkers in Jakarta*, (Jakarta, 1973) pp. 123–71.

43. Hugo "Population Mobility in West Java" p. 521.
44. McGee and Yeung *Hawkers in Southeast Asian Cities* pp. 33, 112.
45. Dorodjatun "Ekonomi Abang Becak" 50.
46. Moir & Wirosardjono *The Jakarta Informal Sector* p. 74.
47. DKI *Kaki Lima—Hasil Pencacahan Pedagang Kaki Lima di DKI*, (Jakarta, 1978) p. 37.
48. DKI, data collected by the Kelurahan of Kebun Kacang, (Jakarta, 1981).
49. See also Collyer, L. G. "Report on the Food Markets—Fruit and Vegetables, Meat and Rice", (Jakarta, 1972) p. 5; Forbes "Development and the 'Informal' Sector" pp. 113, 156, 165; Hugo "Population Mobility in West Java" p. 560.
50. Although in 1977/78 the becak was more expensive (Rp.100/1 litre of rice) than a bus, Bemo or Opelet (Jitneys) (Rp.50/0.5 litres of rice) for longer distance (2 Kilometers or more) travel, it was the cheapest and most convenient means of carting market produce for short distances along back streets.
51. Dick "Urban Public Transport" Part I pp. 71–2, Part II p. 73; Hidayat, "The Urban Informal Sector Survey of Java: Some Preliminary Findings", Colloquium on Rural-Urban Relations and Development Planning in Asia, (Japan, 1977).
52. Mintz suggests that in parts of urban Africa and the Caribbean, economic growth has forced women out of petty trade and into unskilled wage work such as domestic service which has caused a drop in social status, financial independence and mobility: Mintz, S. W. "Men, Women and Trade", *Comparative Studies in Society and History*, Vol. 13: 1971: pp. 247–69.
53. *Kompas*, 21 October 1977, 27 November 1977, 18 February 1978, 21 June 1978; *Jakarta Post*, 27 April 1983, 3 June 1983, 10 April 1983.
54. Universitas Indonesia *Laporan Hasil Survey Profile Pedagang Kaki Lima di DKI Jaya*, (Jakarta, 1976) pp. 26–8; see also Hidayat *Penelitian Sosial Ekonomi* pp. 153, 235.
55. DKI *Kaki Lima* pp. 30–3.
56. In the late 1970s, the yearly rents in official markets ranged from a minimum of Rp.150,000 (1304 litres of rice) for a second floor kiosk of 1 × 2.5 metres to over Rp.2,000,000 (17,391 litres of rice) on the ground floor for a kiosk of 5 × 2.5 metres (*Kompas*, 22 June 1978; *Jakarta Post*, 27 January 1983). Additional daily charges for market administration, rubbish collection and night security amounted to Rp.500–700 (4–6 litres of rice). See also Forbes "Development and the 'Informal' Sector" pp. 106–11.
57. Tomasoa, 1978: pers. com.
58. *Jakarta Post*, 6 January 1984. See also Krausse "The Kampungs of Jakarta" p. 58; Universitas Indonesia *Laporan Hasil Survey* p. 28; Forbes "Development and the 'Informal' Sector" pp. 106–11; Praginanto "Pak Parto Pengusaha Warung Tegal", *Galang*, Vol. 1, No. 1: 1983: p. 45.
59. *BPS, Indikator Ekonomi*, 1983.

60. See Mintz for the Caribbean and Africa and Moser for Bogota on the rise in prices and stagnant or declining position of petty traders, especially women, as a consequence of the modernization and streamlining of urban marketing: Mintz, S. W. "The Role of the Middleman in the Internal Distribution System of a Caribbean Peasant Economy", *Human Organization*, Vol. 15, No. 2: 1956: pp. 21–2; Mintz, S. W. "Internal Market Systems as Mechanisms of Social Articulation" in *Proceedings of the 1959 Annual Spring Meetings of the American Ethnological Society*, (Seattle, 1959) pp. 24–5; Mintz "Men, Women and Trade"; Moser, C. "The Dual Economy and Marginality Debate and the Contribution of Micro Analysis: Market Sellers in Bogota", *Development and Change*, Vol. 8, No. 4: 1977: pp. 479–87.

61. There is disagreement in the literature about the impact of modern retailing and the rise of the middle class on petty trade. While Moser ("The Dual Economy and Marginality Debate" pp. 473, 478, 486) for Bogota and McGee (*Hawkers in Hong Kong* pp. 171, 185–86) for Hong Kong support my findings, Tokeman for Santiago and Waworoentoe for Bandung argue that petty traders remained viable in the face of formal sector competition: Tokeman, V. E. "Competition Between the Informal and Formal Sectors in Retailing: The Case of Santiago", World Development, Vols. 6, 9 and 10: 1978: 1187–1198; Waworoentoe, W. *Hawkers and Vendors in Bandung*, (Bandung, 1974) p. 27. Forbes suggests that some petty traders were "conserved" whilst others were "destroyed" depending upon the nature of the goods sold: Forbes, D. "Petty Commodity Production and Underdevelopment: The Case of Pedlar and Trishaw Riders in Ujung Pandang, Indonesia" in Diamond, D. and McLoughlin, J. B. (eds.), *Progress in Planning*, Vol. 16, No. 2: 1981: 107–78.

62. For a young, attractive and intelligent kampung girl, prostitution was the easiest route, at least temporarily, into the formal sector. Most prostitutes were self-employed and their work was unpredictable, but they rapidly gained resources. Equally quickly, however, these girls lost their wealth and slumped back into poverty.

63. Sethuraman *Urbanization and Employment* 2.8, 7.4, 7.10.

64. See also Hidayat (*Penelitian Sosial Ekonomi* pp. 96, 235) and Sannen for the irregularity of construction work in Bandung: Sannen, Ad. M. H. "Mandur and Tukang: The Functioning of Informal Subcontractors and Building Workers in the Construction Sector of Bandung" in Nas *The Indonesian City* pp. 220, 227. 90 percent of the construction workers had irregular jobs.

65. According to Padco, 90 percent of the housing was built by residents themselves rather than government or large private firms. It is difficult to determine, however, whether most of this housing was built by the home owner or small gangs of local construction workers because kampung dwellers tended to say they built their own houses even when they employed a builder: Padco, "Perumnas Policy Review and Background Materials for Pelita III Planning", *Consultants Report World Bank*, Vol. 2, (Washington D.C., 1977) p. 41.

66. Suryo, D. "Social and Economic Life in Rural Semarang under Colonial Rule in the Later 19th Century", Ph.D Thesis, Monash University, 1982, pp. 135–58.
67. The composition of this category was unclear. It certainly did not include household food stalls. (Sethuraman *Urbanization and Employment* 7.4)
68. Sethuraman *Urbanization and Employment* 2.8–2.9, 7.5, 7.21.
69. Moir & Wirosardjono *The Jakarta Informal Sector* p. 7.
70.

The Type and Number of Services in Ibu Imah's Neighbourhood 1979

Type of service	Number
Unskilled service	
Household stalls*	22
Water seller	4
Laundresses	7
Domestic servant	7
Skilled services	
Dressmaker	5
Masseur and healer	5
Midwives	2
Total	52

Source: As Table 3.
* stalls could be included under petty trade thus bringing the number of petty traders in the neighbourhood to 89 instead of 67.

71. Moir and Wirosardjono *The Jakarta Informal Sector* pp. 106, 129–30.
72. DKI *Hasil Survai Sosial Ekonomi DKI*, (Jakarta, 1981).
73. *BPS, Indikator Ekonomi, Pekerja Sektor Informal di Indonesia*, 1986: p. 60. 76. *Ibid*, 1978: 28, 31,
74. In 1961 payments in kind (rice, sugar, fish, cooking oil, kerosene, soap, transport, housing etc.) to compensate for the freeze in money wages, were estimated to make up from 66 to 87 percent of government workers' total income (Johnson *Business Environment in an Emerging Nation* pp. 93–5).
75. See also Manning, C. "Pockets of Privilege Amidst Mass Poverty: Wages and Working Conditions in Indonesian Industry" in Jellinek, L., Manning, C. and Jones, G. *The Life of the Poor in Indonesian Cities*, (Melbourne, 1978) pp. 17–31.
76. Although legislated, not all of these benefits were received by the lower-level officials such as sweepers, cleaners, guards etc.
77. See also Manning "Pockets of Privilege" pp. 17–31.
78. Pinches ("Anak-Pawis" pp. 252–54) writing about the Philippines stressed the insecurity of wage work even in large-scale multinational firms. "Nearly half of his sample who in 1979 had full-time jobs (mainly in large firms) were without regular work" in 1982.

79. Cole, W. E. and Sanders, P. D. "A Modified Dualism Model for Latin America", *Journal of Developing Areas*, Vol. 6, No. 2: 1972: 185–98; Moser "The Dual Economy and Marginality Debate".
80. Dick, 1985: 71–90.
81. DKI, 1979c: 59.
82. Sethuraman, 1974: 1.3; PCD, 1973: 3, Tables VII, VIII.
83. Critchfield, 1973a: 9; Sritua Arief, 1977: 31; The National Times, 4–9.6.1973: 47.
84.

Population Growth in Jakarta by District Showing Decline in Central Jakarta and Tanah Abang

District	1971	1980	% of Population Increase/Decrease
Central	1,275,436	1,236,876	−3.02
Tanah Abang	253,809	239,004	−5.8
North	616,777	976,045	+36.8
West	828,179	1,231,188	+32.7
South	1,051,843	1,579,795	+33.41
East	801,021	1,456,750	+45
Total	4,574,056	6,480,654	+29.42

Sources: DKI (1979: 19)
          DKI (1980a: 1, 22)

4

The Penetration of Government

Although Kebun Kacang was at the heart of Jakarta, until 1970 government seemed to have almost no presence there. The Ministry of Interior and the city government offices, which were supposed to control and order most citizens' lives, were within walking distance. Yet, in the early 1970s, a person could live in the neighbourhood for many months without being aware of the government. Kampung dwellers satisfied their own basic needs of housing, work and amenities in their own way. After the mid-1970s, however, government welfare programs began to have an impact.

Kampung dwellers, in turn, had no positive expectations of government. Bitter experience had taught them to distrust government programs. Most Kampung dwellers had never been informed of the government's welfare programs or understood how they could benefit by them. Most of the policies with which they were familiar, such as becak, trader and kampung clearance, had hurt.

Until 1920, urban kampungs remained outside the sphere of municipal administration and were self-governing under *adat* customary law and the Government Regulation of 1854.[1] During the first two decades of the Ethical Policy, from about 1900, when concern with the welfare of the indigenous population encouraged the extension of government into village affairs, urban kampungs were completely overlooked. In the 1920s, however, legislation was passed transferring control of internal kampung affairs to the municipal administration.[2] The timing of this legislation seems to have been related to growing fears on the part of the European elite of the spread of disease. Rapid population growth in the city had brought new European suburbs such as Menteng into close proximity with overcrowded and unsanitary Indonesian kampungs.[3]

In 1920 plans were laid for a Kampung Improvement Program in Java's major cities. The scheme was inspired by engineers who wanted to implement similar physical improvements to those applied in the densely populated centres of European cities in the late nineteenth century. The essential task was to provide access to a safe drinking water unpolluted by sewerage. Due, however to mismanagement, lack of funds, the onset of the Depression and delays, the impact of Kampung Improvement was disappointing.[4] Kebun Kacang, then still a pocket of market gardening, seems to have benefitted from the provision of a large well.[5]

Between 1942–1945 the Japanese were frustrated by their lack of control over the kampung population and what to them seemed to be indiscipline and disorganization. They introduced an urban neighbourhood administrative system, the *Tonarigumi*, which most scholars view as the first officially sponsored administrative network at the kampung level.[6] Based on the organization of urban neighbourhoods in Japan, the Japanese tried to establish units which were meant to register and control all people in the neighbourhood and serve as a vigilance corps.[7] These units were not set up in all areas and many kampung dwellers remained totally unaware of them. By 1970, kampung dwellers in Ibu Imah's neighbourhood could not recall the *Tonarigumi* and only vaguely recall the *Gumicho*, the *Tonarigumi* headman.

In the four years between the Japanese surrender and Dutch recognition of Indonesia's Independence in December 1949, there appears to have been no effective municipal control of kampung affairs. Until the first Dutch military action of July 1947, the Republican Balai Agung claimed to control the municipal affairs of the Indonesian population. Thereafter, a symbolic control was maintained from the Republican General Hospital at Salemba and, after August 1948, from an informal public health clinic in Menteng and a few unofficial Republican schools.[8] Although there is scant information on what was happening to kampung dwellers during these years, it seems likely that they were very much left to their own devices. After substantial out-migration from the city during the confusion and turmoil of 1946, when the Dutch were re-asserting their control, settlement of inner-city land continued apace. The occupation of land by newcomers had accelerated during the Japanese occupation when kampung dwellers had been encouraged to cultivate vacant urban land to overcome the dire food shortage. Inner-city land settlement was further encouraged by the Republicans to restrict Dutch access to these areas.[9]

For almost a decade after Independence in 1949, the municipal government had difficulty in obtaining control over the use of central city land. In the early 1950s, Kampung dwellers' occupation of the land between Jakarta and Kebayoran Baru, a new satellite suburb, held up the completion of Jalan Thamrin, the six lane highway. The rules and regulations governing land occupancy and registration remained confused. Kampung dwellers were not aware of the extent of their legal title to land. Yet a government which espoused human rights, self-determination and freedom could not simply expropriate the homes of its citizens, many of whom had just fought a war of independence on its behalf. Furthermore, the government was burdened by the numerous other tasks of daily administration and lacked the resources to develop such land. It was obliged to provide alternative land and assistance to those it forced away. The resettlement procedures were time consuming, cumbersome and expensive.

It was only during the 1950s that kampung dwellers' interests were defended by a vocal municipal council which although not representative, espoused their point of view.[10] During the elections of 1955 and 1957, political parties, trade unions and women's groups wooed voters and kampung dwellers had channels through which their grievances were aired. In 1956, the municipal council authorized the enforcement of restrictions upon the operations of petty traders, which were viewed as "cluttering the streets and lowering the tone of the city". Nevertheless, the council was unwilling to allow traders to be cleared from the streets until alternative trade locations were provided.[11]

After 1959, the return to the Constitution of 1945 placed much greater power in the hands of the President. Sukarno, a civil engineer by training, dreamed of Jakarta becoming one of the world's great cities and was impatient with the slow progress of the 1950s. In 1960, he increased the powers of the Mayor, retitled him Governor, released him from the authority of the municipal council and made him directly responsible to the President. Nevertheless, the Jakarta Master Plan, completed in 1960 and addressing major problems such as transport, water supply, industry and green belts, was allowed to lapse. Instead, manpower and resources were diverted to complete various prestige projects in time for the Asian Games in 1962. City planners could now clear away kampungs without having to worry about opposition. Their power had been enhanced by the declaration in 1957 of Martial Law. Whereas it had taken over half a decade to move 500 people from the path of Jalan Thamrin in the early fifties, it took only two years to move 47,000 people to make way for the Asian Games Complex. Although both the Master Plan and Sukarno had proposed slum clearance and the building of multi-storey flats, no such project was attempted.[12]

Members of Ibu Imah's neighbourhood knew nothing about the

Master Plan or Sukarno's dreams of slum clearance. They did not even distinguish between the earlier and more lenient Parliamentary period (1949–1959) and the later and more authoritarian period of Guided Democracy (1959–1965). In their memories, the government had left them alone, enabling them to set up their houses on vacant central city land and to work in small scale income earning activities. If government demolished their homes for some of Sukarno's grandiose schemes, they could readily move elsewhere but still remain near the city centre. Central city space was still abundant, kampung dwellers possessions were few, and their simple bamboo houses were easily resurrected. Many of those who had came to Kebun Kacang in the late 1950s and early 1960s had previously lived in other nearby sites.

During Sukarno's period kampung dwellers could recall only the literacy and cooperative programs. They remembered that informal illiteracy eradication courses were held in local prayer houses or wherever there was space. Most kampung dwellers were at first reluctant to attend these classes because they felt too old, embarrassed or lazy. When attendance picked up, however, the local headman in Imah's neighbourhood charged a fee for a program that was supposed to be free. Immediately the numbers attending the course declined. Nevertheless, in the city as a whole, the estimated literacy rate had risen from 12 percent in 1930 to 64 percent in 1961.[13]

According to the government's cooperative scheme instituted in 1959, government-controlled shops and kampung cooperatives were supposed to provide basic commodities such as rice, cooking oil, sugar, salt and tea at fixed prices to all ration card holders. The program was designed to bypass Chinese retail outlets which were blamed for the unfair price rises.[14] In Ibu Imah's neighbourhood, the cooperative's manager disappeared with the goods and the kampung dwellers' financial contributions. Nevertheless, through this system some kampung dwellers managed to accumulate rice and textiles which they then sold on the black market. Officially, however, it was recognized that a lack of capital, experienced staff and an inadequate delivery system caused the program to run into difficulties.

Governor Ali Sadikin

In 1966, after the Coup in 1965, Sadikin, a dynamic former Marine Corps commander and Minister of Shipping, was appointed Governor of Jakarta by Sukarno. To the position he brought the dreams of Sukarno, but he also came to epitomize the New Order's administrative efficiency. He confronted enormous problems. The city's infrastructure, designed to serve half a million people in the 1930s, had been badly run down, but now had to cope with a population at least ten times as large. Yet, essential improvements in housing, education and health facilities would only lead to a further influx of newcomers. Thus, before improvements could take place, migration had to be curtailed.

Sadikin seemed to have a systematic approach to solving these problems. A reinvigoration of the kampung administrative system was to be followed by the registration of all the city's inhabitants and restrictions placed on the entry of any newcomers. Unregulated self-employed jobs such as petty trade and becak driving were to be banned from the main streets of Jakarta, so making the city even less attractive to prospective migrants and forcing those who were already in the city illegally back to their village homes. Only after the population growth of the city had been brought under control, could welfare programs have a beneficial effect.

In 1966–67 Sadikin tried to reinvigorate the kampung administrative system. Previous governors, such as Sudiro in 1954, had tried unsuccessfully to revitalize the system established by the Japanese.[17] According to Logsdon, the local leadership system was supposed to provide a link between the kampung dwellers and the government. Information was to be conveyed through these local units from the government to the people and back to the government again. Kampungs were to organize their own civil defence, social welfare (ie. collection funds for the poor, orphans and bereaved), prayer house construction, cleanliness, health and mutual aid.

In order to lessen the city government's financial and administrative burden, Sadikin tried to stimulate community development from below. He encouraged competition between urban neighbourhoods, much as existed between villages in rural areas. Community projects were to be given orders of merit from Siaga (just prepared), Swadaya (showing some effort), to Swasembada (self-supporting). All these activities were to be coordinated by the City's Community Development Committee (Lembaga Kerja Pembangunan Masjarakat Desa Khusus Ibu Kota-LKPMDK).

In reality, however, neither the Rukun Tetangga (neighbourhood association), Rukun Warga (community association) nor LKPMDK functioned as intended. The LKPMDK was not recognized by the citizens of Imah's neighbourhood or Jakartans in general.[18] The RT and RW system remained spottily organized and little utilized. In the 1970s it still failed to provide a means of communication between the government and the people. In most cases, policies issued by government were not conveyed by headmen to their kampung dwellers. Even less often were the wishes of the kampung dwellers conveyed via the headman and subdistrict chief (lurah) to the government.

Until 1968, people coming to Jakarta had required identification and a permit to travel, though these documents were not rigorously policed. After 1968, however, every citizen coming to the city had to register and obtain a Jakarta Identity card. Compulsory registration was closely tied to the government's decision of 1970 to close the city to most newcomers. Officially no one was to reside in the city without proof of regular employment, fixed accommodation and a Jakarta Identity Card.[19] In practice this policy proved impossible to enforce.

The difficulties of implementing the closed city policy were well illustrated in Ibu Imah's neighbourhood. The local headman continued to rent out rooms to people who were temporary migrants from the village with no fixed work, accommodation or identity cards. He ignored government policy by issuing identity cards to newcomers who wished to stay. The headman's flouting of the rules meant that kampung dwellers felt free to rent rooms to friends and relatives from their village.

Aware that the flood of migrants to Jakarta could not be stopped just by administrative decree, in 1971 Governor Sadikin began to restrict the main occupations in which temporary migrants found employment, specifically becak driving and petty trade. Both occupations had long frustrated city planners as eyesores and causes of traffic congestion, which was now acute. The aim was not just to force many temporary migrants back to the village, but by making life difficult for them in the city, Sadikin hoped that the news would travel back to the villages, so deterring further migration.

Except for the anti-becak measures, Ibu Imah's neighbourhood did not feel the impact of the closed city policies until the mid-1970s. By 1972, only four becak drivers remained. Despite the anti-trader legislation, as late as 1975 petty traders were still thriving. Thereafter, the legislation began to be enforced in the central city area with disastrous consequences for the livelihoods of traders in Ibu Imah's neighbourhood.

Concurrent with the extension of control over the city's population, in 1969 the Jakarta government initiated a Kampung Improvement Program. This was followed in the early 1970s by a pilot family planning program involving the setting up of many health clinics. The building of schools became a high priority. In the mid-1970s, a low interest credit scheme was launched. A concern with welfare seems to have been part of the rationale for the closed city policies. This concern was given new urgency by the Malari riots in Jakarta of January 1974. Although it was in large measure a dispute between different elites jockeying for power and manipulating the urban poor to their own advantage, government officials were suddenly made very much aware of the stark gap between the city's rich and poor. There were attacks against Chinese stores, burning and looting of shops and supermarkets and smashing of Japanese cars. Partly as a reaction to this, the nation's second five year plan (1974–1979) emphasized equality and the promotion of indigenous business. By the mid-1970s international agencies such as the World Bank, United Nations and ILO were also encouraging the government to look at the plight of the urban poor.

Kampung Improvement

The kampung Improvement Program reached Kebun Kacang in 1977–1978. The local headman opposed it on the grounds that it would destroy his extra rooms and a toilet which encroached onto the pathway. Most kampung dwellers were unaware of the program paved roads. The growing density of kampung housing meant that the laying of pipes for water and sewerage would have been technically difficult and very expensive. Furthermore, concrete paths and drains had an obvious appeal to planners because they were so highly visible.

The kampung Improvement Program reached Kebun Kacang in 1977–1978. The local headman opposed it on the grounds that it would destroy his extra rooms and a toilet which encroached on to the pathway. Most kampung dwellers were unaware of the program or of the headman's opposition to it. The few who asked about it were told that the government would demolish parts of their homes to make way for the new path, without paying compensation. In the end, the new paths and drains were laid in a richer neighbouring community, some of whose members had requested the program in the first place, while only five houses in Imah's neighbourhood were directly affected.

The path was built one metre above the existing walkway which made it difficult for kampung dwellers to get into and out of their homes. It aptly reflected the relationship between the government and the people. Guards had to prevent some hostile residents from obstructing the work of the construction gang. When the gang withdrew the neighbourhood had lost its only available area of open space. Some houses had been partially demolished to make room for the path. Their owners, who received no compensation, were told they were making a worthy sacrifice for the good of the entire community. Houses which abutted on to the path had to construct

steps up to the path so that the residents could get out of their front
doors. There were sound reasons for building the path above ground
level, for the area was flooded every year. But the waters now
accumulated in the homes instead of on the pathway. Nevertheless,
the kampung now had its first all-weather path. The kampung dwellers began using it immediately and few of them doubted its value.
Yet none of them believed that the government had constructed the
path for their benefit. They believed someone in authority and a
building contractor had colluded to profit from the pathway.

Health and Family Planning

Among kampung dwellers' basic needs, the city government gave
high priority to health and family planning. Health care was not a
new program. During the 1950s, the government had undertaken an
impressive array of public health measures, establishing hospitals and
clinics, carrying out mass vaccinations against smallpox and innocu-
lations against tetanus and typhus, and spraying DDT to combat
malaria. As a result, the city's mortality rate had fallen from an
estimated 20 per thousand in 1935/37 to 14 per thousand in 1955.[20]
Family planning, however, was something new. The program had
been introduced at the national level in 1967 and the Jakarta administration, under Sadikin, was one of the first to implement it.[21] Both
the health and family planning programs emphasized the building of
clinics. These were unfamiliar to kampung dwellers, however, and
took some years to gain acceptance.

In the mid-1970s, most members of Imah's neighbourhood were
still unaware or frightened of modern medicine, despite the fact that
there were at least three polyclinics within twenty minutes' walking
distance of the neighbourhood. These fears were mainly based upon
rumours and the unknown. Mothers threatened their children with
injections if they misbehaved. As most women hardly left the neighbourhood, a twenty minute walk, carrying a sick child and then
queuing for many hours at the clinic, seemed long and troublesome.
They feared the cost. Most did not realize they could get medical
treatment free of charge if they had a document from the headman
proving their inability to pay. But those who knew realized that the
document from the headman entailed a fee which was as much as
they would have had to pay at the clinic without it. Some kampung
dwellers claimed that only old, unwanted drugs were used. Others
feared the impersonal nature of the clinic's nurse and doctor who had
little time to talk and treated everybody in the same way, with an
injection. They preferred the more familiar and flexible traditional

healer. When they were eventually forced into government hospitals because their disease had progressed too far, they often died, which only confirmed the kampung dwellers' worst suspicions about western medicine.

Throughout the 1970s, the headman failed to promote the family planning program to the kampung dwellers. Although at the outset he had been informed of the program by the local government, he failed to pass on this information. His sixth wife continued to become pregnant and, after six children, joined the program only when all headmen's wives were instructed to set a good example. Even then, most of her neighbours remained unaware, fearful of, or uninterested in the program.[22]

Education

In line with national policy, the Jakarta administration also gave high priority to education. As with public health, education had involved a massive effort in Jakarta after Independence. According to census figures, literacy rates for residents over the age of ten had risen from 12 percent in 1930 to 64 percent in 1961.[23] Unlike the 1950s, however, when there had been much grass roots adult education, in the 1970s state education was directed exclusively to children. As in the case of health care and polyclinics, education seemed to involve a preoccupation with buildings. For many kampung dwellers, cost and complicated enrolment procedures prevented them gaining access to these schools.

In Imah's neighbourhood in the early 1970s, schooling beyond the first two to three years was still viewed as a luxury which few kampung dwellers could afford. They expected their children to become artisans or petty traders and felt once they had learnt the basic skills of reading and counting further education would be of little use. Despite the official policy of universal free primary education, most families in the neighbourhood sent their school age children to a locally run Islamic school, which they claimed provided a better and cheaper education. At government schools there was a long waiting list and children had to enrol a year or more in advance. Many lacked the necessary birth certificate and the enrolment fee of up to Rp.30,000 (260 litres of rice) in 1978. Their children were tested for admission and, if they had not attended a kindergarten, usually failed. To enrol at a kindergarten cost Rp.25,000 (217 litres of rice), and then there were additional monthly fees. The Islamic school, by contrast, seemed actively to recruit kampung children and there was no initial enrolment fee.[24]

Small Scale Credit

Perhaps the best example of the gap between the good intentions of government and the reality of kampung life was the small scale credit scheme. The first scheme, Kredit Investasi Kecil (KIK), had been launched in 1974 after the Malari riots to encourage local entrepreneurs and to break the stranglehold of private and predominantly Chinese money-lenders.[25] In 1978, a report found that because of the large minimum borrowing and the collateral requirements, less than 0.1 percent of Jakarta's petty traders made use of the city's official credit facilities.[26] To overcome these shortcomings, in 1977 the government introduced the Canda Kulak (Small Traders' Credit Scheme) which provided loans of under Rp.50,000 (500 litres of rice) with no collateral requirements. Few kampung dwellers, however, were informed about the scheme.

In Imah's neighbourhood, only three kampung dwellers made use of the Canda Kulak, which was set up in a local school less than five minutes' walk from their homes. Most did not know such facilities existed. Those who were familiar with the low interest (12 percent per annum) credit scheme felt that the loan procedures were complex and cumbersome. Forms had to be filled in to prove identity, residential status, and the productive use to which the money would be put. These forms had to be collected from the Canda Kulak office and then signed by the headman. Getting signatures from the headman entailed the expenditure of not only time but also money. Kampung dwellers were not willing to spend many hours filling out forms and negotiating with officials for a loan. Most urgently needed money for a debt, medical expense, school fee or trade and could not wait the two to three weeks it took to obtain a loan. But the government's loans were not supposed to be used for such unproductive purposes. The office was only open at restricted hours once a week and manned by impersonal staff who usually issued loans of less than half of what the kampung dweller had requested (i.e. Rp.5000 or 10,000 instead of Rp.15,000 or 25,000).

The private moneylenders were much more convenient for the kampung dweller even if they charged an exhorbitant interest rate of over 300 percent per annum. They came to one's home upon request. They lived in the community or went from door to door each day. No collateral, proof of Jakarta citizenship or guarantee of how the money would be spent was required. The money was issued the day after the loan was requested. All the lender needed to know was that the person borrowing the money really lived in the area and would not run away. The moneylender was personally familiar with the borrower. Little paperwork was involved. The debtor received a receipt for each repayment. The debtor told his creditor that he wished to delay repayment if he felt unable to pay for one or two days. Although kampung dwellers paid a high interest for this money-lending service, its flexibility, ease, door-to-door and personalized style suited them.

Local Leadership

As the lowest official of the government's salaried administrative hierarchy, the *lurah* was supposed to convey government policies to the kampung dwellers and to pass kampung dwellers' views back to government. The *lurah* of Kebun Kacang, however, rarely met the local headmen or people of Ibu Imah's neighbourhood. *Lurahs* were moved to a new position every few years and the *lurah*, a military man who was appointed in 1980, evidently never set foot in Kebun Kacang. The previous lurah was said once to have entered Ibu Minah's neighbourhood to attend a fair.[27]

Although the *lurah* was ultimately responsible for the registration and welfare of the kampung dwellers, he received his salary and promotion from the higher levels of government and thus directed his attention and most of his time to meeting with higher officials. His subordinates were left with the job of communicating government policies to local headmen. Even these lesser officials met local head-men only once or twice a year, at large meetings held at the Kelura-han office. These meetings were meant to convey government policies and programs to the kampung headmen who were then meant to convey them to the kampung dwellers. But the *lurahs'* uninformed and poorly motivated subordinates were unable to convey policies to the local headmen. Leaders at each level silently acquiesced with instructions from above, which they often did not understand, dis-agreed with or had no intention of implementing. Consequently, as policies were conveyed through the administrative hierarchy, they were distorted and changed at every level.

The headman was a part-time, unpaid official chosen by consensus among household heads to represent a neighbourhood of between 40 and 60 households. He was the critical link between the government administration and the kampung dwellers, assisting the *lurah* while at the same time being expected to protect the people who had chosen him. If government policies harmed his constituents he was expected to shield them against such policies. Most kampung heads did this in practice whenever they had nothing to gain by implementing government policies. But if the government coopted them by infor-mal financial incentives and other benefits they helped to implement its policies.

In Ibu Imah's neighbourhood, the position of headman seems to have been passed from father to son. The election was little more than a formality. Since Harjo's leadership during the 1940s and 1950s, Imah's kinship group had monopolized the position. Tole (1960s–1977), and then Sugi (1977–81), succeeded to the position. A rival candidate was put forward by some of the central Javanese in the neighbourhood as a successor to Tole in 1977, but he lost out to the block vote of Imah's kin group.

Tole, who was barely literate but had served as a guard or policeman under the Dutch and Japanese, was viewed as appropriate for the job. He could not be intimidated by government officials. He had the necessary *jagoan* (tough) qualities for leadership. This was illustrated when Tole prevented the military from searching Imah's neighbourhood for communists in 1965. His refusal to take heed of the "closed city policies" enabled kampung dwellers to continue inviting their village relatives to the neighbourhood. But the very bold and stubborn qualities which enabled him to turn a blind eye to government instructions also served to undermine welfare programs such as health, family planning and kampung improvement.

Tole's job as local headman came without an official salary and he felt compelled to charge the kampung dwellers a fee for whatever service he provided. It was a well-established procedure and most kampung dwellers expected to pay a fee of from Rp.200 to Rp.500 (2–5 litres of rice in 1977).[28] For most kampung heads in Jakarta such work and income was only a side line activity. They performed other types of income-earning activities throughout the day and only turned to their RT responsibilities at night, on Sundays or before departing for work in the mornings.[29] For Tole, however, it was his main activity and source of livelihood.

Tole's performed a multitude of functions. His most important function was to organize the roster for night security. Every young adult male was supposed to spend some evenings guarding the community. Tole took up a monthly collection of Rp.200 (2 litres) per household to pay for the guards' coffee, uniforms and honorarium (Rp.1000/10 litres per guard per week). Those kampung dwellers who wished to avoid night duty paid him an extra fee. Tole registered newcomers who came to stay in the neighbourhood and received cigarette money from those who did not want to be registered. He sold Jakarta identity cards to those who wanted them, even though the government had forbidden their issue to newcomers. He was notified at the birth of a child, a death or marriage, and for a fee issued the necessary documents. He provided building permits to kampung dwellers who wished to rebuild their homes on what was considered government or reclaimed land. He served as an intermediary in the buying and selling of neighbourhood houses, for which he received a commission. Despite all these transactions and documentation, Tole's official records of who lived in the neighbourhood were notoriously unreliable. Many of his dealings with his constituents were not entered in the official records, for as he disingenuously reminded them, to register officially at the Kelurahan entailed additional expenses. For many kampung dwellers, no higher authorization or registration seemed necessary.

Upon his father's death, Sugi inherited his leadership position. In the kampung dweller's eyes, Sugi was a rogue much like his father. His similar tough qualities were viewed as useful for leadership. He had led street gangs in his youth and was not frightened of anybody. His main appeal, however, was that he did not interfere much in the neighbourhood. Sugi minded his own business and that appealed to the kampung dwellers. He had little time for the neighbourhood and insisted that leadership had been forced upon him and was not rewarding.[30] Unlike his father, who had survived on the money he gained from being kampung head and the rent of several rooms and a toilet, Sugi earned most of his living outside the community. He worked as an electrician for the National Electricity Corporation during the day and as a private electrician after hours. He was therefore hardly ever at home. During the evenings, his wife frequently had to tell kampung dwellers that he was away. It was never clear whether he was doing night duty or having an affair, but kampung dwellers suspected the latter.

Because Sugi was hardly ever in the neighbourhood and could not be bothered with the mundane chores of leadership, he delegated the work to two almost illiterate and otherwise unemployed young men. Their main function was to collect the monthly administrative fee of Rp.500 (5 litres of rice in 1977) from each of the households. Some kampung dwellers felt reluctant to pay the fee because they did not know what it was for. Ostensibly it was for rubbish collection, security, burials and administration.

Until the late 1970s there was no proper rubbish collection system in the community. Throughout the 1970s kampung dwellers continued to throw their refuse into the Cideng canal, even though they had been told not to do so by government officials when it was dredged in 1974. Some households who lived closest to the stinking canal took it upon themselves to police the kampung dwellers. But there were always some who surreptitiously continued to dump their rubbish in the canal. After considerable frustration and annoyance Sugi eventually hired two men with a push-cart to collect rubbish from the community each day and paid them some or most of the money which had been collected for this purpose. It was difficult to tell what role government played in organizing this new system. Most services or improvements in the kampung were made by individual households.[31]

A Voluntary Worker

Bridging the gap between the kampung dwellers and the state was very difficult. Ibu Kino—a Dutch educated lower middle class Minangkabau who lived in an adjacent "upgraded" community, took it upon herself to "uplift" the kampung dwellers of Ibu Imah's neighbourhood. As her husband provided an adequate income from his textile trade in Tanah Abang market, she had sufficient time and resources to devote herself to voluntary work. It was not clear what motivated her. She claimed her richer friends and relatives thought she was crazy. She seemed to be driven both by an individual desire to help the poor as well as a wish to gain public recognition.

In the mid- to late 1960s, the prayer house was the focus of Ibu Kino's organizational activities. Prior to this, the prayer house had been a mere shack, tucked away between the shanties which hardly anyone ever visited. Ibu Kino encouraged kampung women to decorate it and established a women's *mushollah* association to which she invited outside speakers. Along with some other middle class women she set up a school in a vacant building nearby for the neighbourhood's poorest children. She was able to help and encourage some poor parents such as Badrun, Dini, Samilah and Wira to give their children an education. Her confidence, education and contacts enabled her to arrange for enrolment fees at government schools to be waived for bright children who had completed her primary school and whose parents could not pay.

In the mid-1970s, Ibu Kino's activities were recognized by the Department of Social Welfare. She was given kerosene stoves and sewing machines to distribute to the poor of Ibu Imah's neighbourhood. Those such as Sani, Samilah, and Wira who received these handouts were thrilled, but those who failed to receive them were jealous and accused Ibu Kino of favouritism. Thus, increased resources and recognition by the authorities of Ibu Kino's social work gave rise to tension within Ibu Imah's neighbourhood.

As Ibu Kino's ties with the Department of Social Welfare grew over the decade, the kampung dwellers increasingly viewed her as representing the interests of the government rather than themselves. She was one of the notables in the area who had requested kampung improvement which had caused difficulties for the less well-off in the community, who had been forced to rebuild their houses to the level of the new pathway. She encouraged kampung women to attend the family planning clinic but her brusque manner alienated them. She came into their homes and suggested that they accept contraception even when they had no children, were too old or beyond child bearing age. Many maintained that the cookery, sewing and self beautification courses Ibu Kino promoted were for the middle class with money and leisure and not for poor overworked kampung dwellers like themselves. They felt that Ibu Kino was imposing programs upon them which were inappropriate to their immediate daily needs. To Ibu Kino's chagrin, only one or two attended the classes. Privately she confided that the kampung women lacked motivation, diligence or the will to improve their lives.

Recognition of Ibu Kino's welfare work increasingly came from the State rather than the kampung and seemed to drive a wedge between her and the kampung dwellers. Because of her other secular commitments around the city she was accused of neglecting the prayer house. Burhanuddin's wife Ibu Sum, a member of Imah's clan, took over Ibu Kino's role as the head of the women's Islamic community. Members of Imah's kinship group, especially the headman, accused Ibu Kino of associating with Christians. They may have felt that her secular activities threatened their power base in the neighbourhood. They accused her of being a government stooge and surreptitiously forcing non-Islamic values, family planning, women's and children's education on kampung dwellers.

Hostile rumours circulated about Ibu Kino. It was said her two daughters had become pregnant before marriage while her son was a drug addict. She was not fit to advise kampung dwellers if she could not bring up her own children. Ibu Kino told me that her dedication to the kampung had been her children's undoing. Instead of uplifting the kampung dwellers her own children had been dragged down by the kampung environment. Other allegations were that the teacher rarely attended the school Ibu Kino had organized and so the children of the poor merely did Ibu Kino's household chores rather than school work. She was accused of pocketing resources from the Department of Social Welfare which should have been for the community. It should be noted, however, that Ibu Kino lived austerely and there was no evidence of this.

Frustrated by the kampung dwellers and pleased at the recognition she gained for her work from the city's authorities, Ibu Kino was driven further and further away from the very people she had originally wanted to help. By the 1980s, she was spending more time at social gatherings with wives of the *lurah*, mayor and governor than with kampung dwellers. Like Octavia Hill in London in the late

1800s, she blamed the poor for their own poverty.[33] She had tried to reeducate them but failed because she did not fully appreciate the basic economic insecurity of their lives.

Despite Ibu Kino's apparent failure to reform the neighbourhood she may have played some role in altering the kampung dwellers' perceptions about education and health. In 1980 she had shown a film about conception and child-birth which had a major impact on the kampung women many of whom did not seem to understand the process. My own efforts to take kampung dwellers to the polyclinic may have paved the way for others to follow. After one person received cheap and successful treatment, the message spread from house to house and other people followed.

Leadership in an Adjacent Neighbourhood

The problems of leadership and organization in Ibu Imah's neighbourhood are highlighted by the very different situation in the adjacent neighbourhood of Ibu Minah, where two relatively wealthy, educated and religious men had more success than either Ibu Kino or Sugi in organizing and leading their kampung dwellers. From the mid-1960s Haji Endi and later his son, Haji Eddy, tried to reform the poor neighbourhood. Although they could have afforded to live in a richer middle class suburb, they consciously chose to live in the kampung because they appreciated its intimate and village-like qualities. Compared with other kampung dwellers they were relatively well-off landowners from Bogor. They wished to spread the message of Islam and like Ibu Kino, started by upgrading the prayer house and setting up men's and women's Koran reading groups in the late 1960s.

Poorer neighbours soon began to ask them for advice and assistance and Haji Endi was chosen to act as kampung head and Haji Eddy as neighbourhood head. They gave loans of money and administrative services free of charge and often refused payment if it was offered.[34] To help overcome the periodic crises that struck households in the neighbourhood, they established a rotating credit society to which all contributed. In addition, five wealthier members in the kampung were recruited to seek donations from outside the area for the neighbourhood's poor. When any household experienced serious difficulty, they could borrow funds from this common pool without paying interest. Money was also raised for orphans and widows so that each year, at Lebaran, they received gifts of food, money and clothing. On occasion, perhaps once a year, the children were taken by bus for a picnic to Haji Endi's place in Bogor. Most of the children had never seen the countryside and were thrilled by the experience. Funds were pooled to buy crockery and chairs for festivities which could then be used by members of the community as they were required. A trade fair was organized to celebrate the new year and display the various skills of the craftsmen and women in the neighbourhood. Some cooked special dishes, others wove baskets, made wooden cabinets or sewed clothes. These artifacts were laid out for sale along the main pathway running in front of Haji Endi's house and the *lurah* was invited to attend.

When young men in the community began to drink, loot and make a noise in the middle of the night, Haji Endi encouraged the formation of a youth group. He appointed the main culprit as leader, saying that he would only learn by being given responsibility. To keep the young men occupied and teach them to drive, a secondhand car was provided by one of the community's wealthier patrons. The car soon fell into disrepair, however, and the young men returned to being a nuisance.

In the early to mid-1970s, gambling was the rage. Many men freely admitted that they frittered away their daily earnings in the hope of making a sudden windfall. If they did make money, it was soon spent on buying drink and food for friends. To most kampung dwellers' surprise, Haji Endi suggested that the leader of the gambling ring replace him as kampung head. Again, his rationale was that only by giving the main culprit a position of responsibility could he be made to toe-the-line and stop himself and others gambling. This approach worked.

My information about Haji Endi and Haji Eddy's efforts at leadership and community organization largely came from themselves or their close friends and so may have provided too glowing a picture of what they actually achieved. The young people, widows and orphans, who lived close to Haji Endi's and Haji Eddy's house, felt they had helped them through many difficulties. The further one went from their houses, however, the less impact their efforts had. Less than a 100 metres away Endi and Eddy were hardly known, except for when they returned from a trip to Mecca and everybody lined the pathway to welcome them home.

The gambler, Kastranadi, who had been appointed kampung head did his job tolerably well and gained respect from the community. He was constantly available for his neighbours' needs because he made a living from a stall in the community. He could type and do the necessary paper-work because of his earlier experience working in the Department of Labour. Along with Haji Endi, he became increasingly involved in the prayer house and helped to collect and organize the community funds. But there were trials ahead which were to prove beyond his courage, intellectual and leadership capacities.

Signs of Change

Members of Ibu Imah's neighbourhood had long been pleased to be remote from government. They had chosen their leaders on their ability to keep government at bay. During the 1970s, however, this isolation was broken down. The power of the State became more evident and penetrated further and further into kampung dwellers' lives. They felt increasingly powerless to resist this penetration. The government's attempts to close the city to newcomers and to restrict street-side occupations made their lives more difficult and insecure. Only towards the end of the 1970s did kampung dwellers begin to perceive some of the benefits of such programs as kampung improvement, health and education.

In Imah's neighbourhood, development programs reached the kampung only when the local headmen were bypassed. After 1978, the government began to use radio and television as alternative channels for conveying information about welfare programs to the people. By 1980 there were signs that kampung attitudes were changing, especially with regard to health and education. Rather than consulting the traditional healer, attending the cheap government polyclinic became the norm. Rather than going to Islamic schools, government schools were suddenly viewed as more desirable, having higher standards and lower fees. Most kampung dwellers now viewed schooling as a basic necessity rather than a luxury. By 1980 even the poorest family was determined to give at least some of their children an education. Most parents tried to get their children into a government school and only turned to private or Islamic schooling if they failed to do so.

The main reason for this sudden shift in kampung dwellers' attitudes seemed to be television. In 1978, commercial advertising which had dominated Indonesian television was banned and there was a concerted effort to make programs more educational. The government used the media to promote birth control, hygiene, kampung improvement and other such programs. This alerted kampung dwellers to the benefits of literacy and to the existence of jobs they had not dreamed of. Kampung dwellers devoured not only the government's announcements but news of the world outside. They developed a clearer conception of Indonesia and the world composed of different countries. They learned about each one on the news and saw the differences between them. Although they remained doubtful and suspicious of government, gradually they began to learn of the services the government was offering, even to kampung dwellers like themselves.

Informal leaders also helped to convey government policies to the people, but in Ibu Imah's neighbourhood, the efforts of one voluntary welfare worker were obstructed by other locally elected leaders. Furthermore, from the kampung dwellers' point of view, as Ibu Kino became more and more identified with officialdom, it was not entirely clear that she had their best interests at heart. By contrast, the cooperation between formally elected and informal leadership in Ibu Minah's neighbourhood resulted in more effective community organization and action. This was especially evident in the organization of various funds to help the poor and activities which revolved around Islam and the prayer house.

If kampung dwellers were to benefit from government programs and to lessen their insecurity, they needed effective local leadership. But a socially aware, concerned and active local leadership such as existed in Ibu Minah's neighbourhood was uncommon. Cynically, even if a leader demonstrated civic mindedness, concern and responsibility, kampung dwellers always suspected his motives. They distrusted their leaders and most assumed they were motivated by self-aggrandisement and self-gain.

Without trusted and dynamic leaders, kampung dwellers found it extremely difficult to cooperate amongst themselves. They were confused by the political system and did not know where to focus their grievances, or which government department or official to contact to express their problems. They lacked the necessary contacts or patrons in high places to get policies initiated, implemented or changed. This became evident in 1981 when the community was threatened by demolition. The thug-like qualities, self-interest and greed of people like Sugi defeated the moral uprightness and courage exemplified by people like Haji Endi and his son. As we shall see, even if their were a few civic-minded leaders, when it came to making major decisions affecting the life and death of the community it was the rogues who gained the upper hand.

1. Krausse "The Kampungs of Jakarta" p. 35.
2. Frederick "Indonesian Urban Society" pp. 91–2, 236–42; Cobban "The City on Java" p. 139.
3. As Krausse ("The Kampungs of Jakarta" in Wertheim *The Indonesian Town* p. 35) notes, " . . . social and health conditions in the kampungs

of Jakarta and other cities were brought to the attention of authorities through the reports of Tillema, Westerveld, and Karsten.". See also Bogaers, E. and de Ruijter, P. "Ir. Thomas Karsten and Indonesian Town Planning" in Nas *The Indonesian City* p. 74.

4. For Kampung Improvement in Jakarta in the 1920s see Wertheim, *The Indonesian Town* pp. xi, xv, 20 and Abeyasekere, *Jakarta* pp. 121–22. See also Cobban, J. L. "Uncontrolled Urban Settlement: The Kampung Question in Semarang (1905–1940)", *Bidjragen tot de Taal-Land-en Volkenkunde*, Vol. 130, No. 4: 1974: 403–27 for Semarang; see Frederick "Indonesian Urban Society" pp. 88–90 for Surabaya; see Polle' & Hofstee "Urban Kampung Improvement" pp. 117–19 for a brief overview.

5. There is evidence that Kampung Improvement was planned in Kebun Kacang in 1929 (Gemeente Batavia rec'd f66, 187). See *25 Jaren Decentralisatie 1905–1930*, p. 173.

6. Milone, P. D. *Urban Areas in Indonesia: Administrative and Census Concepts*, (Berkeley, 1966) pp. 36–7; Cobban "Uncontrolled Urban Settlement"; Krausse "The Kampungs of Jakarta" p. 36; Logsdon, M. "Leaders and Followers in Urban Neighbourhoods: An Exploratory Study of Djakarta, Indonesia", Ph.D Thesis, Harvard University, 1975, p. 56; Abeyasekere *Jakarta* p. 142. According to Frederick, in 1931 in Surabaya the Dutch had tried unsuccessfully to impose a precinct (*wijk*) system over and above the existing kampung mutual aid societies (*sinoman*).

7. According to Frederick ("Indonesian Urban Society" pp. 91–94, 236–42, 431–39), however, in Surabaya kampungs continued to defend their autonomy and to resist the imposition of these new administrative units.

8. Cribb "The Nationalist World of Occupied Jakarta" pp. 96–7.

9. Abeyasekere *Jakarta* pp. 197–205; DKI *Karya Jaya* p. 107.

10. Abeyasekere *Jakarta* pp. 204–5.

11. Abeyasekere *Jakarta* pp. 198–9; DKI *Karya Jaya* pp. 41, 73, 91.

12. Abeyasekere, *Jakarta*, pp. 198, 201–7.

13. Abeyasekere, *Jakarta*, p. 179.

14. Tan, T. K. (ed.) *Sukarno's Guided Democracy*, (Brisbane, 1967); Mackie *Problems of the Indonesian Inflation*; Johnson *Business Environment*.

15. Geertz, C. *The Social History of an Indonesian Town*, (Cambridge, Mass., 1965); Cohen, D. J. "Politics in a Jakarta Kampung: A Local History" in *Proceedings Conference on Modern Indonesian History, July 18–19*, (Ann Arbor, 1975) pp. 196–200.

16. Cohen ("Politics in a Jakarta Kampung") shows how as national political conflicts intensified between 1960 and 1965, parties of the left and right competed for supporters by offering land, jobs and clothes. In Surabaya, for example, the Communist-dominated municipal council granted legal title to squatters (Steele "Origins and Occupational Mobility of Lifetime Migrants" p. 80).

17. The system was based around the *Rukun Tetangga* (RT) (neighbourhood

association) and *Rukun Kampung* (RK) (community association). The RK was later renamed *Rukun Warga* (RW) (citizen's association) (*Madjalah Kotapradja*, 30 April, 1955).

18. Logsdon "Leaders and Followers in Urban Neighbourhoods" p. 56, 67, 192–3.

19. For the legislation see *Lembaran Daerah Khusus Ibu-Kota Djakarta*, 1970, No. 35. For further references to the closure of the city see Critchfield, R. "The Plight of the Cities: Djakarta—The First to 'Close'", *Columbia Journal of World Business*, July/August: 1971: 89–93; Williams, J. B. "Sadikin Closes Jakarta", *Insight*, Feb. 1973: 16–20; Cohen "Poverty and Development in Jakarta" pp. 26–7, 34; Krausse "The Kampungs of Jakarta" p. 92.

20. Abeyasekere *Jakarta* pp. 180–1.

21. Hull, T. H. and Mantra, I. B. "Indonesia's Changing Population" in Booth and McCawley *The Indonesian Economy* p. 270.

22. Logsdon ("Leaders and Followers in Urban Neighbourhoods" p. 151) found that RTs passed on information mainly when they were asked for it by the kampung dwellers.

23. Abeyasekere *Jakarta* p. 179.

24. These figures are not based on any official scale of fees from the Department of Culture and Education (*Departemen Pendidikan dan Kebudayaan*) but come from field notes collected between 1978 and 1980.

25. World Bank *Indonesia: Appraisal of Small Enterprise Development Project*, (Washington D.C., 1978) pp. 9–14; World Bank *The Urban Poor in Jakarta—Strategies for Integrating World Bank Projects*, (Washington D.C., 1977) Annex 1.4.

26. DKI *Kaki Lima* p. 28.

27. From Logsdon's description ("Leaders and Followers in Urban Neighbourhoods" pp. 113–28, 151, 157, 163–70, 180–91, 197–9, 247–9) the role of the Lurah seemed ambiguous. He was the main link between the government and the people and yet, was remote from them and their local headman.

28. As Logsdon ("Leaders and Followers in Urban Neighbourhoods" pp. 172–4) suggests, the payments headmen received hardly covered the cost of the ink and paper they used. However, I found headmen often withheld their services if payment was not forthcoming.

29. Logsdon ("Leaders and Followers in Urban Neighbourhoods" p. 64) found that although RTs needed to devote all their time to headman-ship, most devoted an average of only 7 to 8 hours a week because they had to spend the rest earning a livelihood.

30. Logsdon ("Leaders and Followers in Urban Neighbourhoods" pp. 77–8) suggested that the attraction of local leadership was not money but rather social status and prestige.

31. As late as 1975 Krausse ("The Kampungs of Jakarta" pp. 77–8) found that 80 percent of Jakartan residents lived outside the reach of basic public services.

32. N. Sullivan "Masters and Managers" pp. 301–5.

33. Stedman-Jones *Outcast London*.
34. This accords with Logsdon's ("Leaders and Followers in Urban Neigh-
    bourhoods" pp. 172–3) findings in richer suburbs where RTs and RWs
    were embarassed to accept payment for administrative services.
    Although some households in Ibu Minah's neighbourhood were richer
    than Ibu Imah's, others were much poorer.

5

Demolition (1981)

The penetration of government culminated in the demise of Kebun Kacang as a Kampung. In 1981 both Ibu Imah's and Ibu Minah's neighbourhoods, together containing over 736 households and 3500 people, were demolished. For the first time, members of the entire area came together to fight against the impending destruction of their homes, their last bastion of security against a hostile and rapidly changing world. Because of intense distrust and lack of leadership and organization, this unity did not last for long. In the end, the community was demolished in accord with government plans and despite kampung dwellers' opposition.

The rehousing project was the Indonesian government's attempt to tackle the world-wide problem of what to do with "slums". The fundamental question is how much governments should intervene in providing housing for the poor. On the one had, they are accused of doing too little and neglecting the poor. On the other hand, they are attacked for intervening in the wrong way, raising the cost of living and destroying local initiative. City planners, with their concern for physical appearances, are offended by the sight of slums. They see them as chaotic, unsightly and lacking in amenities. Their answer is to bulldoze slums and replace them by higher standard housing. But demolition of slum communities, even if they are replaced by flats, has often reduced the total housing stock and simply moved the housing problem from one area to another. Richer residents tend to move into the new apartments, whilst the poor crowd into the remaining pockets of inner-city slums, or create new shanty towns on the edges of cities.

City planners and engineers have a very different perspective of slums from the communities that live in them. For the former, the slums are a poverty trap, while for the latter, they are places of hope. The planners view these communities as eyesores. They are especially offended by the contrast between the modern high-rise city and the low, irregular, tightly packed makeshift houses. The urban poor, by contrast, view their neighbourhood as home. They have spent years carefully building and improving their houses from whatever materials they can scavenge or buy. Their homes are their refuge from a rapidly changing and ever-threatening world. They value not only their homes but the social networks which have gradually evolved. For many, the income-earning opportunities within the neighbourhood are their only, even if insecure, source of livelihood.

The Jakarta planners' decision to destroy Kebun Kacang was based on their view of it as a "slum". The planners ostensibly aimed to rehouse poor kampung dwellers in fully serviced flats at the city centre near their places of work. In fact the project resulted in the destruction of the kampung homes and their replacement by flats which less than a quarter of the households felt they could afford. The remainder, mainly the poorer, fled to the city's periphery, far from their former homes. The project epitomized the discrepancy between the proclaimed good intentions of policy and its ultimate impact.

The Evolution of a Housing Policy

The kampung Improvement Program initiated by the Jakarta City government in 1969 was the first attempt since Independence to deal with the awesome problem of improving the environment of Jakarta's poorest and most densely populated areas. The provision of better public facilities was often followed by a spate of private investment in home improvement. Although enlightened, the Program had some major shortcomings and was incapable of improving the tiny, tightly packed houses or of providing them with better amenities. It concentrated too much on the upgrading of footpaths and drains rather than on the kampung dwellers' houses or their most urgent needs of clean water and sanitation.

In 1974 the Indonesia government established Perumnas to help provide low-cost housing throughout Indonesia.[1] From the mid-1970s, Perumnas embarked on a program of building serviced "core" houses. These were single rooms of 21 to 36 square metres on 90 square metres of land, each individually serviced with water, sanitation and electricity. In Jakarta the units were erected on the city's periphery and were reserved mainly for public servants and the military. A few units were later offered to the general public but, because they were located so far from work opportunities, they had limited appeal to the lowest income groups for whom they were originally intended. From 1979 the Jakarta City government, and later Perumnas, began to explore other options. In February 1981 Perumnas completed construction of 960 flats in the Tanah Abang area of Jakarta. The price of these flats made them accessible only to families with an average income of over Rp.100.000 (480 litres) per month which excluded at least 80 percent of the city's population.

Following the President's instructions, in March 1981 Perumnas was directed by the Minister of Public Works to begin a new program that would cater for the city's lowest income group.[2] The plan was to rehouse a poor central city kampung community in flats on land where the community already lived, close to its income-earning opportunities. Kebun Kacang was chosen as the site for the pilot project.

Kebun Kacang qualified as a low income area. It had no water or sewerage supply and inadequate rubbish collection. It was subject to flooding during the monsoons. It was one of the few central city areas not to have benefitted from the Kampung Improvement Program. Its houses were too densely packed together and the path widening component of the Kampung Improvement Program would have destroyed too many homes. This meant that the community was at once urgently in need of improvement and, at the same time, lacking in the ten year security of tenure supposed to be granted to areas that had benefitted by Kampung Improvement. Only 12 percent of the houses had legal title.[3]

The official justification for the program was that an unhealthy and fire-prone slum would be replaced by much better housing and amenities. The program would raise the inhabitants' standard of living and reduce inequality in line with the President's Instructions for Repelita 111 (1979–1984). Perhaps the most compelling reason for the choice of Kebun Kacang, however, was that it was such a highly visible eyesore. The office buildings, embassies and hotels along the main thoroughfare of Jalan Thamrin all looked down upon it. Planners were embarrassed by the discrepancy in height and appearance between the ramshackle kampung houses and the multi-storey buildings all around. Besides, such a central location for this novel program would help demonstrate to the world that the Indonesian government, like that of Hong Kong and Singapore, cared about its urban poor.

City planners believed that expensive central city land should no longer be occupied by "slums". In the past Kebun Kacang had been neglected by government because it was located in low lying swamp land and frequently flooded. With the growing shortage and expense of central city space, however, it was beginning to be viewed as a prime location. Officials felt that by building multi-storey flats the land would be used more efficiently and permit a higher population density. With denser inner-city housing; central city depopulation, suburban sprawl and traffic congestion caused by people commuting back and forth to work each day would be curtailed.

Implementation of the Program

Kampung dwellers first heard of the project in May 1981 when rumours began to circulate that Kebun Kacang was threatened with demolition. Nobody knew where the information came from or whether to believe it. Such rumours had circulated around the community for years. Most kampung dwellers had long assumed that their neighbourhood would one day suffer the fate of other nearby communities which had been forced to give way to multi-storey office blocks. But the kampung dwellers pushed such speculation from their minds. Then in July 1981, day after day, a helicopter was seen hovering over the area. Kampung dwellers assumed a film was being made for television. They did not realize their homes were being photographed and mapped for the government's rehousing program.

In August 1981, all kampung dwellers were called to a mass meeting in their neighbourhood and informed by the Minister of Public Works, Directorate General of Housing, Mayor of Central Jakarta and other dignitaries from the Jakarta City government and Perumnas, of government plans to knock down their homes and build flats. The officials laid out maps, diagrams and models of the proposed units. They insisted that it was not a demolition program but "urban renewal" (*permajaan*), a word with which kampung dwellers were unfamiliar. They were told that all kampung dwellers who lost their homes would be entitled to a ground or first floor unit. The flats would be four stories high and 18 or 36 square metres in size. They would be completely selfcontained with piped water, electricity, gas and sewerage. The officials were non-committal about the size of monthly instalments, but hinted that they would be similar to payments in the Tanah Abang flats. An initial down-payment would have to be made which would be at least 5 percent of the total cost of the flats. The units not taken up by the kampung dwellers could be hired out to university students to help cover building costs.

After the meeting, terror and panic immediately spread through the kampung. Even though the policy makers had promised they would be rehoused, kampung dwellers knew the meaning of demolition. They doubted the good intentions of government and were sure that talk about flats was just a ploy to get them out of the area. They knew that government programs in the past were always beyond their financial capacity and mainly intended for the rich and middle class. If this project was really intended for them, why had university students been mentioned as future tenants?

Despite official explanations, most kampung dwellers failed to understand the nature of flats. Many were too frightened or too busy to attend the mass meeting. Some local headmen had failed to inform their kampung dwellers that a meeting would be held. Many who attended the meeting were too timid to approach the charts, models and maps on display. Those who looked, studied them upside down or sideways. They had never before attended a mass meeting which was meant to convey information directly affecting their fate, nor seen or had to interpret such diagrams. Dominated by a deep sense of fear, they found themselves unable to concentrate. After the meeting they relied on ill-informed neighbours to explain what had been said and the information was distorted as it passed from person to person. Many sat in their homes, paralysed, not knowing what to do, who to ask or what to think.

Had they been asked, kampung dwellers would have explained that housing was not their major problem. Most already owned their own homes at the city centre and, apart from occasional maintenance or improvements, did not have to spend money on accommodation. Over the years, most households had improved their own homes. Even among those who rented, many had paid a constant rate for over twenty years and it was less than 5 percent of their monthly income. Kampung dwellers were not unduly concerned by the low standard of their houses or the lack of amenities. Although their amenities were austere and they had to carry or pay somebody to deliver water, kerosene or whatever else they needed to their homes each day, the flexibility of this system enabled them to cut down on overheads whenever they ran out of cash. They simply bought less water or kerosene or delayed making their payment until a later date. Most had never had piped water, gas or toilets within their homes and did not appreciate their convenience. They worried mainly about the extra cost these amenities would entail.

The absence of a secure job and insufficient income most worried the kampung dwellers. From one month to the next, they did not know whether their jobs would still be viable. From one day to the next, they did not know how much they would earn. They had never been able to guarantee a certain amount of income one month in advance. Now they were being asked to guarantee payment for housing and amenities, which could amount to 50 percent or even more of their current income, for the next twenty years. Nor had they ever envisaged paying so much.

The kampung dwellers worried also about the design of the proposed flats and the regulations governing their use. They suspected that once the flats were built government would forbid them operating their cottage industries and trades from within their homes. They would be without even the insecure jobs and incomes they had had in the kampung. Without sufficient income for food, they would find it even more difficult to pay for flats. When demanding monthly flat instalments government officials would not take hardship into account. If a household failed to pay, it could be thrown out of the units.

To the extent that housing was a concern, kampung dwellers valued space more than anything else. They preferred more living space to a higher standard of housing and improved amenities. The size of the proposed 18-square-metre flats was smaller than 70 percent of the existing kampung houses.[4] In households of up to 15 people, where married children and village relatives frequently came to stay, these flats would permit less than 1.5 square metres of space per person. Accommodation would no longer be provided for extended families or guests from the village.

Kampung dwellers had numerous other concerns. The ill and elderly worried how they would walk up four flights of stairs to the cheapest units which were only to be located on the highest floor. What would they do with their large heavy kampung furniture which would not fit or be allowed in the flats? How would they hold festivities where numerous neighbours and relatives had traditionally been invited to their homes? How would they dry their washing or prevent gas exploding? They even worried about the use of showers or unfamiliar Western-style toilets.

No attempt was made to alleviate the kampung dwellers' fears. Most government officials may not even have been aware of what was troubling the kampung dwellers. Officials never bothered to ask kampung dwellers about their needs or to make sure that they had sufficient resources for the proposed flats. Many of the issues that concerned kampung dwellers had been raised in three official reports on the problems of flat housing in Indonesia but had been either not read or not taken seriously by those planning the project.[5] Some officials from the Jakarta City government who had been involved in compiling these reports were aware of kampung dwellers' hostility to flats, but felt powerless to oppose the President, the Minister of Housing or Perumnas.

Perumnas actually reinforced kampung dwellers' worst fears by issuing a document implying that all those who lacked sufficient

resources to pay for flats were to move to the city's periphery. It
announced the various housing options in unfamiliar jargon.[6] Kampung dwellers were invited to move into the recently completed
Tanah Abang flats at a total cost of between Rp.5,000,000 and
Rp.8,000,000 (24,000–38,000 litres of rice). Alternatively, they could
move to the edges of Jakarta where serviced 21 square metre units or
vacant plots of 90 square metres were available at between
Rp.1,500,000 to Rp.2,000,000 (7100–9500 litres). Or they could leave
the project altogether, take their compensation and rehouse themselves as they pleased. No reference was made to the Kebun Kacang
flats which were ostensibly to be built on their land for their benefit.
Finally and most importantly, the document advised all those on low
or irregular incomes not to apply for the Tanah Abang flats.[7]

The pamphlet directly contradicted what the policy makers had
announced at the first mass meeting. It served to confirm the kampung dwellers' worst fears that they were being forced out of their
central city homes. The document appeared to have been prepared
for the Tanah Abang project and lower level officials implementing
the project only altered a few words and recirculated it in Kebun
Kacang, assuming that the two projects were identical. They did not
seem to realize that the project intended for Kebun Kacang was a
special rehousing scheme for the poorest kampung dwellers and not
commercial housing for the middle class.

The first press report on the project stated that, according to the
Perumnas director of housing, "75 percent of the kampung dwellers
were willing to accept flats".[8] The press failed to give any coverage of
the kampung dwellers' misgivings and fears. Its reports did not reveal
the contradictions that were emerging between the statements of the
policy makers and the actions of those implementing the project. Not
only were there differences between key officials in the Jakarta City
government and Perumnas, but policy makers had failed to convey
their plans to officials at the lower levels of the bureaucracy.

Faced with a threat to their survival in the city, the kampung
dwellers began to organize. Previously each neighbourhood of approximately 40 households had no sense of belonging to the wider
area of 16 neighbourhoods which were earmarked for demolition.
Most kampung dwellers had gone about their daily lives in their own
way without the time, inclination or energy to care about events
beyond their immediate neighbourhood. Islamic meetings had
brought some members of the area together, but these only resulted
in numerous small and unrelated clusters of individuals.

The three prayer houses which had served for purely Islamic
purposes were transformed into meeting halls for discussions on
demolition. Sixteen headmen and nineteen other more politically

aware or educated members of the area chaired the meetings and were chosen to act as representatives of the community in its confrontation with the government.[9] A delegation from the kampung tried to approach the *lurah* to find out about land and house compensation. The *lurah*, however, refused to meet them, saying that he had no further information on the project. Despite kampung dwellers' opposition to the flats, they allowed officials from the Jakarta City government's Department of Lands to enter the community and measure their land and houses.

A day or two before a second mass meeting in mid September, a confidential government document on compensation was leaked to the kampung by somebody who worked in the municipal administration.[10] The document, signed by the Governor, stated that those with the rights to use land (*Hak Pakai*) would be paid Rp.60,000 per square metre. Those with other rights to the land would be paid a percentage of ownership rights (Hak Milik) in accordance with the Governor's decision of 1972.[11] In that decision seven different legal titles were spelt out and these were further subdivided into 12 categories.

An estimated 88 percent of the community had no legal tenure and thus could hope to be paid only at the lowest rate of Rp.25,000 per square metre or 25 percent of those with full ownership rights.

At the second mass meeting on the 15th September, officials read out the leaked document. They read out endless lists of varying compensation rates for land of different legal titles, houses of brick, timber or bamboo, fences, terraces, tress, telephones, business permits, electricity, water connections and water pumps. Even though the kampung spokesmen had access to the leaked document, the majority of kampung dwellers did not. So the legal terminology and speed of presentation only served to confuse them. After the oral presentation they were little wiser than before and still had no idea how much compensation they would each receive. The proposed prices for flats and sites and service units, however, were clearly spelt out by the officials. Each kampung dweller was handed a sheet of paper on which the prices were shown.[12] The Tanah Abang flats were to cost approximately Rp.6,000,000 (29,000 litres of rice) while the sites and service units would cost from Rp.1,500,000 (7100 litres). So the kampung dwellers were left not knowing precisely how much they would receive, but feeling they would have to pay a sum well beyond their reach for alternative housing.

At the end of this second meeting with officialdom, almost six months after the project had first been planned, the first sign of kampung resistence was openly expressed. One kampung spokesman, Asep, stood up and told the officials that the kampung dwellers would not be bullied into submission. He said kampung dwellers rejected both the compensation and the flats. They objected to the government's authoritarian style of imposing a program without prior consultation. The kampung dwellers were not opposed to the beautification of the city but they did not want it to be at their expense. All they demanded was just compensation so that they could rehouse themselves adequately elsewhere. They were not in a position to think about, let alone discuss alternative rehousing choices when they did not know how much compensation they would receive or felt it to be inadequate. The kampung spokesmen put forward a document which stated that the kampung dwellers would accept no less than Rp.250,000 (1200 litres of rice) per metre for all members of the community irrespective of legal tenure.[13]

The dignitaries were shocked by the spokesman's aggressively forceful words and the cheers from surprised and elated kampung dwellers which followed. The officials appeared not to have anticipated such hostility to their "welfare rehousing program". Whilst planning the project for the past five months, they had accepted without question the *lurah's* assurances that he had informed the kampung dwellers and that there was no opposition to the project.[14]

While officials and kampung dwellers remained at loggerheads during the rest of September and most of October, five of the most educated kampung spokesmen launched a sophisticated press campaign to present the kampung dwellers' point of view. They claimed the *lurah* had tried to intimidate them into accepting the project and that both he and Perumnas had tried to force them to take sites and service units on the edges of the city if they did not want to accept flats. The kampung spokesmen drew attention to the Minister of Interior's decree of 1975, which specified that all regional governments had to negotiate land takeovers with the inhabitants concerned.[15] They insisted that their compensation claim of Rp.250,000 per square metre was reasonable, especially considering Kebun Kacang's strategic location and the fact that registered land just 100 metres away was worth from Rp.350,000 to Rp.500,000 per square metre.[16] They espoused the kampung dwellers' concern about the loss of their homes, jobs, proximity to the city centre, social ties and the disruption of their children's schooling. They argued that it was not worth talking about alternative accommodation until the issue of compensation was resolved. They sent deputations to the Governor, Minister of Interior, Minister of Public Works and to the Jakarta legislative assembly requesting that the Governor's decision on compensation be revised. They also sent a delegation to the Indonesian Legal Rights Assistance Bureau (*Lembaga Bantuan Hukum*—LBH).

Government officials responded by both reassuring and castigating the kampung dwellers. They promised the kampung dwellers that they would be rehoused in the flats in accordance with their financial capacity. Again and again they stressed that it was not a "demolition" scheme but a "rehousing" project and the kampung dwellers would not be hurt. Allowances would be made for trade in flats and the other shortcomings kampung dwellers saw with the program. Those unable to pay instalments would be allowed to rent at minimum rates.[17]

Other government officials, however, chastised kampung dwellers for rejecting the project and simply focusing upon the compensation they would receive.[18] The kampung dwellers were attacked for being short-sighted, self-interested and standing in the way of an innovative government welfare scheme. The Mayor of Central Jakarta and the Vice Governor of the city suggested that opposition to the project and demand for higher compensation stemmed from individuals who were not even living in the area. These cunning outsiders, it was claimed, just wanted to make a profit out of the project by helping kampung dwellers to obtain higher compensation in return for a commission.[19] In fact, some more educated and courageous individuals within the community made these demands and there was no evidence that outsiders were involved. The *lurah* stated that considering the quality of the kampung dwellers' land their claims for higher compensation were absurd.[20] The Governor asked the kampung dwellers to be thankful that the government wanted to improve their lot.[21] And the Vice Mayor of Central Jakarta claimed that "if his house was being renovated he would not only have to pay for it but also be grateful".[22]

As the impasse continued into late October, most kampung dwellers were still unfamiliar with the details of the project and unable to trust the government. Some officials in turn could not understand why the kampung dwellers were opposing their well-intentioned project. Others were convinced that the kampung dwellers had to accept their greater wisdom and some sacrifices for the common good. In frustration, I went in search of the program's directors to try and clarify the kampung dwellers' position. I persuaded the head of Perumnas's Planning and Feasibility Section to go into the area and see for himself why the kampung dwellers objected to the project.[23] Until this time, not one official had bothered to find out directly about the kampung dwellers' living conditions or desires.

Upon entering Kebun Kacang the planner (Duddy Soegoto) was surprised by the good quality of the kampung houses. He saw that many had just been renovated. He had not realized that over 50 percent of the people used their homes as places of work. Nor had he been aware of the great disparity between the rich and poor with the rich living in large, 50 to 100 square metre good quality houses, and the poor thrilled to have shelter for which they did not have to pay. Some had recently invested up to Rp.2,000,000 (9500 litres of rice) in their homes while others paid less than 5 percent of their monthly income on rent. It was clear to Soegoto that the government flat building program could not cater for such varying capacities and needs. He expressed concern as to whether the proposed rehousing scheme would in fact benefit most members of the area.

Nevertheless, because the program had the backing of President, Minister and Director General of Public Works and Minister of Housing, there was no turning back. Soegoto made representations to the Ministerial level and was granted a larger central government subsidy (Rp.1,8 billion) for the project bringing its total estimated cost to Rp.4 billion (US$6,000,000), but he could not alter the fundamental design of the project. Too many key agencies and people in authority had a stake in its success. Perumnas had already geared up its large administrative staff, engineers and contractors to design and build the flats. The Jakarta City Government had members of its staff on the project's payroll. The best Soegoto could do was make the project more amenable to the kampung dwellers' needs: he set about lowering the flat prices and changing their size, conditions of use and payment.[24]

Soegoto invited the kampung spokesmen to a discussion at Perumnas. Transport and a meal were provided along with a slide show on rehousing. Soegoto promised that all Kampung dwellers would be entitled to flats, even those who were too poor to pay. Any kampung dweller who initially rejected a flat, perhaps through ignorance or fear, would be entitled to change his mind once the flats were built and he could see what they looked like. Instead of the 18 and 36 square metre units, he proposed more varied sizes of 21, 42 and 51 square metres. Instalments were to be paid in a flexible manner, either monthly, weekly or daily. The cost of the cheapest 21 square metre unit was lowered to Rp.9.600 (46 litres of rice) a month, approximately 16 percent of most kampung dwellers' earnings. Those who were too poor to buy flats could rent at nominal rates (Rp.8000 per month). Free temporary accommodation with water, electricity and sanitation was to be provided while the flats were being built over a period of 6 to 12 months. An allowance of Rp.65.000 would be paid to all registered households for the hardship endured as a consequence of demolition. The original rate of compensation, however, could not be altered. If that rate was raised, then the cost of the flats would also rise.

Disagreement emerged amongst the kampung spokesmen as to whether to support the revised project. Asep insisted that he was the kampung dwellers' main spokesman and they all accepted the project.[25] Other kampung spokesmen, however, claimed that Asep was no longer their spokesman and that most kampung dwellers still found the government's offer of compensation unacceptable.[26] It was rumoured that Asep was ingratiating himself with the authorities in exchange for large sums of money and guarantees of a large ground floor flat. Other spokesmen claimed that over 50 percent of the community would not be able to pay for the flats, even at the lower rates, and would be squeezed out of the area. These spokesmen were not interested in the special subsidized prices of flats but continued to demand higher compensation so that kampung dwellers could rehouse themselves adequately elsewhere without having to rely on government. In addition, they felt that if they returned to the kampung from the Perumnas meeting backing the project, then they would be accused by the people of having sold out to the government.

The overworked officials within Perumnas, including Soegoto, were unaware of the schism amongst the kampung spokesmen and mistakenly assumed that their project had been accepted. Over the following days, the press reported that the project had been accepted by most of the kampung dwellers.[27]

The nature and aims of the project were lost sight of as Kebun Kacang was split asunder by the spokesmen's inability to agree. Within a matter of weeks, the fragile unity of the community in opposition to the project was destroyed. Spokesmen spread contradictory information about the project and kampung dwellers never properly understood the changes which had been made by Soegoto to suit their needs. They remained ignorant of the flat designs, sizes, prices and special conditions guaranteeing every kampung dweller's access to a flat, even if they were very poor. Instead, most continue to assume that the flats were for the middle class.

Whilst most kampung dwellers still did not know what to do, by late November 1981 a few households started to demolish their houses, take their compensation and apply for flats or alternative accommodation. Asep and his aides enticed some kampung dwellers into accepting compensation by promising speedy processing of their claims, first choice of temporary accommodation and an opportunity to apply for a flat without the prerequisite down payment. It was reported that more recent migrants who only rented accommodation in the area were the first to take up the government's offer.[28] They had nothing to lose. They had few social or economic commitments to the neighbourhood. Instead of paying rent they could pay instalments and obtain a flat of their own in a central city area where they could never have bought a home at such a subsidized rate. Those who took their compensation or accepted flats earned the wrath of those who refused to give in. It was felt that those who accepted compensation were destroying the resolve of the community to oppose the project.

Fear that the community was about to be destroyed had repercussions for trade, credit and kampung morale. Previously the economy of the community had been lubricated by borrowings from moneylenders, stall-keepers, traders, neighbours and friends. With the threat of demolition, however, creditors refused to give loans for fear that borrowers would disappear without repaying their dues. Small scale enterprises found it difficult to operate as the chain of relationships between buyers and sellers broke down. Small scale entrepreneurs were called away to attend meetings or seek alternative accommodation and found it difficult to earn an income.

The walls of kampung houses abutted upon one another and the demolition of one house left gapping holes in the next. When one house was torn down, the adjoining houses usually fell into disrepair. The remaining kampung dwellers did not bother repairing or maintaining their houses for they did not know how much longer they would be living in them. Rats and mosquitoes gathered in the rubble. The kampung security system no longer functioned effectively and kampung dwellers were frightened by the strangers who came past their homes fossicking for left over building materials.

By late December, more and more kampung dwellers could no longer bear the indecision, uncertainty and demoralization. The kampung looked unsightly as one stumbled along pathways over pieces of building materials and rubbish. With increasing economic hardship, many were attracted by the prospect of compensation. During this time, government officials stood back and let the community be torn apart by its members suspicion, distrust and fear.

The kampung dwellers seemed increasingly suspicious of one another, their headmen and the government. Confidential documents had been leaked to the kampung headmen which itemized each householders' land title, house size and quality and other items and amenities for which they would be compensated.[29] The government had kept the precise details of compensation a secret and told kampung dwellers only what they could generally expect at the mass meeting in September. The documents had been leaked in the hope that each headman would advise his kampung dwellers how much money they would receive. But many headmen kept the information to themselves and failed to inform their members.

Without telling the kampung dwellers precisely how much compensation they would receive, the headman of Imah's neighbourhood called a meeting where he promised to raise their compensation by

Rp.15,000 per metre if each household guaranteed to pay him Rp.5000 per metre from the increase they received. All members of Ibu Imah's neighbourhood were forced to sign a document agreeing to this proposal. The headman had found Harjo's original land certificate from the 1930s which proved that taxes had been paid to the Dutch. He showed this to the City government's Lands Department, proving that the land they occupied had more legality than was indicated in the municipal records. Although the Jakarta City Administration officially refused to raise the level of compensation, by informal means the compensation was raised from Rp. 25,000 per square metre to Rp.40,000 per square metre. Such manoeuvres by cunning headmen resulted in a desperate search throughout the area for old Dutch land certificates.

If rates of compensation could not be changed by the use of land certificates, neighbourhood headmen tried to manipulate the system by making deals with lower level officials responsible for implementing the project. The officials were offered a share in the spoils if the rates of compensation were illicitly raised. The official figures were simply crossed out in government documents and new figures were written in. Households with strong headmen who had contacts in the right places, money and powers of persuasion managed to have their compensation altered. Jealousy and friction intensified as some households were promised three or four times more than others because of their headman's ability to manipulate the system.

The press did not mention the turmoil in Kebun Kacang but noted that some kampung dwellers were still holding out for higher compensation whilst others had started to take their compensation, knock down their houses and leave the area.[30] One man out of the 3500 people in Kebun Kacang, however, refused to be intimidated by either government officials or local headmen. He refused to accept Rp.25,000 per square metre and believed that if some people could get Rp.60,000 per square metre through underhand deals, he could obtain it by refusing to move. He was not prepared to accept the lowest rate nor give any official or middleman a percentage of the compensation he received. Whilst all other kampung dwellers flocked to take their compensation and demolish their homes, he and his family stood their ground. Thugs employed by Asep tried to intimidate the family into moving by throwing stones on their roof at night. In the end, the recalcitrant family obtained Rp.60,000 per square metre, so their suffering and fear had not been in vain. Kampung dwellers spoke of *Hukum rimba*— the law of the jungle. Men exploited and cheated each other in order to line their own pockets. Even relatives or nextdoor neighbours deceived one another for financial gain.

The press only hinted at the distortions taking place during the payment of compensation. It stated that substantial sums of compensation had mistakenly been paid to people who had left the area years earlier.[31] People who no longer lived in Kebun Kacang, but still had residence permits took advantage of the government's eagerness to get the project moving. In the government's eyes acceptance of compensation was tantamount to acceptance of the project. So some former members of Kebun Kacang obtained official documents signed by the *lurah* entitling them illicitly to receive compensation.[32]

There was further evidence of Kelurahan mismanagement when over fifty Perumnas application forms for the flats, which were meant specifically for the inhabitants of the project area, went missing.[33] They should all have been distributed by the kelurahan to households in Kebun Kacang. Although the press failed to mention it, kampung dwellers believed that the *lurah* and his assistants had made a profit selling these forms to outsiders who wanted to buy flats in the project.[34]

The trickle of kampung dwellers seeking their compensation became a flood as they worried that project funds would run out before they had been paid. Their fears were not unfounded, for some weeks later the government treasurer handling the compensation funds was removed for financial impropriety and many of the cheques he had issued proved to be invalid.[35] It came as a shock to kampung dwellers, unused to cheques or banks, to discover that the piece of paper they held in their hands was worthless. It was reasonable to wonder how all those entitled to compensation would be paid when many people were illegitimately getting their hands on compensation and the compensation rates had been illicitly inflated.[36]

The officials at the compensation office were in no hurry to process kampung dwellers' claims. Their work as compensation officers was over and above their normal course of duty. They arrived late at the compensation office; on some days they did not arrive at all. Without knowing when the office would open, kampung dwellers queued in scorching sun or torrential rain. They were worried that if they were not there when their names were called they would miss out on being paid. After the officials arrived, they ate their lunch, took a siesta or listened to the radio whilst kampung dwellers waited. When the officials started to work, they spent much time fumbling through folders, forms and files. The lucky few to be called into the office to have their claims processed were more often than not told to return the next day because their forms were incomplete or did not have the *lurah's* signature. To get the *lurah's* signature involved more hours of queuing and additional payments.[37]

Ironically, only four months earlier the authorities had been in a rush to get the project implemented and chastised the kampung dwellers for causing delays. Now the position was reversed. While many kampung dwellers were only too eager to take their compensation, demolish their homes and leave the area, the bureaucrats administering the project caused delay. Kampung dwellers believed officials deliberately delayed the processing of their compensation claims in order to get a special bonus paid by the project for the duration of the compensation payments. Many kampung dwellers needed to work each day to feed their families. Others were embarrassed or frightened to take leave from their employers as they waited day after day for their forms to be processed.

Lower level administrators seemed to do their utmost to discourage kampung dwellers from taking flats. Despite the heated dialogue in the press and numerous official statements, the administrators seemed unaware that the project was supposed to be an innovative rehousing scheme. They assumed it was another commercial flat building program along the lines of the Tanah Abang flats and insisted that the Kebun Kacang flats were only for those with regular incomes of over Rp.60,000 per month. They advised kampung dwellers with low or irregular incomes to take their compensation and accept the cheaper core units on Jakarta's periphery or rehouse themselves elsewhere.[38] The sick, aged and poor were told that 21 square metre flats would be available only on the highest floor, even though the latest Perumnas plans clearly indicated 21 square metre units on the lowest level. Kampung dwellers who had decided to trust the policy makers and take flats changed their minds. It emerged that the local administrators had a financial stake in the non sale of flats at subsidized rates to the kampung dwellers. By the use of spare flat application forms and the names of kampung dwellers who had left the project, they could illicitly sell off the flats to richer outsiders at much higher rates.

One enlightened aspect of the project was that bulldozers were not used to demolish the kampung houses. Kampung dwellers were supposed to dismantle their own home within 14 days after receiving compensation and were allowed to reuse or selling the old building materials. Piece by piece, each house was destroyed. Some kampung dwellers, especially the poor, carefully removed tiles, bricks and planks of wood for reuse on their next home. Many of them bought, dismantled and carted away the unwanted homes of the better-off which were built of more durable materials than their own. By the end of March 1982, Kebun Kacang looked as though it had been struck by a bomb. Only then, bulldozers were brought in to level the land and prepare it for flat construction.

Over three quarters of the kampung dwellers failed to accept flats because of the way the project had been implemented and their fears about their inability to pay. Slightly over a quarter accepted sites and service housing on the city's periphery and the remainder rehoused themselves.

Ironically, participation in what was officially regarded as a slum reclamation project gave kampung dwellers a real taste of slum life. Most of the 160 families who accepted flats had to wait two and a half years instead of the promised six to twelve months. In the meantime, they were rehoused nearby by Perumnas on borrowed land in temporary barrack-like accommodation until the flats were built. Most had to put up with conditions that were very much more congested, unhygienic and uncomfortable than their former homes. Although the accommodation was free, families had to squeeze into 8.5 square metres, less than half the space they had had in Kebun Kacang. There was no community organization or leadership to maintain or supervise the use of the free public amenities. The free water and toilets soon fell into disrepair. The washing troughs never functioned and the toilets doubled as places to wash. During the first month the piped water was never turned off and gushed freely from the taps, but later it often ran dry. Kampung dwellers were forced to catch droplets of water in plastic containers throughout the night for use the next day. The communal toilets were not cleaned and people not from the rehousing project used them. Frustrated kampung dwellers who lived near the toilets blocked them with boulders and cement to overcome their stench and illicit use by outsiders. The brick walls of the toilets were soon dismantled and used for other purposes. The few toilets that remained were padlocked. As kampung dwellers overloaded the limited electricity facilities there were frequent blackouts. The thin walls of the flimsy plywood barracks and constant noise destroyed any semblance of tranquillity.

The kampung dwellers' physical privation was overshadowed by doubts, rumours and fears. Although they had agreed to purchase a flat and had paid deposits, all they held was a receipt for the money they had paid. They had no written commitment that the government would supply them with a flat. As the months dragged on in their tiny temporary accommodation, the kampung dwellers found it hard to believe that their receipt would, one day, be translated into a flat. Kampung dwellers constantly recalled the loss of previous homes without compensation or the confiscation of their trading carts and source of livelihood. They began to envy those who had rehoused themselves or moved to sites and service units without a long period of waiting and uncertainty. Many wondered whether they had made the wrong choice and one or two left the temporary accommodation and exchanged their rights to a flat for a sites and service unit on the periphery.[39]

When the flats were almost completed in 1983, those who inspected them were horrified to discover that some had enormous cracks the size of a fist. The kampung dwellers knew that the flats had been built on unstable swamp land and suspected that the heavy four-storey cement walls would collapse. When the cracked flats were dismantled and rebuilt, Kampung dwellers wondered whether they would ever move into them. In the meantime, the kampung dwellers were being ordered to leave their temporary barracks because another government department wanted to use the land. Perumnas's contract for the temporary use of the land had expired months earlier.[40] The Kampung dwellers remained in the temporary barracks where they had lived for two and half years but were confused and demoralized, being instructed to leave and yet unable to move into the flats.

When the flats were eventually completed, they were advertised for commercial sale before the kampung dwellers had been allocated their units. The units were to be sold for between Rp.13,000,000 (US$13,000) and Rp.16,500,000 (US$16,000).[41] These prices far exceeded kampung dwellers expectations. Panic swept the temporary barracks as they believed the flat prices had been altered beyond their reach and that the units were being sold to the Jakartan middle classes. Most kampung dwellers did not understand the concept of "cross subsidy" whereby those flats sold for commercial purposes would help pay for those sold to themselves at lower prices.

Eventually in April 1984, the Kampung dwellers were allocated flats. Most were pleased to move out of the temporary barracks but some were dismayed by the allocation procedures and unanticipated costs. Bud, for example, was not allocated the unit she had applied for. The unit was smaller, on the fourth floor and in the block of flats which had cracked. Others were thrilled to obtain a large unit on the ground floor. After a little resistance by those who felt the flat allocation had been unfair, most passively accepted the flat they were offered. They were only too eager to escape from the insecurity and squalor of the past two and a half years and re-establish a more permanent way of life in the flats. After moving into their units, however, some encountered unanticipated charges for electricty, gas and water connections and additional certificates from the *lurah*. Those who could not bear these financial burdens eventually left the flats.

The 200 families who moved to sites and service core units had the advantage of being able to settle straight into their new homes without the trauma of a long wait in temporary accommodation. They had the choice of three alternative housing sites 15 to 20 kilometres south, east or west of Jakarta. Most chose the location closest to the village from which they or their relatives had come over twenty years ago. Thus it was no coincidence that those from Ibu Imah's kingroup chose Depok whilst those from Ibu Minah's neighbourhood mainly chose Tangerang.

The first six months proved the most traumatic in many kampung dwellers' lives. The 21 square metre core units were in disrepair. They had walls with holes in them, broken windows and lacked doors. There were rumours of theft and kampung dwellers did not dare leave their units for fear their newly acquired sideboards, tables, televisions sets and chairs would be stolen. Each unit had a privy but none had been dug to the required depth of three metres. In some cases, the floor level of their units stood below that of the toilet and washing area so the water and sewage ran into their homes.

All these problems could be repaired by the kampung dwellers themselves, but Perumnas officials insisted that they had to have permission to make any alterations. Perumnas was actually responsible for the building and maintenance of these units, which had stood empty for at least two to three years. If kampung dwellers made written application for any repairs that needed to be made, Perumnas promised to attend to them. Kampung dwellers soon found, however, that unless bribes were paid to the local Perumnas officials, their written and oral requests for repairs went unheeded. Kampung dwellers even believed that the units had been intentionally vandalized by people associated with Perumnas, so that extra income could be made out of the repairs.

Some kampung dwellers had hoped that by chosing sites and service units on the edges of the city they would have fewer troubles with officialdom. Nevertheless they could not entirely escape bureaucratic interference. Whilst kampung dwellers rebuilt their units Perumnas officials intervened, demanded to know why the toilets were being moved from their original location and why the units were being changed without prior permits. Perumnas officials made money out of the permits they sold. They also tried to dictate how the units were to be redesigned and the type of building materials to be used. Timber and bamboo, for example, were forbidden and only batako bricks were to be used.[42] Officials resented kampung dwellers bypassing Perumnas and doing the work themselves.

Over half of the kampung households rehoused themselves. Most bought land or dilapidated houses on the private market on the city's periphery or moved in with relatives. They carefully salvaged the building materials from their kampung homes and bought planks and tiles from neighbouring houses in Kebun Kacang which were then reused for their houses elsewhere. A wealthier minority rehoused themselves in kampungs near the city centre similar to Kebun Kacang. Some of them soon discovered that these new homes were also destined for demolition and that they had no greater legal title than they had had in Kebun Kacang.

Rehousing starkly revealed the powerlessness of the urban poor. For years they had felt powerless, but in the past had seldom had to confront government directly. With demolition, however, the government intruded right into their homes. Attending meetings, having to comprehend the contradictory words of policy makers, reading and filling in forms, obtaining signatures and dealing with petty bureaucrats suddenly dominated their lives as never before. Most kampung dwellers doubted the government's good intentions and did not know what to expect or how to react.

For the first time in the kampung's existence, its members tried to organize. Meetings were held and spokesmen were elected to represent the community. The press provided the only outlet for the kampung dwellers to express their opposition to the project. Five of the more educated kampung dwellers were able to launch a sophisticated press campaign. When a few of the kampung's key leaders turned to support the government, however, the fragile unity of the kampung dwellers was destroyed. The community split asunder with one kampung dweller distrusting another.

The demolition of Kebun Kacang marked a dramatic turning-point for most kampung dwellers and yet, in many ways, the loss of their homes fitted with the perpetual turmoil of their lives. More unusual was the fact that the kampung dwellers were offered substantial compensation and alternative housing in central city flats or sites and service units on the edges of the city. Whilst a minority were able to accept and adapt to a new way of life at the city centre, the majority fled to the periphery and tried to reestablish the community and jobs they had lost. Although the kampung of Kebun Kacang was destroyed, for its former inhabitants the struggle for existence went on.

1. *Perusahaan Umum Pembangunan Perumahan Nasional* (National Housing Development Corporation). It was referred to by the World Bank as the National Urban Development Corporation (NUDC). (World Bank) *Fourth Urban Development Project, Indonesia, Staff Appraisal Report* (Washington D.C., 1981) pp. 23–5.

2. Personal Communication with officials of the Jakarta Municipality. DKI and Perumnas officials were under orders to have the flats completed by the Presidential election of May 1982.
3. Data provided by the Lurah of Kebun Kacang to the Governor of Jakarta and forwarded to Perumnas (Data-data Wilayah RW.01 dan RW.03 Kelurahan Kebon Kacang, untuk Rencana Pengembanan Flat Perumnas, (11 and 25 April 1981). Local government records were notoriously inaccurate. Patterns of land tenure were so complicated that it was difficult to determine kampung dwellers' title.
4. The data on the size and number of buildings in Kebun Kacang is derived from "Data2 Peremajaan Lingkungan Kebon Kacang" (Data on the upgrading of Kebon Kacang's environment) Direktorat Agraria, Jakarta Pusat and Kelurahan Kebon Kacang and compiled by Direktorat IV, Pembangunan, DKI September 1981.
5. An official study found that only 4.5 percent of kampung dwellers out of a sample of 500 chose to live in flats: DKI *Malasah Perumahan di DKI Jakarta*, (Jakarta, 1979) pp. 28–9 and 41. It listed why flats had little appeal. This information was included in an official document outlining the Jakarta City Government's housing policies (DKI *Kebijaksanaan Pembangunan* pp. 20–2). Another study conducted by the Institute of Technology Bandung in cooperation with the DKI confirmed these findings: DKI *Study Pengembangan Lingkungan Perumahan Flat Di DKI-Jakarta*, (Jakarta, 1981).
6. This document (Penyediaan Rumah Bagi Penghuni yang Terkena Peremajaan Kota Dilokasi Kebon Kacang Jakarta Pusat—Preparation of housing for those affected by urban renewal in Kebun Kacang) referred to "Rumah Inti" (core units), "Rumah Sub Inti" (sub-core units), "Rumah Susun" (flats), "KPR/BTN-Kredit Pemilikan Rumah/Bank Tabungan Negara" (Mortgage/National Savings Bank), "Pembayaran diatur secara tunai" (cash payment), "Perjanjian Pendahuluan Jual Beli (Preliminary Buyers Contract), "Angsuran Uang Muka" (Down-payment)".
7. Most kampung dwellers could not make a clear distinction between the Tanah Abang or Kebun Kacang flats.
8. *Berita dan Daerah*, 9 September 1981; *Berita Buana*, 10 September 1981.
9. A Letter (Laporan pembentuk panitia peremajaan wilayah RW01/RW03) was sent to the Lurah of Kebun Kacang on 18 August 1981, indicating that on 14 August 1981 a committee consisting of 35 members had been formed.
10. Keputusan Gubernur Kepala Daerah Khusus Ibukota Jakarta, Nomor 903, Tahun 1981 tentang Pengukuhan Besarnja Ganti Rugi Pembebasan Tanah dan Benda Lain yang ada Diatasnya jang Terkena Proyek Pembangunan Rumah Susun Perum Perumnas Di Wilayah Jakarta Pusat, 3 September 1981 (Jakarta Governor's Decision Number 903, 1981 on compensation for land, housing and other objects affected by the flat building project in Central Jakarta).
11. Lembaran Daerah Chusus Ibu Kota Djakarta, 1972. Nomor 18. No. DA

11/3/14/1972.SK Gubernur Pedoman Penetapan Besarnja Penaksiran Ganti Rugi Pembebasan Tanah Beserta Benda Benda Jang Ada Diatasnja Dalam Wilajah Daerah Chusus Ibu Kota Djakarta p. 4 (Jakarta Governor's Decision Number 18, 1972 on compensation for land and other items in Jakarta).

12. "Program Peremajaan Kota" 1198081/TSG/Tsb (The City's Urban Renewal Plan).

13. "Aspirasi Warga RW01 Dan Sebagian RW03 Kelurahan Kebun Kacang Sehubungan Dengan Program Peremajaan Kota oleh Pemerintah DKI Jaya Di Daerah Kebun Kacang" (The People's Aspirations of RW01 and part of RW03 in connection with the program of Urban Renewal) 15 September p.2.

14. Every two weeks from May to November 1981 meetings were held at Perumnas and the minutes recorded in "Risalah Rapat Team Teknis Rumah Susun (Flat) Dalam Rangka Peremajaan Kota DKI Jakarta" (A Summary of meetings held by the Flat Technical Team for Jakarta's Urban Renewal), Perum Perumnas, Jakarta. See Risalah Rapat Team Teknis 20 August p. 2. Also *Berita Buana*, 10 September 1981; *Berita Dan Daerah*, 9 September 1981.

15. *Terbit*, 18 September 1981; *Berita Buana*, 1 October 1981; *Pelita*, 2 January 1981.

16. *Sinar Harapan*, 18 September 1981; *Kompas*, 26 September 1981.

17. *Sinar Harapan*, 23 September 1981; *Suara Karya*, 28 September 1981; *Pelita*, 28 September 1981; *Berita Buana*, 28 September 1981.

18. *Terbit*, 22 September 1981, 29 September 1981; *Sinar Harapan*, 29 September 1981.

19. *Pos Kota*, 2 October 1981; *Merdeka*, 3 October 1981; *Berita Buana*, 3 October 1981.

20. *Pos Kota*, 9 October 1981.

21. *Terbit*, 29 September 1981; *Sinar Harapan*, 29 September 1981.

22. *Suara Karya*, 2 November 1981.

23. Duddy Soegoto, head of Perumnas's Planning and Feasibility Section, was a sensitive and enlightened government engineer. He geniunely wished to know why the kampung dwellers objected to the project.

24. Later, in November 1981, this was presented to the kampung dwellers in a question-answer format—"Tanya Jawab Masalah Peremajaan Kota Di Kebon Kacang—Jakarta" (Question and Answers on the Problems of Kebun Kacang's Urban Renewal) Perum Perumnas, Departemen Pekerjaan Umum.

25. *Suara Karya*, 2 November 1981; *Berita Buana*, 4 November 1981.

26. *Kompas*, 24 October 1981, 31 October 1981; *Terbit*, 31 October 1981.

27. *Kompas*, 23 October 1981, 27 October 1981; *Pelita*, 26 October 1981.

28. *Berita Buana*, 24 November 1981.

29. Daftar: Pembayaran Pembebasan Tanah dan Ganti Rugi Bangunan/ Tanaman di Kampung Kebun Kacang untuk Keperluan Proyek Perum Perumnas Berdasarkan Surat Keputusan Gub. KDKI Jakarta No. 755/Tahun 1981 tgl. 18 Juli 1981 (List: compensation payments for land

and housing cleared for the Perum Perumnas Project in Kebun Kacang based on the Jakarta Governor's Decree No. 755 . . .).

30. *Berita Buana*, 24 November 1981, 4 December 1981; *Kompas*, 27 November 1981; *Sinar Harapan*, 4 December 1981.

31. *Berita Buana*, 7 December 1981.

32. Accurate figures on the number of mispayments are difficult to obtain. Both Perumnas and local government officials were tight-lipped. The press, however, reported that some of the 78 people who initially received compensation did not have rights to it (*Berita Buana*, 7 December 1981) and the kampung was full of rumours that the wrong people had been paid.

33. *Berita Buana*, 7 December 1981.

34. A list drawn up by a number of kampung spokesmen from RW01— "Daftar Orang luar yang Masuk Plat" indicated that at least 12 people from outside the project area had registered for the Kebun Kacang flats and illegally been given temporary accommodation.

35. *Sinar Pagi*, December 1981.

36. A list with 35 names of the inhabitants of RW01 was drawn up—"Daftar Nama-Nama Warga RW.01"—indicating that their compensation had been raised to Rp.60,000 or Rp.40,000 even though their land was "Tanah Garapan" (worth Rp.25,000). An additional 80 households from RW03, not mentioned in the list, had their compensation illicitly raised.

37. *Sinar Pagi*, December 1981.

38. Although local officials did not want to bother much with kampung dwellers' doubts and fears and some had a vested interest in selling the vacant flats to wealthier outsiders, their knowledge of the Tanah Abang project made them sceptical about the kampung dwellers' ability to accept or pay for the units. Based on this experience, some officials may honestly have been giving kampung dwellers the best advice they could.

39. When kampung dwellers eventually moved into the flats only 146 families remained out of the original 160. By November 1986, an estimated 15 percent had left the flats (Field work 1986).

40. A letter to the Secretary of State (Menteri Sekretaris Negara) TN.13.03, 13 June 1981 from the Minister of Public Works, indicated that the land controlled by the Department of Communications would be borrowed by the project for approximately two years (from July 1981 to July 1983).

41. Pengumuman Perum Perumnas Nomor:Dir 4/1182/21/111/84 Tentang Pembukaan Pendaftaran Permohonan Penghunian Rumah Susun Di Lokasi Kebun Kacang Jakarta Pusat, Jakarta 12 March 1984. Direksi Perum Perumnas (A Public Announcement Inviting People to Apply for the Kebun Kacang Flats in Central Jakarta).

42. Hollow friable bricks.

6

Aftermath (1981–1987)

Although for many kampung dwellers the demolition of Kebun Kacang was the most frightening and frustrating experience of their lives, it also presented them with undreamed of opportunities to lead a very different life. Unlike most other demolition schemes which had forced kampung dwellers away from their homes without providing adequate compensation or alternative housing, this scheme not only provided generous compensation for the loss of the kampung dwellers' houses, but also rehousing in highly subsidized and fully serviced flats in the same location. So, for the first time in their lives, kampung dwellers had access to large amounts of cash and the opportunity to buy legal, secure and well-serviced accommodation.

The Opportunity of Compensation

After payment of compensation, most Kampung dwellers suddenly had more cash on hand than ever before. Although they complained that the compensation was inadequate, each householder received considerably more than they would have been able to obtain by selling their homes in the kampung housing market. Before demolition kampung dwellers would have been lucky to have received half the price later offered in compensation. For those who owned their own land and homes, the sums paid in compensation were two to three times their annual incomes. As cash in hand, people suddenly held 100 to over 1000 times their daily incomes.[1] They were not used to handling so much money. Previously most had immediately spent whatever they earned. On the rare occasions when they had more cash than they needed, they bought consumer goods or jewellery or renovated their homes.

The government had assumed that the kampung dwellers would spend most, if not all, of their compensation on alternative accommodation. But the authorities had not allowed for the practical and social pressures that most kampung dwellers were exposed to. Only the educated, better-off and independent few were able to spend most of their compensation on housing for themselves and the surplus on productive enterprises. The majority found their life's assets, or a substantial part of them, were soon consumed fulfilling family obligations, repaying creditors and turning their fantasies into reality. Within a matter of months, little of the compensation money remained.

Kampung dwellers use of compensation was restricted by their economic and social insecurity, limited knowledge of how to invest and previous patterns of behaviour. From my observations, most spent their money according to the following priorities:

1. Day-to-day living during demolition and rehousing
2. Commissions to headmen and brokers for assistance during demolition
3. Repayment of cash debts
4. Social obligations and inheritance
5. Housing
6. Consumer goods
7. Saving in jewellery, land or bank deposits
8. Income-generating activities.

Day-to-day household needs were a most important use of compensation during the turmoil of demolition. The source of many kampung dwellers' income was interrupted and they were forced to rely on some of their compensation for daily survival. Because they were self-employed, battery recyclers, petty traders and becak drivers were especially affected. While having to attend meetings, queue for compensation and seek alternative accommodation, they could earn no income. As the chaos lasted for at least six months, they needed over Rp.200,000 (950 litres of rice) for food, transport, temporary shelter and school reenrolment fees. Those in fixed employment, by contrast, felt embarrassment and awkwardness at having to ask their employers for leave to attend to their rehousing needs, but still received an income.

During the process of demolition, kampung dwellers were obliged to pay for assistance they had received from their headman. To receive compensation, forms had to be filled in and official signatures obtained. Hardly any of the kampung dwellers, especially among the

poorest and illiterate, had ever seen a cheque or been in a bank. They
therefore relied on their headman, or some other broker, to help
change their cheques into cash. Headmen like Sugi who had helped
to raise their members' compensation expected a commission, which
could amount to 10 percent of each kampung dweller's compensation. Sugi, or one of his assistants, openly went to the kampung
dwellers' homes and demanded a commission. If it was not forthcoming, he threatened to make the kampung dweller's life more
difficult by refusing to sign any of the documents the kampung
dweller needed for his move to a new location. Burhanuddin, who
received one of the highest compensations, was forced to hand over
almost half a million rupiah (2400 litres of rice) to Sugi, whilst
Aswan, one of the poorest, reluctantly parted with Rp.100,000 (500
litres) which he badly needed for alternative housing. Only one or
two kampung dwellers managed to avoid this payment by fleeing
from the area immediately compensation was paid, or by insisting
that they had spent it before the headman made his claim. Some
kampung dwellers, however, wanted to make a contribution for they
felt genuine gratitude to their headman for having helped them
during the turmoil of demolition.

With cash in hand, kampung dwellers felt obliged to repay those
who had helped them in the past. As long as their resources had been
tied up in a house, they had been able to avoid discharging obligations that in some cases went back many years. Now obligations to
friends, neighbours and even the deceased could no longer be ignored. One man, for example, spent a quarter of his compensation
on presents of batik and food for relatives who had cared for his
daughters after his wife had died years earlier. He then spent another
quarter of his compensation on a ceremony for his parents, who had
died long ago but had never been given a proper funeral due to lack
of funds.

Creditors who felt they had a right to a share in the kampung
dwellers' compensation made their claims. The Sanis for example,
had debts of up to 15 percent of their compensation for food they had
obtained from four different stalls in the neighbourhood. Bud had to
spend 5 percent of her compensation on a gold ring for her mother
which she had borrowed when her trade went bankrupt. She also had
a longstanding debt with a moneylender for the cost of some house
renovations. Mus spent 15 percent of her compensation on repaying
debts for some batik and jewellery. There was hardly a kampung
dweller without such debts, but the most heavily indebted were the
poorest, who had often run out of cash.

Compensation had sometimes to be divided between several heirs.
For example, five brothers and sisters, some of whom were married

and lived elsewhere had equal inheritance rights to a house even though only one of them lived in it. Each of them received a fifth of the total compensation, leaving the family who lived in the house without sufficient resources to pay for alternative accommodation. They just had enough to place a deposit on a government unit and perhaps buy a little furniture.

Kampung dwellers who for many years had rented the land on which their house stood were also placed in a difficult position. Lukman for example, like many others in the kampung, had built his house on Haji Tejo's land. The compensation on his house provided just enough to build another house elsewhere, but not enough to pay for the land on which it stood.

To ensure security in old age, parents felt obliged to give some of their compensation to their children. Children, in turn, felt entitled to inherit some of their parents' compensation because the kampung house would have passed to them upon their parents' death. Married children who had lived with their parents usually received 5 to 10 percent of the compensation so that they could rehouse themselves elsewhere. Like the Sani's married children, they were often not registered as an independent family, so were not entitled to a government flat or sites and service unit. They either had to move with their parents or rent accommodation elsewhere. Unmarried children received presents such as gold earrings, cassette radios, bicycles or television sets.

Wives who had been deserted or divorced by their husbands were often obliged to pay them a share. Absentee husbands turned up at their former wive's homes and refused to leave until they were paid. Bud's husband, Santo, for example, demanded at least 10 percent of Bud's compensation. Another husband took one third of his wife's compensation. Fathers who had been absent for years suddenly turned up demanding a share of their family's compensation. A few astute kampung dwellers decided not to cash their cheques until their begging relatives had gone away.

By the time the poorest kampung dwellers came to rehousing themselves, more than a quarter of their compensation had often been spent on day-to-day living, commissions, debts and social obligations. Many of those who received little compensation like Agus or Aswan, were invited to rebuild their kampung homes beside their relatives' house. Most of their remaining compensation was given to the relatives for the piece of land on which they were to build and the rest was spent on buying and transporting secondhand timber from the demolished houses of Kebun Kacang to their new locations on the city's periphery. Much of the timber Agus bought, however, proved to be the wrong size and of such poor quality that it could not be used. Others like Lukman's wife did not need to rely on relatives for land for she still had hereditary title to land on the edges of Jakarta. Consequently, they were able to spend most of their compensation on a charming two-storey cottage with a cobbled pathway, toilet and washing facilities which Lukman built with the help of his son-in-law.

Kampung dwellers who received little compensation and had neither hereditary title to land nor relatives to turn to for assistance placed a deposit on a government unit or rented accommodation outside the project. They lacked the resources (from Rp.1,100,000 to Rp.4,000,000/5200–19,000 litres of rice) to buy alternative housing at the city centre or periphery. If they accepted a government flat or sites and service unit, they had to make a minimum downpayment of Rp.75,000 (360 litres) when they received their compensation. People like Wira, who only received a hardship allowance of Rp.65,000, had to raise an extra Rp.10,000 for the deposit and spent all the cash they had on rehousing.

Some kampung dwellers rejected the opportunity to buy either a central city flat or sites and service unit by instalments. They had sufficient resources to buy an alternative central city kampung house or land on the city's periphery. Mus, for example, spent half of her compensation for a partly burnt down house she bought near the city centre. She had discovered the house by word of mouth, real estate advertisements being unknown amongst kampung dwellers. Her crew of ice-cream makers and relatives from her village, working as a team, carefully demolished her recently renovated house in Kebun Kacang. Plank by plank they took the old building materials to the new location. In four days they had completed the new house, which looked identical to the one they had destroyed. As in Kebun Kacang, Mus paid most of her workers in food and the total cost of the land and house came to nearly three quarters of her compensation. Most of those who could afford alternative central city kampung houses like Haji Eddy, however, paid twice as much as Ibu Mus who had been lucky to buy a damaged house from her neighbour. Those who bought land and housing on the city's periphery, by contrast, paid only a quarter as much as such housing cost at the city centre.

Most of the kampung dwellers who received sufficient compensation preferred to pay for their new homes in full, so that they would not be burdened by monthly instalments. Burhanuddin and Lamirah, for example, immediately paid for their sites and service units and so gained legal title and the right to rebuild their new homes as they pleased. They immediately recreated houses as similar as possible to the ones they had lost. They claimed that moving into an identical house lessened the trauma of demolition.

Once kampung dwellers knew how much they would need for rehousing, they could spend the balance of their compensation on house renovations and consumer durables. For the sake of appearances, they added elaborate external porticos to the bare cell-like interiors of their sites and service units. Kampung dwellers claimed it was embarrassing to move into a new neighbourhood with torn or broken furniture. They bought sideboards, lounge suites, television sets and refrigerators. Bud, who still had much of her compensation when she moved into a flat, spent most of it on plastering and painting the walls and tiling the floor. Even the poorest households in the kampung, like the Sanis, were tantalized by the consumer goods at last within their reach. They paid only a minimal deposit on their sites and service unit so that they had money left over for beds, mattresses, pillows and a television set. In one extreme case, a man spent all his compensation on lavish food, white high-heeled shoes and expensive clothing, leaving nothing for his wife and children.

To the extent that kampung dwellers saved at all, they did so in the form of gold jewellery or consumer goods. Consumer goods not only enhanced their social status and prestige, but were viewed as a store of wealth which could be realized in times of need. Virtually nobody put their compensation in the bank. Most neither understood nor trusted banks. Furthermore, Islam prohibited the earning of interest. According to Bud, accepting interest on a bank deposit meant that at death, one would be strangled by snakes in hell. Bud, who under my advice did place the bulk of her compensation in the bank, subsequently withdrew it for flat renovations.

Only a few kampung dwellers invested part of their compensation in income-generating activities, and this was mostly in petty trade. Badrun, for example, spent half of his compensation expanding his household stall in the government sites and service housing estate. After placing a quarter of his compensation on a unit, he bought a refrigerator for his stall and diversified his stocks from the iced drinks he had sold in Kebun Kacang to rice, salted fish, sweets and any other item his neighbours would buy. Dini and Timin received much less compensation, but placed half on a sites and service unit and invested the remainder in Dini's fresh vegetable trade. One or two of the richest kampung dwellers bought or placed a deposit on motor vehicles for public transport. As Burhanuddin's ice-cone making enterprise could no longer operate in the housing estate on Jakarta's outskirts, he placed one fifth of his compensation as a deposit on a vehicle which was used to drive customers from Depok railway station to the government housing estate. The other one or two kampung dwellers who had bought vehicles, initially made a thriving business driving kampung dwellers, their possessions and house building materials from Kebun Kacang to their new sites on the edges of the city. Although those who invested a substantial part of their compensation in income-generating activities had better prospects to look forward to, they could never be sure about the future.

Kampung dwellers' main objectives in their use of compensation was immediate survival, social status and prestige. They continued to spend within the same short term time horizon despite the fact that they suddenly had more cash. Having just lost their homes, they spent a substantial proportion on housing. But contrary to the program's intentions they did not view their compensation as purely for housing. To enhance their social status and prestige, consumer goods had to be bought and social obligations satisfied. Most kampung dwellers did not know how to invest successfully in income-generating activities, but they knew that kinsfolk and friends whom they helped would later come to their assistance in times of difficulty. Unlike investment in income-generating activities, consumer goods were tangible and immediately useful and served as a store of wealth that could be realized in times of need. They felt money was not dissipated or lost if it was put into goods. Only the richer or better educated and informed minority carefully put aside a certain amount of cash in a bank or invested in income-generating activities that could provide longer term economic security.

The Opportunity of Flats

Kampung dwellers were offered the extraordinary opportunity of buying highly subsidized, fully serviced flats at the city centre where their former kampung had been. The flats were to be paid off by monthly instalments over twenty years with interest added to their home loan at the rate of only 5 percent per annum. The monthly instalments ranged from Rp.10,000 to Rp.40,000 (48–190 litres of rice) and were supposed to be no more than 25 percent of kampung dwellers' income. Each flat was self-contained, with its own gas, electricity and water supply. Perumnas was to be responsible for regular rubbish collection, night watch and maintenance of all facilities. A health clinic, school, mosque and meeting hall were to be built nearby.

Not surprisingly, only a fifth of the kampung dwellers (160 households), who were mainly the better-off and better informed, accepted flats. They were the ones who had regular jobs or sufficient income and felt able to meet the regular monthly instalments. Headmen and kampung spokesmen, for example, had better access to government officials and information about the project and trusted the government to rehouse them. They understood the government did not want its first inner city rehousing scheme for the poor to fail. Unlike the less informed kampung dwellers, they believed that if they could not pay for the flats, they would not be forced out. A number of larger entrepreneurs, like Ateng, who needed to remain at the city centre close to their income-earning activities, also accepted flats. A person like Ateng was prepared to take the risk of a very different way of life from the one he had experienced in the kampung. He had not been dependent on the kampung community for his livelihood or security and looked forward to trying flat life surrounded by new middle class neighbours.

The majority, by contrast, who earned less than Rp.60,000 (286 litres of rice) per month or had only irregular jobs, felt unable to pay the regular flat instalments. The becak drivers, ice-cream sellers, battery recyclers and those who had serviced the kampung with water, kerosene, cooked food and laundry services, felt that the flats had destroyed their means of livelihood. Many felt a strong emotional attachment to the kampung and felt socially and economically dependent upon their former neighbours. They objected to the alien and isolating nature of flats. They wished to preserve their social ties with kinsfolk and kampung friends, and some chose to move together to the edges of the city to try to recreate the community they had lost.

The minority of poor kampung dwellers who accepted flats were those who needed to live at the city centre if they were to keep their jobs. They needed to be within walking distance of their poorly paid service sector work because they could not afford the cost of daily transport. Apart from leaving their jobs and moving elsewhere, their only alternative was to rent central city accommodation or pay monthly instalments on a flat. Some had previously been able only to rent accommodation in Kebun Kacang and were in no position to buy an alternative central city kampung house. Eventually they realized that instead of perpetually having to pay rent, it was better to pay instalments on a flat which they could someday own.

Ateng exemplified the type of person who could accept a flat without hesitation. He was one of the richest, most experienced and dynamic people in Ibu Imah's neighbourhood. Whilst most other kampung dwellers vacillated for months, unable to make their minds, Ateng requested not just one but two units in Tanah Abang.[2] One flat was to be used for accommodation, whilst the other was for his cap making enterprise. He did not bemoan the loss of his kampung neighbours or his recently completed brick and glass two-storey kampung house. He believed that the secret of success was to adapt to changing circumstances and to grasp new opportunities.

Bang Ateng immediately saw the advantage of flats. He realized that his enterprise could not survive in the state of turmoil and uncertainty that surrounded the six months of demolition. Without a fixed address near the city centre his cap sewers could not work, his customers could not place orders and his material suppliers would not give credit. Above all, Ateng felt that without a stable base he could not concentrate on his enterprise. Previously when he had tried to set up an enterprise in a village near Bandung he had learnt that he had to be near his raw material suppliers and marketing outlets at Tanah Abang and the offices of central Jakarta.

Bang Ateng was used to handling large amounts of money. In the past he had bought clove trees, rice land, a car and a generator and had rebuilt his village house. He had been in banks and used cheques in his transactions with Chinese storekeepers and government departments. He understood mortgages and interest rates and realized the government was offering him an excellent investment. Thus, he placed all his compensation, which was less than three quarters of his annual income, as a deposit on the two flats.

Being the first of the kampung dwellers to accept the government's offer and demolish his house, he was given speedy and special attention in the processing of his claims and move into the flats. His decision, however, was viewed as treason by other kampung dwellers. They said "he seeks profit and forgets his friends". He was viewed as opportunistic and only interested in his own material advance. For some time kampung dwellers had viewed Ateng with envy as his enterprise prospered and he rebuilt his house and now, before anybody else, he took up the opportunity of a flat. For his part, Ateng felt the kampung dwellers were "stupid" and caught in poverty of their own making. "Here was the kampung dwellers best chance to start a new life and they could not see the opportunities the government was offering".

Wira was poor, illiterate, ill-informed, lacking in confidence and one of the least likely persons to accept a flat. Why she eventually decided to take a flat sheds light on why most other poor people felt unable to do so. Wira dreamed of owning her own home instead of always having to rent accommodation and each year battled to raise the necessary amount. During the 1970s, Wira was forced to move from room to room in Kebun Kacang because each of her new landlords wished to raise their rents. Room rents rose three times faster than the price of rice.

At first, Wira did not recognize the unique opportunity provided by the offer of a government flat. Her automatic response was to take the hardship allowance offered to those who were registered as living in the area but lacking a home of their own, and rent accommodation elsewhere. She was convinced that the flats were intended for the rich and not for people like herself. She feared that on the washerwoman's salary she received from the maternity hospital where she worked, she could not keep up with the monthly instalments. If she failed to pay, she was sure that she would be forced out on the street. Government officials had never shown her any sympathy in the past, so why would they treat her kindly now? She feared the alien and isolating nature of flats, and could not envisage "living alone, high in the sky like a bird in a concrete cage". She wanted to live on the ground, close to her married daughter who had decided to move to sites and service units on the edges of the city. She preferred the space, variety and more self-contained nature of kampung or sites and service housing.

Without my intervention, Wira would certainly not have accepted a flat. I explained that if she moved to the edges of Jakarta, she would spend most of her time and salary travelling to and from work each day and have no money left to rent a room, let alone buy a house. If she rented a room in another kampung close to her place of work, then her hardship allowance would not even cover one year's rent. She would soon be forced to raise the money for an even higher rent. She would never break out of having to rent accommodation year after year. She would never gain the security and pride of her own home. For the first time in her life, Wira could start to buy a house by placing her hardship allowance as a deposit on a flat. As she only had Rp.65,000 (310 litres of rice) and needed at least Rp.75,000 to make a flat deposit, I promised to make up the difference. That deposit ensured that she had temporary accommodation and free water and electricity until the flats were built.[3] The proposed flats would be within walking distance of Wira's work and so she would not need to spend any of her income on travel. She had lived alone in the kampung and so the smallest flat of 21 square metres would suffice. After much indecision, anguish and doubt, Wira eventually accepted the economic rationality of living in a flat, even if it seemed socially and aesthetically unappealing.

Wira's doubts about her ability to pay for a flat, however, may have been well placed. On a number of occasions when unanticipated costs emerged, she had to ask me for assistance. Upon entering the flats, she lacked the resources to transport her possessions and pay for the electricity, gas and water connections. Her flat leaked badly during the monsoon season and she lacked the Rp.100,000 needed for repairs. In 1986, Wira like the other kampung dwellers who had accepted the government's offer of accommodation, had the opportunity to take out a mortgage instead of perpetually paying rent. It was normal for occupants of Perumnas housing to first rent their units for two years and then take out a mortgage for the next 15 to 20 years. The administrative charges for organising the mortgage, however, were prohibitive. Certificates of regular employment, good behaviour and health had to be obtained from ones employer, the police, local government and a doctor. Had I not arranged these things for Wira, over time financial pressures would have forced her to move out of the flat. In the end, I felt Wira's experience of how the real world operated was a better guide to poor kampung dwellers than my calculations based on government promises.

From these two case studies it becomes clear that only kampung dwellers who had access to both sufficient knowledge and sufficient resources could accept the opportunity of flats. Ateng represented the dynamic, well-informed, financially secure and courageous type who immediately recognized and grasped the opportunities the government was offering. Wira, by contrast, was typical of the poor, illiterate and frightened majority who could not accept flats unless an outsider provided the necessary economic logic, resources, administrative know how and foresight to see that it was important to be close to their place of work at the city centre. In short, Wira was the exception that proved the rule.

Kampung Dwellers' Fates

It is hard to generalize about the fate of kampung dwellers after rehousing. Some benefitted and some suffered, and even a statistical survey would only provide a rough and uninformed overview of the range of experiences. Some who invested their compensation in a house close to their place of work like Ateng and Wira, or in income-generating activity like Burhanuddin, Dini, and Badrun, did well. Others like Bud, Mus, Lamirah, Agus, Aswan or Lukman who spent most of their compensation on debts, a house and/or consumer goods and lacked secure jobs or income earning activities near their new homes suffered. Apart from Bud and Mus who were located at the city centre, the others had not considered the difficulties of finding work on the city's periphery, or the time and cost entailed each day in getting to work at the city centre. Those who had homes on the periphery but continued to work at the city centre paid transport costs which could amount to 20 percent of their income and spent up to four hours per day commuting, instead of the ten minutes by foot from Kebun Kacang. Some who obtained work on the edges of the city found that their incomes dropped by more than half.

Although Ateng had initially established his cap making enterprise in the austere and low cost kampung environment, he benefitted by investing in two flats. He could never have obtained equivalent housing or work space in such a central location so cheaply. He had a telephone, parking space and a legal, respectable and accessible address, which fitted the needs of his enterprise. He was no longer awkwardly caught between the world of the kampung and the modern economy. Instead of blocking the narrow kampung pathway with his motorcycle, he bought a truck for distributing his caps and parked it directly in front of his flat. Instead of customers having to go by foot into the kampung's twisted and muddy pathways, they could place orders by telephone. Some of his middle class neighbours, who worked in government or private offices, also placed orders for his caps. Living amongst the middle class, he was no longer envied and ostracised by neighbours for his entrepreneurial success. He had the time and privacy to concentrate on his business. As the flats were fully serviced with gas, water and electricity, he no longer had to rely on poorer neighbours for the delivery of basic services. Kampung neighbours no longer came begging for assistance when they were out of cash. Consequently, his hard earned savings were not continually dissipated.

In her new flat, Wira found that she was within walking distance of her place of work and for the first time could buy a home of her own. She took great pride in her unit and its amenities. Although the monthly cost of the flat and its amenities absorbed over half her income, she learned to budget and lived very austerely in order to make ends meet. She admitted that it was better paying for a flat than spending half her income on travel to work each day and still not being able to buy a home.

Wira's son-in-law, who had taken a sites and service unit on the periphery, found it impossible to find a job and was forced to return to the city centre to seek work. The cost and time taken to commute to the sites and service unit each day to visit his family proved prohibitively expensive and time consuming. They could not save enough to pay the monthly instalments on their unit. Eventually, Wira's daughter and her family moved into Wira's flat. They lived there during the week and returned to their sites and service unit only on weekends, when Wira joined them for some fresh air, space and greenery. Wira was delighted that she and her daughter once again lived together but the congestion in the flat with 6 people in 21 square metres of space was difficult to bear.

After their move to Depok, Burhanuddin's family continued to perform a wide variety of income earning activities in an attempt to maintain the standard of living they had had in Kebun Kacang. They gained an income from the vehicle Burhanuddin had bought with part of their house compensation. His wife, Sum, resumed her Islamic classes in the sites and service area and her son contributed an occasional income from his work as a minor government official. For the first six months after the move they experienced considerable hardship. Later, even though they continued to eat modestly, they were pleased with their new life in Depok and could not understand how they had endured the density, filth, noise, pollution and stench of Kebun Kacang. In the sites and service area all amenities were nearby, including school and health facilities. There was better community organization. Rotating credit societies, sports tournaments and New Year celebrations were organized. In the evenings parents and children played on the sports fields. Families cultivated their own gardens.

By 1986, Burhanuddin had bought a second car and hired two drivers to do the driving. He felt prosperous and too old to work and dedicated himself to religious activities. Along with twenty other wealthier households in their area, Sum and Burhanuddin decided to buy some vacant land from Perumnas and set up an Islamic school. Burhanuddin was the main force behind the scheme and invested much of his time in it.

Badrun, who was one of the few to have invested a large part of his compensation in income earning activity, namely a household stall in the sites and service area, for the first two and a half years succeeded beyond all expectations. His former neighbours pointed to his success in disbelief. In Kebun Kacang he had barely made ends meet. In his new location, he was the only trader to have a large dried-food stall and quickly acquired a large clientele. Like Burhanuddin, they appreciated the much improved environment, the possibility of buying legal accommodation and the opportunity to set up a new business, even though they too had originally bitterly resented the demolition of their kampung home. At the end of 1986, Badrun and his wife's home remained half-finished, but their stall had expanded and their children were doing well at school.

After four years, however, some neighbours began to copy Badrun and set up stalls of their own. Badrun worried that competition could undermine his trade, but believed that if he and his wife worked hard, budgeted carefully and kept their prices below that of their competitors they would continue to prosper. But in 1987 Badrun's tuberculosis returned and he had to undergo regular medical treatment. He could not work so hard. Their refrigerator broke down. Their customers went elsewhere and much to Badrun and his wife's dismay their children were forced to drop out of school.

Dini and Timin, who had lived a hand-to-mouth existence in Kebun Kacang and never had the resources or opportunity to own a home of their own, found, to their surprise, that for the first four years in the sites and service area their trade and construction work was in great demand. There were no other fresh vegetable sellers in the street where they lived and Dini diligently walked long distances to the market to bring back produce to sell to her neighbours who were unwilling to walk so far. Timin, the construction worker, was constantly offered work renovating neighbours' sites and service houses. Dini and Timin no longer had to pay rent but started to buy a sites and service unit by monthly instalments. They were proud about the prospect of owning their own home, even if they lacked the resources to renovate it. Their family could enjoy living in a house which was double the size they had in Kebun Kacang. In addition, they had piped water, private washing and toilet facilities, electricity and a garden, all of which they had never had in Kebun Kacang. After 1986, however, like Badrun's family, they began to experience increased difficulty in earning a livelihood. Population growth brought more successful traders and builders to the area who could outcompete them.

Bud illustrates the difficulties faced by a kampung dweller who accepted a flat but later lost her source of income as a domestic servant. When she moved into the flat, she was saddened by the grey cell-like walls and claimed her aging mother coughed badly because of the dust in the batako bricks. She envied her neighbours who were busily improving their flats and felt embarrassed when she could not invite her visitors to sit on nice chairs. Bud soon spent most of her compensation, which I had encouraged her to put in the bank on house renovations and furnishing. She was immensely proud of her renovated flat and believed she was rising into the middle class.

After her mother died, Bud left her live-in job as a domestic servant to look after her thirteen year old daughter, who was alone and refused to go to school. To get over the depression of her mother's death, Bud withdrew the rest of her compensation and bought a refrigerator, colour television set, lounge suite and sideboards. Without any income from a job, she was forced to accept a boarder to help pay for the flat instalments and amenities. The boarder, however, soon moved out and Bud was left without any income. To cover her rising costs, she was forced to sell her new possessions. Her flat was soon bare.

Bud tried to earn a living preparing and delivering banana fritters to stalls in the flats, an activity which did not differ much from her cake trade in the 1960s. Hawking in the flats, however, made her feel more destitute because she was surrounded by a prosperous middle class and not poor kampung dwellers. In addition, she lived in a flat she did not own and for which she could not pay. In the kampung she had owned her own home and had to worry only about income for food. By late 1986, Bud was just managing to survive by leasing her two bedrooms and sleeping with her daughter on the floor of the living room. She felt sad, embarrassed and oppressed. One year later, she was dead.

Mus, who had run the ice-cream enterprise and communal lodging-house, bought an alternative central city kampung house but found it difficult reestablishing her trade. Before Kebun Kacang's demolition her ice-cream sellers were already suffering from the rise in cost of raw materials, competition from mass-produced ice-creams, government opposition to petty trade and changes in consumer tastes. In the new area, they had the added disadvantage of trying to establish themselves where other ice-cream vendors were already operating. Even though Mus's sellers had to push their carts long distances, they continued to return to their former trade routes near Kebun Kacang. Many of their regular customers, however, had been cleared away with the demolition.

Mus lacked the time, know how or contacts in the city administration to check on the legality of the land she bought. Later she discovered that it, too, was destined for demolition. Mus was frequently ill and began to spend more time in her central Javanese village. Her new lodging-house was frequently empty. It was hard to determine whether this was due to the traumas of demolition, age, exhaustion or difficult economic times. By late 1986, Mus no longer returned to Jakarta. She was seriously ill and spent many months in a hospital in Yogyakarta. The sale of her cows in Klaten helped pay for her hospitalization. Relatives explained that Mus's illness had started with the demolition of Kebun Kacang.

The future of the ice-cream sellers in central Jakarta looked bleak. Some sellers returned to cultivate their land or become labourers in the village. Others tried their luck with hand made ice-creams in other cities of Java or the Outer Islands. Some of the ice-cream sellers' sons turned to construction work rather than ice-cream selling and clustered around new building sites on Jakarta's periphery. With the recession after 1982, however, hand-made ice-creams, like other small scale enterprises seemed to gain a new lease of life. Although Mus no longer came to the city, some of the ice-cream sellers continued to operate from her central city home. Their absolute incomes, however, were not much higher than in 1981.

The fate of Agus, the becak driver, epitomized that of the poorest and least informed. His becak driving had been harassed at the city centre, but he found that work on the city's outskirts was even harder to find. On Jakarta's periphery, becak drivers had to pedal much longer distances over pot-holed roads to earn as much as they had earned at the city centre for a 15 minute drive on smooth asphalt. To break into the circle of becak drivers he needed a relative, friend, personal charm or courage. Tired, old and without a contact, Agus therefore continued to drive his becak in his former location at Kebun Kacang, just beside the construction of the new flats. He returned to his family which remained in Depok only when he had earned sufficient income. Whilst in the city he slept in his becak and ate from a regular stall. His three eldest sons were also forced to go to the city because of the lack of income earning opportunities at Depok. They did the odd jobs they had previously done near Kebun Kacang, stayed with different friends and only occasionally returned home.

When Agus or his three sons did not return home for days on end, Samilah had to find other ways of feeding her family. In Kebun Kacang she had been able to make an income from dress repairs, but in the new location she lacked the regular contacts. When she was unable to find work, she helped in her relatives' mattress making enterprise, but was given only food and a little pocket money. She had fled from this uncomfortable dependence on relatives thirty years earlier, when she had first made her way to Jakarta. Now again, in shame, she was forced to turn to them for assistance when her children were without food. Although initially welcoming, her relatives became reluctant to bear the burden of extra mouths to feed.

In 1982 Agus' becak was confiscated by the authorities. For over twenty years he had worked to buy that vehicle. In despair, he returned to his family in Depok. His wife pawned her sewing machine for Rp.50,000 (240 litres of rice) so that Agus could operate a vegetable stall from their new home. While Samilah repaired clothes, Agus looked after the stall. Within weeks the stall was bankrupt, for Agus had no experience in trade. Crushed, he returned to Jakarta and was forced to rent a becak again. But the Jakarta administration was clamping down on becak drivers and the restricted routes limited his earnings. His journeys home with money for his family became even more infrequent. Samilah was sad that her family was dispersed. In Kebun Kacang they had always stayed together. She suffered increasing sorrow, loneliness and despair of ever improving her life or that of her children.

Ironically, Samilah's family had a larger and more solid house than ever before, but had never felt so helpless and so poor. Samilah's relatives continued to own the land Samilah's family occupied. Samilah worried that in later years a feud would develop over who actually owned the land. In 1985, the land was threatened with demolition. The government planned to dam the river which ran just beside Samilah's house. There was, however, no certainty when demolition would occur.

The one redeeming feature of their move to the periphery was that

Samilah's children, like those in sites and service units, enjoyed a strikingly better physical environment. The children were sick much less often than when they had lived in Central Jakarta. Even though increasing number of people came to settle in the area, the environment was not as congested and filthy as Kebun Kacang. An enormous river surrounded by bamboo groves flowed nearby and Samilah's children ran and played along its banks. The setting was not very different from Kebun Kacang of thirty years earlier, although many large modern brick houses with television aerials now intermingled with the rustic village dwellings.

After five years Samilah's family seemed to have settled into their life on the periphery, even though earning sufficient income still remained a problem. Samilah's determination to educate her children at all costs, however, was beginning to pay off. Her eldest children were coming of age and increasingly helped support the family. Furthermore, as their contacts expanded at Depok, new opportunities became available. The eldest son no longer went to Jakarta but sought income earning activities in Depok. He had contacts with a video cassette hire shop which allowed him to borrow cassettes and hire them to neighbours. In addition, he travelled to Bogor to organize car registration and licences for his neighbours in Depok. The second eldest son commuted daily to Jakarta to work as a driver and car parking attendant. Having a wife and child in Depok, he was reluctant to stay in the city overnight. The third son had changed from shoe-shining to car washing. The fourth and most educated son earned occasional windfalls from the pictures he drew using Islamic calligraphy and decorations he made for weddings out of coconut leaves. Samilah's daughters remained at school despite the battle their mother had paying for their education. The eldest daughter dreamed of being a nurse, but Samilah felt this was unrealistic.

Aswan, the water seller who had married Samilah's sister Ani, initially had parallel experiences to those of Agus' family. He had sought refuge with his sister on the opposite side of the city. He had no legal title to the land he occupied, could barely survive and aged rapidly. When he and his wife had sufficient capital (Rp.5000/24 litres of rice) they hawked green-bean porridge door to door and were lucky to earn Rp.5500 a day, which was less than half of what they had earned in Kebun Kacang. Samilah and her sister Ani had still not been reunited two and a half years after demolition. They were too impoverished to make the journey to each other's home. It was only after Aswan's death in 1984 that Ani first visited Samilah and occasionally stayed with her.

Lukman, the battery recycler observed that since demolition he "had a large house but a small heart". Outwardly, his life looked prosperous but inwardly he felt hollow. After years of struggle, his hopes of ever bettering his life were dashed. His lot, in old age, was worse than his life over 50 years ago. Even his simplest dreams to smoke a cigarette or drink a cup of coffee could not be realized. When dealing in batteries in Kebun Kacang he had been able to afford fish, mangoes and other delicacies. Now he did not even have the money to visit his 90 year old mother in the village. Previously he had seen her at least once or twice a year.

Lukman had spent the little compensation he received on a television set and rebuilding his house on inherited land on the edges of Jakarta. Lacking capital to restart his battery recycling business, which he believed could again thrive on Jakarta's periphery, he busied himself in the garden. He and Rohani ate whatever they produced, which largely consisted of cassava roots and spinach. To add variety and cash, Lukman began to rear chickens, but suddenly they fell ill and Lukman quickly distributed them to Rohani's relatives to eat before they died. Lukman himself nearly died of cholera. His wife lacked the money for medical treatment and the hospital where he was treated refused to release him until his medical debts were paid. The initial warm welcome of Rohani's relatives turned to indifference. They were too busy trying to satisfy their own material aspirations to worry about Rohani's and Lukman's needs.

Lukman and Rohani's area seemed to be experiencing a speeded up version of the changes that had overtaken Kebun Kacang. Within a couple of months the dirt lane running past their new home was covered by asphalt. Rohani was pleased, for not only would the value of their land rise but she hoped more customers would come to the stall she had just established. Builders from central Java came to work in the area, renovating homes and building offices. Some of these newcomers ate at Rohani's stall and she offered them accommodation. The subdivision of land, construction boom, new migrants, and increase in small scale income earning opportunities was tantalizingly reminiscent of Kebun Kacang's recent past.

Escape Route or Poverty Trap?

Looking back, some kampung dwellers (Ateng, Wira, Burhanuddin) recognized that the demolition of Kebun Kacang had given them a new lease on life. This was initially also true for Badrun and Dini but four years later things started to go bad again. For people like Bud, Mus, Agus, Aswan and Lukman, the destruction of the kampung temporarily provided them with large amounts of cash and material possessions, but then threw them back into poverty.

The kampung dwellers who benefitted from the project already had secure jobs and sufficient incomes to pay for their new accommodation and amenities, or were able to find more lucrative employment in the new locations. On the periphery some small scale income earning activities which had suffered in Kebun Kacang, were again able to thrive. The rapidly growing population and lack of transport and retail outlets provided them with new opportunities. It was difficult to know, however, how long the opportunities on the city's periphery would last. As the city continued to spread would the same forces which had first boosted and then undermined small scale enterprises in Kebun Kacang also affect these peripheral areas?

The kampung dwellers who did not benefit from the project remained trapped by insecure jobs and a way of thinking and behaving which prevented them from taking advantage of the new opportunities. The project showed that giving poor urban dwellers large amounts of cash and the opportunity to buy a house did not necessarily overcome their poverty. With these resources their priorities were distorted away from the urgent need of earning sufficient income to spending money on social obligations, housing, renovations and new possessions. Soon they discovered they had large solid houses, amenities and many material possessions, but no secure source of income. Their material possessions—and in some cases even their homes—had to be sold to provide for their daily food needs. They were then thrust back into the very poverty they had been trying to escape.

1.

Compensation Payments, Average Daily Cash Holdings and Annual Income (selected households)

Household	Compensation payment in Rp.	Typical daily cash holdings in Rp.	Ratio of compensation payments to typical daily cash in hand	Annual income in Rp.	Ratio of compensation payments to annual income
H. Eddy	9,000,000	7000	1300:1	2,700,000	3:1
Burhanuddin	7,615,000	7000	1000:1	2,700,000	3:1
Mus	3,393,000	3000	1000:1	1,080,000	3:1
Ateng	2,425,000	10,000	243:1	3,600,000	0.67:1
Bud	2,355,350	1665	1414:1	594,000	4:1
Badrun	1,958,350	2000	1000:1	720,000	3:1
Sani	1,198,350	1500	800:1	540,000	2:1

Agus	1,172,000	1500	780:1	540,000	2:1
Aswan	1,025,000	1000	1000:1	360,000	3:1
Lukman	500,000	2000	250:1	720,000	0.7:1
Dini	250,000	1500	160:1	540,000	0.5:1
Wira	65,000	650	100:1	240,000	0.3:1
Tukirah	65,000	500	130:1	180,000	0.4:1

This table was derived partly from Daftar: Pembayaran Pembebasan Tanah dan Ganti Rugi Bangunan/ Tanaman di Kampung Kebun Kacang untuk Keperluan Proyek Perum Perumnas Berdasarkan Surat Keputusan Gub.KDKI Jak.No 755/Tahun 1981 tgl.18 Juli 1981 and from my own field work.

2. He did not want to wait six to twelve months until the flats in Kebun Kacang were built.

3. In the end, the flats took over two and a half years to build. Had Wira rented private accommodation at the city centre like some of her neighbours, she would have spent over Rp.700,000 for housing and amenities instead of Rp.75,000. Financial pressures eventually forced those who rented on the private market out of the city centre.

7

The Wheel of Fortune

Kebun Kacang: The Jakarta Context

The changes encountered by the inhabitants of Kebun Kacang affected the lives of most kampung dwellers in Jakarta. They lived through a transition from a rural to an urban environment and experienced rapid changes in social values, interpersonal ties, patterns of income earning and their relationship with government. Although kampung dwellers' social ties cushioned them against the vagaries of the outside world, these bonds were fragile and often dissipated their wealth and perpetuated their poverty. Although kampung dwellers' small scale income earning activities could thrive for a brief period, they were soon undermined and mobility into more secure and adequately paid jobs proved very difficult. Government became more and more intrusive with mixed results for kampung dwellers. All of them suffered from the demolition of their homes. Although the experience of demolition was not unusual, the government's intention to rehouse the kampung dwellers in cheap inner-city flats was new for Indonesia. This more enlightened program, however, still resulted in most kampung dwellers being squeezed out of the central city area. Only a minority could take advantage of the new opportunities offered by government to improve their lives.

The first kampungs to feel the transformation from a predominantly rural to an urban way of life were those located near the city centre. From the early 1900s the heart of Jakarta moved progressively southwards, from the old colonial town of Batavia to Merdeka Square near Kebun Kacang. After Independence in 1949, Jakarta experienced a population boom. Poverty and the difficulty of life in

170

the countryside drove increasing numbers of people to the town. Kampungs like Kebun Kacang, which in the 1920s and 1930s had been rural backwaters, suddenly became part of the modern metropolis. They changed from being sparsely populated swamps and vegetable gardens to shanty towns.

The development boom of the late 1960s and 1970s was nowhere more evident than in central Jakarta. Inner-city kampungs like Kebun Kacang prospered because of their proximity to big construction projects. As the large scale capital-intensive sector was not yet well established, the small scale labour-intensive enterprises, from which most kampung dwellers earned a livelihood, filled the vacuum for construction, transport, manufacturing and retail services. A symbiotic relationship existed between the kampungs and the city, with the former providing cheap labour and the latter, income, hope and the possibility of escape from the poverty of the countryside. The higher incomes in the town enabled many kampung dwellers to educate their children, renovate their homes and buy consumer goods.

In the late 1970s, however, the complementary relationship between the kampung and the city began to break down. Kampungs at the city centre like Kebun Kacang were the first to feel the effect. As the modern city engulfed these neighbourhoods their inhabitants' income earning activities were squeezed. Dramatic changes in the demand and supply of goods and services undermined their livelihoods. Small scale income earning activities were rapidly made obsolete by the growth of larger scale, capital-intensive enterprises and the spread of a centralized and more efficient government bureaucracy. Daily press reports described the removal of petty traders and becak drivers from the streets and the demolition of urban neighbourhoods to make way for highways, government and private offices, recreation centres and luxury housing estates.

By 1981 Kebun Kacang's survival at the heart of Jakarta had become an anomaly. Whilst neighbouring kampungs had been demolished to make way for Jalan Thamrin, Hotel Indonesia, Sarinah department store, and numerous other multi-storey buildings, Kebun Kacang had been bypassed. Many poor people had sought refuge there after the demolition of homes elsewhere. The authorities seemed to hesitate to act against this long established and densely populated neighbourhood. The low lying and formerly swampy land of Kebun Kacang made it unattractive as a construction site. Eventually, however, Kebun Kacang was chosen as the first inner-city rehousing project. It was to serve as a model for Indonesia's other poor and densely populated urban neighbourhoods.

The processes of change which affected Kebun Kacang over the

172 THE WHEEL OF FORTUNE

past thirty years are now occurring on the city's periphery. Village land is being subdivided and market gardens are giving way to houses. Villagers who made a living mainly from their land have turned to renting and selling accommodation to newcomers who work in trade, transport, cottage industry or jobs in offices or factories. The newcomers include the inhabitants of former central city kampungs like Kebun Kacang as well as new migrants from rural areas. The increase in population and economic development on the edges of the city have created new opportunities for small scale income earning activities which were no longer viable at the city centre.

Kebun Kacang: The Indonesian Context

Kebun Kacang and other kampungs in Jakarta are not necessarily typical of those in other Indonesian cities. John Sullivan, for example, in his study of a lower-class neighbourhood at the heart of contemporary Yogyakarta, rejected what he interpreted as excessive emphasis on poverty, insecurity and flux in the literature on the urban poor.[1] He found a stable, ordered and integrated society with effective community organization reinforced by the State. Kampung dwellers were not merely the pawns of external forces but controlled and improved their lives by close social ties and community co-operation.[2] Although aware of exceptions, John Sullivan asserted that his findings were valid for "a major proportion of Indonesia's urban population."[3]

The contrasts between Sullivan's and my portrayal of kampung life can perhaps be explained by the two cities' very different experience of development. Since 1949, Jakarta has been the focus of national development. Yogyakarta, by contrast, until the early 1970s experienced economic stagnation and net outmigration. Over the decade 1961 to 1971, Yogyakarta's rate of population growth was the lowest of all the main cities of Indonesia.

Even though Yogyakarta's population growth accelerated over the decade 1971 to 1980, as late as 1979 the population and housing density in Sullivan's district at the centre of the city had varied little for two decades. The kampung's population growth rate "had been an insignificant 0.1 percent".[4] From this perspective, the social stability and cooperative nature of kampung life in Yogyakarta may not have been typical of Indonesia's larger and faster growing cities.

Nineteenth-Century London—A Precedent?

The experience of Kebun Kacang and modern Jakarta is not without precedent. Similar processes were taking place in London (and other western cities) over one hundred years ago. During the first half of the nineteenth century London's population grew rapidly from less than 1 million to 2.5 million.[5] Central London experienced a great influx of petty traders and a proliferation of casual labouring and street-side occupations.[6] In the 1850s it was estimated that there were 45,000 to 100,000 pedlars.[7] Income earning for the poor was very insecure with great seasonal variations.[8]

From the 1860s, external pressures began to force the casually employed poor from their inner-city residences. Rising rents and competition from mass-produced goods from the industrial north harmed London's many small workshops.[9] Government and middle class hostility together with economic and spatial pressures destroyed poor peoples' jobs and homes. The middle class, for example, increasingly regarded pedlars as a nuisance dirtying the streets and making a noise.[10] In response to this hostility, government legislation banned pedlars and other street-side occupations. Throughout the century, other pressures such as the construction of markets, roads, railways, commercial and government offices, banks and warehouses forced the urban poor to crowd closer and closer together in utterly miserable living conditions.[11] There was a growing separation between the rich and poor as the former escaped the filth and stench by moving to more salubrious suburbs on the city's periphery.[12] Although the poor were ruthlessly cleared from their homes, they were tied to central London by the lack of work on the city's outskirts and lack of cheap, reliable and convenient transport.[13]

The slum clearance and urban renewal programs in London of the 1860s and 1870s are also reminiscent of contemporary Jakarta. City planners viewed the slums of London as eyesores and anachronisms in an age of rapid change. They wished to beautify the city and assumed that rehousing the poor in model houses or flats would raise their standard of living. As in Kebun Kacang, however, most of the original inhabitants were not rehoused by the government but suffered the loss of their homes and simply huddled closer and closer together, while the better-off occupied the newer and more expensive accommodation. As in Jakarta, the poor bore the brunt of demolition schemes which decreased rather than increased the city's housing stock.[14]

Although the similarities between nineteenth century London and twentieth century Jakarta are striking, they should not be overdrawn. Firstly, the changes which occurred in London, initially attracting and then repelling the poor from the city centre, spanned the entire nineteenth century, whereas in Jakarta they happened within a period of thirty years. Secondly, there are marked differences in the size and rate of growth of population. While Jakarta's population took only twenty years to grow from under one to nearly five million, London's took 100 years. The number of petty traders in Jakarta in the 1970s was estimated to be up to 500 times that of London's a hundred years earlier. Thirdly, there are marked differences in the rate of labour absorption. In London the small scale sector eventually faded away. The problem of under or unemployment all but disappeared during the First World War as most of London's casual workers were absorbed in large scale manufacturing to provide for the needs of the wartime economy.[15] In Jakarta, however, the possibility of most of the casually employed being absorbed by the modern sector seems remote. Jakarta's informal sector persists, despite the boom and bust of small scale enterprises in Kebun Kacang and central Jakarta during the 1970s. Its role has been reinforced by the recession of the early 1980s. Jakarta seems to fit the argument of writers such as McGee and Lewis who have argued that the small-scale sector will persist, because there is no other way for the urban and rural poor to earn a livelihood.[16]

Scholars suggest that Third World cities like Jakarta now face much greater problems than London of a century ago.[17] While their populations are both larger and growing at a faster rate, the technological revolution of the twentieth century has slowed down the rate of labour absorption in modern industry.[18] The problems of providing employment, housing and basic amenities for their massive urban populations are therefore correspondingly greater. Meanwhile, the aspirations of the twentieth century urban poor are rising. Compared to their counterparts in London of one hundred years ago, they have access to better education, mass communication and knowledge of the outside world. They have seen the life of the rich on their television screens and know what is to be had.

Contemporary Asian Cities

Within contemporary Asia, the contrasting experiences of urbanization are mirrored in Singapore, Hong Kong and Manila. On the one hand, Singapore and Hong Kong exemplify those countries which, through industrialization, have been able to raise the standard of living of their inhabitants. On the other hand, Manila manifests the major problems of growing poverty existing side by side with the penetration of capitalism.

Although the basic processes of change—rapid economic growth, spatial transformation and increasing government penetration—seem rather similar, their impact has differed markedly. The three cities experienced the destruction of central city slums and small scale income earning activities. In the case of Hong Kong and Singapore, the capital-intensive sector was able to absorb most of those pushed out of labour-intensive activities so successfully that during the 1970s, they even experienced labour shortage.[19] In Manila, by contrast, the poor have been pushed out of their small scale income earning activities without adequate alternatives being provided. Under and unemployment remain major problems. Although industrialization occurred and there was a move of poor people from the small to the large scale sector during the 1970s, this appears to have only been a temporary phenomenon. The jobs in factories proved no more secure than employment within the small scale sector.[20] Consequently, a large proportion of the city's population are still forced to eke out a livelihood from the small scale sector, which is continually harassed by hostile government policies and competition from large capital intensive firms.

Housing programs within the three cities present similar contrasting experiences. Hong Kong and Singapore stand out as examples of cities which have been able to house a majority of their populations in multi-storey apartment blocks.[21] This, however, was not always the case. During the 1960s, their inhabitants lived in slums that were probably worse than those in many other Third World cities. Currently, in Manila, an estimated one quarter to one third of the city's population of over six million live in shanty town or slum communities. These communities are viewed with hostility by the elite and continually threatened with demolition to make way for highways, office blocks and industry.[22] Since the mid-1970s, the government, with the backing of the World Bank, has adopted a number of more enlightened rehousing schemes for the urban poor, but only a minority of the population has benefitted.

The experience of Jakarta seems to have more in common with Manila than Hong Kong and Singapore. The city governments of Jakarta and Manila have tried to adopt labour creation and public housing schemes but have been handicapped by their rapid population growth. Without a rural hinterland, Hong Kong and Singapore have been better able to restrict the influx of unskilled labour.[23] Although these city-states have other social problems related to a loss of community and contact with the natural environment, most of their inhabitants have experienced a rising standard of living while inequality has also declined. In Jakarta and Manila, by contrast, whatever advances have been made in the provision of employment and housing have quickly been outstripped by population growth and the influx of poor peasants from the countryside.

Poverty

The literature on the urban poor focuses upon the lack of material resources. It suggests that the main problem of the poor is low income and a lack of possessions. In Ibu Imah's neighbourhood, however, destitution was unusual. Even the poorest could feed and clothe themselves. Under normal conditions these people were not in dire need. Only during the Japanese occupation did kampung dwellers experience absolute poverty. Then even basic necessities such as food and clothing were unavailable. During the colonial period or the decade after Independence, kampung dwellers lived austerely. They had few possessions but felt fortunate to be part of the town. Their aspirations were limited and capable of satisfaction.

Ironically, as kampung dwellers prospered during the 1970s, their sense of impoverishment and dissatisfaction increased. Their aspirations rose dramatically and became increasingly difficult to fulfil. Hard work was no longer sufficient to satisfy their basic needs. Moreover, jobs were harder to find. At the same time, a few kampung dwellers were becoming richer and buying modern consumer durables like television sets and motorcycles. Those who lacked possessions experienced envy and shame. Their sense of poverty was intensified by the highly visible and growing gap between the city's rich and poor.

Even within Ibu Imah's poor neighbourhood there was considerable variation in wealth. Some households earned more than ten times that of others. Whilst one kampung dweller like Ateng had a new two-storey brick house with colour television set, two motorcycles and numerous other possessions, his neighbour Agus had a dingy shack without water, electricity or other amenities. Although at any one time, income and possessions provided the best indication of a kampung dweller's wealth, this could also be very misleading for most kampung dwellers gained and lost possessions quickly.

From the kampung dwellers' point of view, the constant feature of their lives was not so much low income or few possessions but insecurity. Everything seemed to be in a state of flux. They did not know for how long they would have their jobs, incomes, homes or possessions. During the late 1970s, lucrative jobs in cottage industry or petty trade rapidly became obsolete. Incomes which had been many times more than a household needed for food suddenly dropped to bare subsistence. When fortunes turned sour, possessions which had been useful, provided pleasure or served as an insurance against disaster and a source of prestige had to be sold. Even their homes, many of which had only recently been renovated, were demolished to make way for a government rehousing scheme.

Human relationships were transient. Although social networks provided some protection against the vagaries of life, they were also fragile. Kampung dwellers had lost contact with parents, brothers, sisters, husbands and wives. Relatives, neighbours and friends who had helped one another in times of need suddenly left. Kampung dwellers put forward distrust and deception as the main reason why they could not pool resources for productive purposes, even within a single household. Husbands and wives were reluctant to hold their earnings in common for fear that one would deceive the other. Their insecurity was consequently enhanced by their inability to cooperate.

Not only human relationships but also values were in flux. A constant tension existed between kampung dwellers' need to share their few resources and their need to stand apart to prevent the dissipation of their wealth. They were torn between the traditional values of sharing and reciprocity and modern values of cash exchange. They were caught between two worlds, that of the community and that of the city. They were being pushed out of the community but had not yet gained access to the more formal institutions of the city.

Before the 1970s, when government mainly left kampung dwellers to cater for their own needs in their own way, they did not feel so powerless. Indonesia's stagnant economy and Jakarta's weak administration intruded little into their lives. They created jobs, homes, amenities and social security for themselves. The government passed legislation with welfare objectives, but except in the fields of health and education its programs were largely ineffective. Policies were readily bypassed and kampung dwellers chose local headmen who could keep government at bay.

After the 1970s, however, kampung dwellers' sense of powerlessness increased as government penetrated further into their lives. Their autonomy and scope for individual initiative in work and housing were increasingly restricted by an expanding bureaucracy and modern economy. Kampung dwellers had no positive expectations of government, for past experience had taught them that its policies hurt. The closed city policy, anti-becak and anti-trader legislation and kampung demolition schemes of the 1970s gave them little reason to believe otherwise. Kampung dwellers were therefore slow to take advantage of such welfare programs as polyclinics and primary education. Other policies which were ostensibly meant for their benefit, such as small scale credit and rehousing, were distorted beyond recognition in their implementation as low level officials and middlemen lined their pockets at kampung dwellers' expense.

The demolition of Kebun Kacang left kampung dwellers bewildered. Many did not understand what the government intended and did not know to whom to turn for advice and assistance. They were intimidated by government meetings, obstructionist bureaucrats and official documentation. Their ignorance and fear meant that they failed to recognize, let alone grasp, the new opportunities. What little unity existed between them in opposition to the government's rehousing scheme soon broke down. In contrast to the middle class, they lacked the necessary contacts, capital, time and knowledge of government. They lacked the leadership and ability to organize to defend their own interests. But most of all they lacked trust in each other to work together for a common purpose.

The Causes of Poverty

Few problems have been more vexing to social scientists than the causes of poverty. The literature on poverty is polarized. On the one hand there are those who believe in the "culture of poverty", which attributes the persistence of poverty, at least partially, to the culture of the poor.[24] This culture enables the poor to survive under great duress but at the same time perpetuates that very poverty. The poor seldom maintain jobs for long. The little they earn is soon spent on necessities. Anything left over is dissipated on luxuries for display or shared with others to enhance their social status and prestige. They live it up when times are good in the expectation that tomorrow will be bad. People are fatalistic about improving their lot and rarely invest in ways that would raise their future income. Human relationships are distrustful and even the family unit is fragile, so that it is difficult to pool resources for mutual benefit. Childhood is brief and education minimal. This way of life is passed on from generation to generation and becomes a self-perpetuating phenomenon, a vicious circle from which it is difficult to escape.

The structuralist view, by contrast, blames society for the poverty trap.[25] The poor have initiative, ability and the desire to improve their lot but are constrained by the economic and political structures of society. The insecurity of their jobs and incomes makes all other aspects of their lives vulnerable. Even those who have regular jobs receive so little income for their long and arduous hours of work that they are lucky to pay for their basic daily needs, let alone save for the future or make risky investments. In a society dominated by cash, the poor are priced out of education, homes and amenities. Their petty enterprises are destroyed by large capital-intensive firms. Their low cost self-made communities are forced to give way to large scale capital-intensive and bureaucratic developments. Lack of resources prevents them from adequately educating their children. The few who do, find that their children still lack the necessary capital, contacts or confidence to get secure, well paid jobs. The lack of an inadequate and secure income reduces their mobility and reinforces their restricted view of the world. They are unaware of and unfamiliar with alternative choices and opportunities. If they are aware, they find most are beyond their reach. The poor are trapped by the structure of society, from which there is little hope of escape. Their choice is to retreat into the world of religion which makes life more bearable, or to destroy the social and economic structures which imprison them.

Which of these two theories is valid has profound implications for the analysis of poverty. The culture of poverty thesis suggests that the search for the causes of poverty is almost futile, for poverty itself breeds poverty. The theory is ahistorical. It does not explain why poverty came into being in the first place but only why it persists. This is attributed to individual attitudes and behaviour that are passed on from generation to generation. The other view, by contrast, tries explicitly to identify the causes of poverty and virtually assumes that those causes are external to individuals and their immediate communities. The focus of the latter view is therefore upon structures and processes.

Kebun Kacang provided much evidence to support the "culture of poverty" hypothesis. Poverty itself did seem to acquire a momentum of its own. Families tended to be unstable. The bond between husbands and wives was often weak. Children were born into broken families and soon dropped out of school. Among teenage girls premarital pregnancies were common and young men were forced into marriage before they could support a family. Both within and between families, people distrusted one another and resources could not be pooled for productive purposes. Fatalism and despair were pervasive. As one kampung dweller said, "what was the use of battling if whatever you achieved was simply taken away". This view of life was self-fulfilling. People coped as best they could from day to day, regarding the future as beyond their control.

The rehousing project provided the strongest evidence of the existence of a "culture of poverty". Even after constraints such as lack of resources were lifted, most kampung dwellers were unable to take advantage of new housing opportunities. Their former attitudes and patterns of behaviour still held sway. The large sums of money received in compensation were used in the old way to satisfy immediate needs, their desire for consumer goods and social obligations. Kampung dwellers thereby gained instant gratification and enjoyed a momentary affluence but jeopardized their future and perpetuated their poverty.

Nevertheless, the history of Kebun Kacang also revealed a good deal more dynamism than the culture of poverty would suggest. During the 1950s and 1960s employment was not difficult to find and the kampung population grew rapidly. With the economic boom of the early 1970s, kampung dwellers enjoyed unprecedented prosperity. Their aspirations rose and their energy seemed to increase. By diligence and hard work they believed they could improve their lives. They hoped to educate their children to gain more secure and prestigious jobs. After the mid-1970s, however, for many kampung dwellers things began to turn sour. When their efforts to improve their lot proved abortive, they slumped back into fatalism and apathy.

Whether kampung dwellers displayed hope and energy or fatalism and apathy therefore depended very much upon the opportunities open to them. The availability of these opportunities was very little within their own control. In the main, opportunities were created or destroyed by external forces. The growth of Kebun Kacang from a vegetable garden in the 1920s to a shanty town in the 1950s was stimulated by the economic and demographic growth of the city. Being at the centre of the city its inhabitants felt the full impact of economic stagnation and then economic growth. During the 1950s and 1960s they benefitted from the vacuum in the production and distribution of goods and services. From the mid-1960s to early 1970s, the shanty town's inhabitants prospered as the modern metropolis rose up around them. But during the mid-1970s, a dramatic change in the demand and supply of goods and services combined with physical, demographic and political changes at the city centre undermined their trades. As the city engulfed the neighbourhood, their income earning activities and homes stood in the way of development. The symbiotic relationship between the kampung and the city turned to antagonism. The kampung dwellers either had to leave the area or change their way of life to become part of the modern metropolis.

The structuralist and "culture of poverty" theories therefore reinforce rather than contradict each other. The causes of material poverty, insecurity and powerlessness cannot be understood without considering both external economic and political conditions as well as individual attitudes and patterns of behaviour. Sixty years of Kebun Kacang's history has revealed a constant struggle between its inhabitants' efforts to build a better life for themselves and the many forces pitched against them. It is the mesh between external forces and peoples' attitudes and behaviour which creates the vicious cycle of poverty. The structuralist theory helps explain why poverty comes into existence in the first place, while the "culture of poverty" helps explain why most people find it hard to escape from poverty even after at least some of the external forces have ceased to oppress them.

Kampung Dwellers' View of History

Kampung dwellers had a sophisticated view of history. Unlike the optimistic middle class, kampung dwellers did not view their history as simply a progression to greater security, affluence and happiness. For them, history was full of contradictions: material progress went hand in hand with the loss of social stability, contentment and tranquillity. Human relationships were impoverished by the struggle for self-enrichment and self-advance. Wealth and material possessions insulated people from one another. Intimate relationships fell apart. New income-earning opportunities suddenly arose and equally suddenly disappeared. The kampung community had come into existence, and then existed no more. Homes which had just been rehabilitated were demolished. A government which seemed cruel was also benevolent. Increased hopes and opportunities for a better future existed side by side with increased frustration, disappointment and despair.

Kampung dwellers were well aware that they were living through a period of rapid transformation, although at times history did seem to repeat itself. Within their own life time the oldest inhabitants had seen a market garden transformed into a densely populated kampung and finally multi-storey flats. They experienced a clash of values, fluidity of social ties, transcience of income-earning activities and extremes of poverty and wealth. Government which had long seemed unimportant, suddenly became intrusive. They felt that the more ordered and tranquil rural existence of half a century earlier had given way to a period of tremendous change and turmoil.

Metaphorically, kampung dwellers depicted their life as a "revolving wheel" (*roda yang berputar*). Sometimes they were on top and sometimes underneath this wheel. Sometimes they were doing well and at other times they were doing poorly. Another analogy they used was the rise and fall of waves (*turun ombak, naik ombak*), suggesting that their passage through life was a rough one, full of ups and downs. In recent times, the fluctuations in personal fortunes seemed to increase—the wheel turned faster and the waves grew bigger.

Even though this story has only been about one kampung in Jakarta similar experiences of social disintegration, economic boom and bust, rising aspirations countered by despair are being experienced by people elsewhere. In Bud's last words to me she said "we come into this world with nothing and we leave with nothing". Although possessions and wealth made life easier, ultimately it was the human bonds that gave meaning to kampung dwellers' lives.

1. J. Sullivan "Back Alley Neighbourhood" pp. 1–7, 34, 36, 50–2.
2. Guinness (*Harmony and Hierarchy* pp. 42–53, 171–76) also found "a remarkable cohesiveness" amongst the inhabitants of another kampung in Yogyakarta.
3. J. Sullivan "Rukun Kampung and Kampung" p. 327.
4. J. Sullivan "Back Alley Neighbourhood" p. 6.
5. Quennell, P. (ed.) *Mayhew's London*, (London, 1984) p. 18.
6. Green "Street Trading in London" pp. 130–9; Stedman-Jones *Outcast London* pp. 53–126.
7. Green "Street Trading in London" p. 137.
8. Stedman-Jones *Outcast London* pp. 33–51.
9. Stedman-Jones *Outcast London* pp. 19–32.
10. Green "Street Trading in London" pp. 138–46.
11. Stedman-Jones *Outcast London* pp. 161–3; Green "Street Trading in London" pp. 140–6.
12. Stedman-Jones *Outcast London* p. 166.
13. Stedman-Jones *Outcast London* pp. 152–71, 207–9.
14. Stedman-Jones *Outcast London* pp. 179–214.
15. Stedman-Jones *Outcast London* p. 336.
16. McGee "The Persistence of the Proto-Proletariat" p. 261; Lewis, W. A. "Unemployment in Developing Countries", *The World Today*, Vol. 23, No. 1: 1967: pp. 21–2.
17. McGee "Beach-heads and Enclaves".
18. Armstrong and McGee "Revolutionary Change"; Reissman *The Urban Process* pp. 158–65.
19. Oshima, H. "Perspectives on Trends in Asian Household Income Distribution: An Overview with Special Reference to Indonesia", *Ekonomi dan Keuangan Indonesia*, Vol. 30, No. 1: 1982: pp. 100–1.
20. Pinches "Anak-Pawis" pp. 248, 252, 298.
21. Dwyer *People and Housing*; Drakakis-Smith, D. W. *High Society Housing Provision in Metropolitan Hong Kong 1954 to 1979: A Jubiliee Critique*, (Hong Kong, 1979).

22. Pinches "Anak-Pawis" pp. 70–6, 139–45.
23. Oshima "Perspectives on Trends in Asian Household Income Distribution" pp. 100–1.
24. Lewis "The Culture of Poverty" pp. 19–25.
25. Gilbert *Cities, Poverty, and Development*; Lloyd *Slums of Hope?*

Character List

ADE	The third youngest wife of Santo, Bud's husband. She lived in the village of Parung approximately 30 kilometers south of Jakarta where Jaya often stayed.
AGUS	Samilah's husband, who came to Jakarta from Parung in the 1950s. He had lost his family and all his possessions during the war and, after working as a charcoal seller for a Chinese storekeeper, became a becak driver.
ANI	Aswan, the water-seller's twelfth wife and Samilah's elder sister. She was a domestic servant and belonged to one of the poorest families in the neighbourhood.
A'ON	Head of a large stable Central Javanese household. A Bank worker with seven children whose wife cooked and sewed.
ASEP	The kampung dwellers' spokesman during demolition. He could be charming, courageous but had no moral scruples. At times he behaved like a thug.
ASWAN	The husband of Ani and one of the two main water-sellers in the neighbourhood.
ATENG	The cap entrepreneur from a village near Bandung who came to Kebun Kacang with virtually nothing in 1972 and by 1978 had established a very successful enterprise. Ateng was one of the first kampung dwellers to accept the government's offer of flats at the city centre.
BADRUN	A member of Ibu Imah's clan who ran a household iced-drink stall together with his wife. Formerly he had worked as a vegetable gardener and then vegetable seller. Later he prospered in the sites and service units.
BANI	A becak driver and brother of Canil and said to be a thief. In 1981, after the kampung's demolition, Bani

184

	accepted a sites and service unit at Depok. Unable to pay, he illicitly sold the unit and moved back to his wife's place of origin in the hills near Bogor.
BUD	A very successful cooked-food seller in the early 1970s who later went bankrupt and was forced to become a domestic servant. She was the first wife of Santo, who by the late 1970s had two other wives—Nanti and Ade. She was my main informant.
BURHANUD-DIN	An ice-cone manufacturers, pensioned government accountant and second or third husband of Sum, the Islamic teacher and member of Imah's clan. He had a family of eight children, two of whom were adopted from relatives. An additional six unrelated circular migrants worked in his house.
CANIL	A seller who lived with his two younger brothers having lost his mother and been deserted by his father who lived with another woman elsewhere. One of Canil's brothers worked as a becak driver and the other shined shoes. These young men were sometimes referred to as thieves by other kampung dwellers.
DARMO	Tukirah's mother, a widow, who lived with her unmarried children. She ran a tiny household stall which frequently went bankrupt. Her daughters washed clothes for neighbours and, after 1978, worked in a pen factory.
DINI	Had a household stall selling fresh vegetable and was married to Timin the construction worker. They did not have a home of their own but had rented a room from Ibu Imah for over 20 years. With their six children, they lived a hand to mouth existence in very cramped conditions. After demolition, they moved to a Depok sites and service unit and their life improved.
FATMA	Ibu Imah's daughter and Timah's sister. She supported herself by selling porridge in the mornings and rice cakes in the afternoon. In addition she was a masseur and traditional healer and loved by the frustrated youth of the kampung who gathered at her house to eat and sing. She had married three times and her last husband, a construction worker seemed to frequently be visiting another wife in Sukabumi.
GANI	Kuntil's husband, Suli's brother and one of the first people to buy land from Imah in the 1940s. After obtaining accommodation in Kebun Kacang, he invited his wife and relatives to join him in selling car parts.
HAJI TEJO	A landlord who pegged out and sold much of the land in Kebun Kacang to newcomers. He died before I arrived in Kebun Kacang but his children who lived elsewhere still had rights to much of the land there. At

the time of demolition they received the largest compensation (over Rp.27,000,000/US$41,221).

HARJO Imah's husband. A vegetable gardener who prospered and invited relatives to help him cultivate the land in Kebun Kacang. Later, when the land was taken up by shanties, he and his colleagues became vegetable traders and employees of the Jakarta City Government. In 1968 he died from tetanus.

IJAH Adopted into Imah's clan after her parents died and before 1975 married to a prosperous rice merchant. After her husband's death, Ijah became impoverished and was forced to rent out her house to circular migrant cap sellers from Bandung. In 1979 she married a cousin who was irregularly employed and had another wife in Bogor.

IMAH The oldest person in the neighbourhood, a midwife and one of my three informants for the early period of Kebun Kacang's history. She married Harjo and was the mother of seven children, most of whom after marriage continued to lived next-door to each other. Imah's clan of 23 related households dominated my sample and monopolized the secular and sacred leadership of the neighbourhood.

ITIN A member of Kuntil's clan who became increasingly prosperous after 1978 and distanced his family from his relatives. Itin worked in a private office as a typist and research assistant.

KINO A middle-class reformer who tried, often in vain, to uplift the kampung dwellers.

KOMAR Ateng's brother-in-law and also a cap making entrepreneur, but not as successful as Ateng.

KUNTIL Gani's wife who had come from Bogor in the 1950s and set up one of the first temporary lodging-houses for trader migrants selling ices. Her large house was gradually subdivided amongst relatives and friends, many of whom took part in the car parts trade. In 1979 Gani died and Kuntil's two married children and their offspring continued to live with her. She gained extra resources by preparing meals and washing clothes for her brothers, who lived next-door.

KUNTO The neighbourhood's main water seller. He also worked as a sweeper and rubbish collector for the DKI.

LAMIRAH Formerly a relatively well-off widow who ran an unsuccessful household stall next-door to her brother, Badrun. All of her deceased husband's compensation was absorbed in the stall and house improvements. Lamirah survived only because of the patronage of her relatives from Imah's kinship group.

LUKMAN | Lived in Ibu Minah's neighbourhood. He had walked to Batavia in the late 1930s. He performed odd jobs for the Dutch, drove a becak during the Japanese occupation and was the first to start recycling batteries in Kebun Kacang. He was one of my three main informants for Kebun Kacang's history.

MANDROPPI | Lamirah's brother who had a regular job looking after engines at the Tanjung Priok docks. His wife had seven children, was illiterate and ran an unsuccessful cooked-food stall. After 1978 their three daughters married, had children and lived in their parents' home. Initially their husbands were irresponsible and the daughters were forced to seek a livelihood by selling snacks or working in a pen assembly or soft-drink factory whilst their mother looked after their babies. Later two of their husbands found regular work and became more responsible.

MARYATI | Sugi, the second headman's, wife. She was related to Menik, her husband's father's young wife. To overcome her sadness at having no children, Maryati adopted two of Menik's children.

MENIK | Married at 14 to Tole (part of Imah's clan), the neighbourhood's elderly headman. She had six children, two of whom were adopted by Tole's first son Sugi after Tole died in 1976. Menik then supported her remaining four children by operating a cooked-food stall. Her eldest son sold newspapers to pay for his schooling whilst her two little daughters carted water and ran errands.

MIMI | When deserted by her husband in 1975, she moved to live with and assist Bud.

MINAH | Born in Kebun Kacang in the 1920s. She was from one of the wealthiest and long-established families in the area and provided me with details about Kebun Kacang's history.

MUS | Arrived in Jakarta from Klaten, Central Java in the 1950s. She bought part of Bud's house and in the 1960s set up a communal lodging-house and ice-cream making enterprise. She was married to Sentot.

MUSTAPHA | The head of the prayer house, part of Imah's clan and Sum's father. His married son and children shared the same house.

NANTI | The second wife of Santo and junior wife to Bud. She came to live in Bud's house after the mid-1960s and was the backbone of Bud's enterprise.

NANO | Head of a better-off family from Central Java which lived in the neighbourhood but was not really part of it. In order to be accepted by their neighbours they in-

	itially shared some of their luxuries but later distanced themselves.
PUTRO	The first Central Javanese to rent and then buy a house from Ibu Imah in the 1950s. She then introduced many other Central Javanese to the area and served as a real estate broker for Ibu Imah. Like her deceased husband, she was a traditional healer.
SAMILAH	Married to Agus, the becak driver, and mother of eight. She arrived in Jakarta from Depok as a child in the 1950s and followed her sister Ani into domestic work.
SANI	A very poor Jakarta City Government sweeper and guard. His married daughters were deserted by their husbands and he was forced to support them and their children.
SANTO	A jack-of-all trades who had travelled widely. He could repair radios and becaks and had built a large trader's cart for Bud, his first wife. He later had two other wives (Nanti and Ade). He died shortly after demolition.
SARWOTO	Putro's son-in-law, a Central Javanese and "jack-of-all-trades". He helped renovate many of the houses in Kebun Kacang. After demolition he built himself a house on the edges of Jakarta.
SENTOT	Mus's husband the ice-cream maker and seller who had another wife and family in a village in Klaten, Central Java.
SITI	A deserted mother of seven who survived by cooking snacks and sewing clothes. Later her husband became more responsible and divided his income evenly between his two wives and thirteen children.
SUGI	Maryati's husband, a member of Imah's clan and the son of Tole. He became headman after Tole died.
SULI	Gani's brother's wife who, after her husband died, was left to fend for her seven children. She set up a breakfast stall and each of her children made some contribution to the household either from shoeshining, water carrying or newspaper selling. Occasionally relatives who lived nearby provided some assistance but they were also struggling to make ends meet.
SUM	Burhanuddin's wife, women's Islamic teacher and kitchen utensil and shawl trader. She took over the running of the prayer house from Ibu Kino.
SUNDARI	The daughter of Ibu Putro who worked as a washerwoman at a local maternity hospital. Sundari's husband, Sakri, worked in a construction company until it went out of business and then tried unsuccessfully to become a gado-gado seller. He then turned his talents to traditional healing.

SUTI   Suli's daughter whose husband was Agus, the becak driver's brother. Suti and her husband ran a mobile noodle-soup stall in front of a government office along Jalan Thamrin. They also raised rabbits for sale and Suti worked as a seamstress.

TIMAH   One of Ibu Imah's daughters and Fatma's sister. Her husband, a driver, was rarely at home though he occasionally made a contribution. Timah supported herself by dealing in furniture which she sold on credit to the kampung.

TIMIN   Dini's husband and a construction worker who had performed many different jobs like trade and becak driving. His family was one of the poorest in Kebun Kacang but after they moved to Depok life became easier.

TOLE   Menik's husband, Sugi's father and the local headman who died in 1976. He sabotaged the illiteracy campaign of the 1960s and the Kampung Improvement Program of the 1970s, but he protected the kampung dwellers against harassment during the turmoil of 1965/66.

TUKIRAH   A young washerwoman in the neighbourhood, who was forced to marry into Tukinem's household due to pregnancy. Her husband rarely contributed money and she did local chores to earn a livelihood.

UDIN   He lived just beyond the seventy-seven households and as a construction worker had taken part in the renovation of many of them. His father had formerly been a soldier for the Dutch. Udin travelled widely throughout the 1950s and was well informed.

WIRA   An illiterate Central Javanese who had one surviving child from three unsuccessful marriages. She supported herself and child by domestic work, selling cooked-food and washing clothes. She had never owned a home of her own and the flat-building program presented her with her first opportunity to buy a unit. Previously she had always had to rent.

Appendix

Average Yearly Retail Price of Rice (Medium Quality) in Jakarta, 1953–1982

Year	Rupiah price of Rice/litre
1953	1.8
1958	6
1959	5.3
1960	6
1961	10
1962	30
1963	53
1964	140
1965	305
1965 (Sept)	1100
1966 (Feb)	4500
1966 (Apr)	7000
1968	43
1969	32
1970	36
1971	36
1972	41
1973	58
1974	65
1975	82
1976	97
1977	101
1978	115
1979	150
1980	180
1981	210
1982	240

Derived from: Tan, *Sukarno's Guided Democracy*, p. 150, Mears, *The New Rice Economy of Indonesia*, p. 496 and Field work in Kebun Kacang 1972–82.
Note: From 1978 the kampung prices which have been used were 5–10 percent above the figures provided by Mears.

Foreign Exchange (US$1.00) in Jakarta, 1968–83

1968		– Rp.414
1969		– Rp.378
1970		– Rp.382
1971		– Rp.420
1978	Dec	– Rp.632
1981	Dec	– Rp.655
1982	Dec	– Rp.697
1983	Jan	– Rp.701
1983	Mar	– Rp.980
1983	Dec	– Rp.998

Source: *Indikator Ekonomi*, 1973: p. 103, 1980: p. 114, 1983: p. 38.

Bibliography

Newspapers and Periodicals

Berita Buana, Daily, Jakarta.
Berita Dan Daerah, Daily, Jakarta.
The Evening Star and News
Insight, Hong Kong.
Kompas, Daily, Jakarta.
Merdeka, Daily, Jakarta.
National Times, Weekly, Sydney.
Pelita, Daily, Jakarta.
Pos Kota, Daily, Jakarta.
Sinar Harapan, Daily, Jakarta.
Suara Karya, Daily, Jakarta.
Sinar Pagi, Daily, Jakarta.
Tempo, Weekly, Jakarta.
Terbit, Daily, Jakarta.

Official Publications

Indikator Ekonomi, Monthly, BPS, Jakarta.
Pekerja Sektor Informal di Indonesia, BPS, Jakarta, 1986.
Some Data About Djakarta, DKI, Jakarta, 1972.
Karya Jaya, DKI, Jakarta, 1977.
Gita Jaya, DKI, Jakarta, 1977.
Penghapusan Becak Di Jakarta, DKI, Mimeo, Jakarta, 1977.
Kaki Lima—Hasil Pencacahan Pedagang Kaki Lima di DKI, DKI: Kantor Sensus & Statistik, Jakarta, 1978.
Hasil Survey Tenaga Kerja Di Kecamatan Miskin DKI-Jakarta 1978/1979,

Kanwil. Dit.-Jen. Bina Guna, DKI: Kantor Sensus & Statistik, Jakarta, 1978/1979.

Masalah Perumahan di DKI Jakarta, DKI: Lembaga Penelitian Kemasya-rakatan dan Lingkungan Bekerjasama Dengan Team Studi Perumahan Direktorat IV, Jakarta, 1979.

Kebijaksanaan Pembangunan Perumahan Pemerintah Daerah Khusus Ibu Kota Jakarta, DKI: Direktorat IV, Jakarta, 1979.

Penduduk Propinsi DKI Jakarta, DKI: BPS & Kantor Statistik Propinsi, Jakarta, 1980.

Buku Data, DKI: Departemen Tenaga Kerja dan Transmigrasi, Jakarta, 1980.

Hasil Survey Tenaga Kerja Sub-Sektor Industri Kecil DK-Jakarta 1979–1980, DKI: Kanwil. Dit.-Jen. Bina Guna, Kantor Sensus & Statistik, Jakarta, 1980.

Data collected by the Kelurahan of Kebun Kacang, (Unpublished), DKI, Jakarta, 1981.

Hasil Survai Sosial Ekonomi DKI, DKI: Kantor Statistik Propinsi, Jakarta, 1981.

Study Pengembangan Lingkungan Perumahan Flat Di DKI-Jakarta, DKI: Lembaga Afiliasi Penelitian dan Industri Institut Teknologi Bandung & Direktorat IV DKI, Jakarta, 1981.

Short Guide Djakarta-Bogor-Bandung, Republic of Indonesia, DKI: Ministry of Information, Jakarta, 1981.

Perumnas Policy Review and Background Materials for Pelita 111 Planning, Consultants' Report World Bank (PADCO), Mimeo, Vol. 2, Washington D.C., 1977.

Kampung Improvement Programme, Jakarta, Indonesia, IBRD and IDA, PCD (Planned Community Development Ltd.), Washington D.C., 1973.

Watts, K. et al. *Rentjana Pendahuluan/ Outline Plan Djakarta Raya*, Jakarta, 1957.

The Urban Poor in Jakarta—Strategies for Integrating World Bank Projects, Mimeo, World Bank, Washington D.C., 1977.

Indonesia: Appraisal of Small Enterprise Development Project, Mimeo, World Bank, Washington D.C., 1978.

Fourth Urban Development Project, Indonesia, Staff Appraisal Report, World Bank: Projects Department East Asia and Pacific Office, Washington D.C., 1981.

Secondary Sources

Abeyasekere, S. "Overview of the History of Jakarta 1930s to 1970s" in Abeyasekere, S. (ed.). *From Batavia to Jakarta: Indonesia's Capital 1930–1980*, Melbourne: Centre of Southeast Asian Studies, Monash University (1985) 1–24.

Abeyasekere, S. (ed.) *From Batavia to Jakarta: Indonesia's Capital*

1930–1980, Melbourne: Centre of Southeast Asian Studies, Monash University, 1985.

Abeyasekere, S. *Jakarta: a History*, Singapore: Oxford University Press, 1987.

Abrams, C. *Housing in the Modern World*, London: Faber Press, 1966.

Abu-Lughod, J. and Hay, R. (eds.) *Third World Urbanization*, Chicago: Maaroufa Press, 1977.

Amin, S. *Unequal Development: An Essay on the Social Formation of Peripheral Capitalism*, Sussex: Harvester Press, 1976.

Anderson, B. and McVey, R. *A Preliminary Analysis of the October 1, 1965 Coup in Indonesia*, Modern Indonesia Project Cornell University, Ithaca, 1971.

Armstrong, W. R. and McGee, T. G. "Revolutionary Change and the Third World City: A Theory of Urban Involution", *Civilizations*, Vol. 18, No. 3: 1968: 353–78.

Arndt, H. W. "Economic Disorder and the Task Ahead" in Tan, T. K. (ed.) *Sukarno's Guided Democracy*, Brisbane: Jacaranda Press, 1967, 129–40.

Arndt, H. W. "Survey of Recent Developments", *Bulletin of Indonesian Economic Studies*, Vol. 5, No. 2: 1969: 1–16.

—— "Survey of Recent Developments", *Bulletin of Indonesian Economic Studies*, Vol. 7, No. 2: 1971: 1–18.

—— "Survey of Recent Developments", *Bulletin of Indonesian Economic Studies*, Vol. 10, No. 2: 1974: 1–34.

Atma Jaya *Hawkers in Jakarta*, Vol. 1, Jakarta: Pusat Penelitian Atma Jaya, 1973.

Bianpoen "The Pattern of Settlement in Densely Populated Areas of Jakarta", Seminar on Urban Community Problems, Jakarta, November 15–17 1976.

Bienefeld, M. "The Informal Sector and Peripheral Capitalism: The Case of Tanzania", *Institute of Development Studies Bulletin*, Sussex University, Vol. 6, No. 3: 1975: 53–74.

Bloomberg, W. Jr. and Schmandt, H. J. (eds.) *Power, Poverty, and Urban Policy*, Urban Affairs Annual Reviews, Vol. 2, Beverly Hills (Calif.): Sage Publications, 1968.

Boeke, J. H. *Economics and Economic Policy of Dual Societies as Exemplified by Indonesia*, New York: Institute of Pacific Relations, 1953.

Bogaers, E. and de Ruijter, P. "Ir. Thomas Karsten and Indonesian Town Planning, 1915–1940" in Nas, P. (ed.) *The Indonesian City: Studies in Urban Development and Planning*, Dordrecht: Foris, 1986: 71–88.

Boland, B. J. *The Struggle of Islam in Indonesia*, The Hague: Martinus Nijhoff, 1982.

Booth, A. and McCawley, P. (eds.) *The Indonesian Economy During the Soeharto Era*, Kuala Lumpur: Oxford University Press, 1981.

Booth, C. *Life and Labour of the People in London*, London: Macmillan, 1902.

Breese, G. W. (ed.) *The City in Newly Developing Countries: Readings on Urbanism and Urbanization*, New Jersey: Prentice-Hall, 1969.

Breman, J. "A Dualistic Labour System? A Critique of the 'Informal Sector'

Concept", *Economic and Political Weekly*, Vol. 11, Nos. 48, 49 and 50: 1976: 1870–6, 1905–8, 1939–44.

Bromley, R. and Gerry, C. (eds.) *Casual Work and Poverty in Third World Cities*, Chichester: John Wiley, 1979.

Bulsara, J. F. *Patterns of Social Life in Metropolitan Areas—with particular reference to Greater Bombay*, Bombay: Gujarat Research Society, 1970.

Castles, L. *Religion, Politics and Economic Behaviour in Java: The Kudus Cigarette Industry, Cultural* Report Series No. 15, Yale University: New Haven, 1967.

Chayanov, A. V. *The Theory of Peasant Economy*, Homewood (Illinois): Dorset Press, 1966.

Cobban, J. L. "The City on Java: An Essay in Historical Geography", Ph.D Thesis, Berkeley: University of California, 1970.

—— "Uncontrolled Urban Settlement: The Kampung Question in Semarang (1905–1940)", *Bidjragen tot de Taal-Land-en Volkenkunde*, Vol. 130, No. 4: 1974: 403–427.

Cohen, D. J. "The People Who Get in the Way: Poverty and Development in Jakarta", *Politics*, Vol. 9, No. 1: 1974: 1–9.

—— "Politics in a Jakarta Kampung: A Local History" in *Proceedings Conference on Modern Indonesian History*, Madison: Wisconsin University, 1975. See also Ann Arbor: University Microfilm International, 1982.

Cohen, D. J. "Poverty and Development in Jakarta", Ph.D Thesis, Madison: Wisconsin University, 1975.

Cole, W. E. and Sanders, P. D. "A Modified Dualism Model for Latin America", *Journal of Developing Areas*, Vol. 6, No. 2: 1972: 185–98.

Collyer, L. G. "Report on the Food Markets—Fruit and Vegetables, Meat and Rice", Jakarta: Special Projects Department, City of Jakarta, 1972.

Connell, J. et al. *Migration from Rural Areas—The Evidence from Village Studies*, Delhi: Oxford University Press, 1976.

Cribb, R. "Political Dimensions of the Currency Question 1945–1947", *Indonesia*, No. 31, April: 1981: 113–36.

—— "The Nationalist World of Occupied Jakarta, 1946–1949" in Abeyasekere, S. (ed.) *From Batavia to Jakarta: Indonesia's Capital 1930–1980*, Melbourne: Centre of Southeast Asian Studies, Monash University, 1985, 91–108.

Critchfield, R. *Hello, Mister! Where are you going?* Part 11, New York: The Alicia Patterson Fund, 1970.

—— "The Plight of the Cities: Djakarta—The First to 'Close'", *Columbia Journal of World Business*, July/August: 1971: 89–93.

—— "Desperation grows in a Jakarta Slum", *The Christian Science Monitor*, 12 September 1973.

—— "Jakarta: Asia's First Closed City", *The Evening Star and News*, 10 April 1973.

Crouch, H. *The Army and Politics in Indonesia*, Ithaca: Cornell University Press, 1978.

Dapice, D. O. "Trends in Income Distribution and Levels of Living 1970–75" in Papanek, G. F. (ed.) *The Indonesian Economy*, New York: Praeger, 1980, 67–81.

de Jesus, C. M. *Child of the Dark—The Diary of Carolina Maria de Jesus*, London: Souvenir Press, 1962.

de Kadt, E. and Williams, G. (eds.) *Sociology and Development*, London: Tavistock Publications, 1974.

Dennis, N. "The Popularity of the Neighbourhood Community Idea" in Pahl, R. E. (ed.) *Readings in Urban Sociology*, Oxford: Pergamon Press, 1968, 74–92.

Dewey, A. *Peasant Marketing in Java*, New York: Free Press of Glencoe, 1962.

Dick, H. W. "The Rise and Fall of Dualism: The Indonesian Inter-Island Shipping Industry" in Fox, J. J. et al. (eds.) *Indonesia: Australian Perspectives*, Canberra: Research School of Pacific Studies, Australian National University, 1980, 349–72.

—— "Urban Public Transport: Jakarta, Surabaya and Malang Part 1 & 11", *Bulletin of Indonesian Economic Studies*, Vol. 17, Nos. 1 and 2: 1981: 66–82, 72–88.

—— "Survey of Recent Economic Developments", *Bulletin of Indonesian Economic Studies*, Vol. 18, No. 1: 1982: 1–38.

—— "The Rise of a Middle Class and the Changing Concept of Equity in Indonesia: An Interpretation", *Indonesia*, No. 39, April, 1985: 71–92.

Dick, H. W. and Rimmer, P. J. "Beyond the Formal/Informal Sector Dichotomy: Towards an Integrated Alternative", *Pacific Viewpoint*, Vol. 21, No. 1: 1980: 26–41.

Dorleans, B. "Etude Geographique De Trois 'Kampung' a Jakarta", Department of Geography Publication No. 3, Paris: University of Sorbonne, 1976.

Dorodjatun Kuntjoro Jakti "Ekonomi Abang Becak", *Tempo*, 29 January: 1972: 50.

—— "Alternatif Baru Pertumbuhan Kota di Dunia Ketiga: Sebuah Pemikiran", *Widyapura*, Vols. 1, 7 and 8: 1977: 33–40.

Drakakis-Smith, D. W. *High Society Housing Provision in Metropolitan Hong Kong 1954 to 1979: A Jubilee Critique*, Hong Kong: Centre of Asian Studies, University of Hong Kong, 1979.

Dwyer, D. J. *People and Housing in Third World Cities: Perspectives on the Problem of Spontaneous Settlements*, London: Longman, 1975.

Eames, E. and Goode, J. G. *Urban Poverty in a Cross-Cultural Context*, New York: Free Press, 1973.

—— *Anthropology of the City—An Introduction to Urban Anthropology*, New Jersey: Prentice-Hall, 1977.

Epstein, A. L. *Politics in an Urban African Community*, Manchester: Manchester University Press, 1958.

Erve, H. van der "Composition and Recruitment of Construction Labour in Semarang, Indonesia", Urban Research Working Paper No. 9, Amsterdam: Free University, 1986.

Evers, H. "Urban Subsistence Production in Jakarta", Paper read at a Seminar Fieldstudies in Southeast Asian Development, Singapore: ISEAS, 15–19 November 1979.

Feith, H. *The Decline of Constitutional Democracy in Indonesia*, Ithaca:

Cornell University Press, 1962.
—— "The Dynamics of Guided Democracy" in McVey, R. (ed.) *Indonesia*, Southeast Asia Studies, Yale University, New Haven: HRAF Press, 1963, 309–409.
—— "President Soekarno, the Army and the Communists: the Triangle Changes Shape", *Asian Survey*, Vol. 4, No. 8: 1964: 969–80.
Forbes, D. "Urban-Rural Interdependence: The Trishaw Riders of Ujung Pandang" in Rimmer, P. J. et al. (eds.) *Food, Shelter and Transport in Southeast Asia and the Pacific*, Canberra: Research School of Pacific Studies, Australian National University, 1978, 219–36.
—— "Development and the 'Informal' Sector: A Study of Pedlars and Trishaw Riders in Ujung Pandang, Indonesia", Ph.D Thesis, Melbourne: Monash University, 1979.
—— "Production Reproduction and Underdevelopment: Petty Commodity Producers in Ujung Pandang", Paper delivered at the Jubilee Anzaas Conference, Umilaide: 12–16 May 1980.
—— "Petty Commodity Production and Underdevelopment: The Case of Pedlar and Trishaw Riders in Ujung Pandang, Indonesia" in Diamond, D. and Mcloughlin, J. B. (eds.). *Progress in Planning*, Vol. 16, No. 2: 1981: 107–78.
Fox, J. J. et al. (eds.) *Indonesia: Australian Perspectives*, Canberra: Research School of Pacific Studies, Australian National University, 1980.
Frank, A. G. *Capitalism and Underdevelopment in Latin America: Historical Studies of Chile and Brazil*, New York: Monthly Review Press, 1967.
Franklin, S. H. "System of Production: Systems of Appropriation," *Pacific Viewpoint*, Vol. 6, No. 2: 1965: 145–66.
Frederick, W. H. "Indonesian Urban Society in Transition: Surabaya, 1926–1946" Parts 1 and 11, Ph.D Thesis, University of Hawaii, 1978.
Gans, H. *The Urban Villagers: Group and Class in the Life of Italian-Americans*, New York: Free Press, 1965.
Geertz, C. "The Rotating Credit Association: A 'Middle Rung' in Development", *Economic Development and Cultural Change*, Vol. 10, No. 3: 1962: 241–64.
—— *Peddlers and Princes: Social Development and Economic Change in Two Indonesian Towns*, Chicago: University of Chicago Press, 1963.
—— *The Social History of an Indonesian Town*, Cambridge (Mass.): M.I.T. Press, 1965.
—— *The Religion of Java*, Chicago: University of Chicago Press, 1976.
Geertz, H. *The Javanese Family: A Study of Kinship and Socialization*, New York: Free Press, 1961.
Gerry, C. "Petty Production and Capitalist Production in Dakar: The Crisis of the Self-employed", *World Development*, Vols. 6, 9 and 10: 1978: 1147–60.
Gilbert, A. "The Housing of the Urban Poor" in Gilbert, A. and Gugler, J. (eds.). *Cities, Poverty, and Development: Urbanization in the Third World*, Oxford: Oxford University Press, 1982, 81–115.
Gilbert, A. and Gugler, J. *Cities, Poverty, and Development: Urbanization in the Third World*, Oxford: Oxford University Press, 1982.

Glassburner, B. *The Economy of Indonesia: Selected Readings*, Ithaca: Cornell University Press, 1971.

Green, D. R. "Street Trading in London: A Case Study of Casual Labour 1830–1860" in Johnson, J. H. et al. (eds.) *The Structure of Nineteenth Century Cities*, London: Croom Helm, 1982. 129–51.

Grenville, S. "Monetary Policy and the Formal Financial Sector" in Booth, A. and McCawley, P. (eds.) *The Indonesian Economy During the Soeharto Era*, Kuala Lumpur: Oxford University Press, 1981, 102–22.

Guinness, P. *Harmony and Hierarchy in a Javanese Kampung*, Singapore: Oxford University Press, 1986.

Gugler, J. (ed.) *The Urbanization of the Third World*, New York: Oxford University Press, 1988.

Gutkind, P. C. W. "The Energy of Despair: Social Organization of the Unemployed in Two African Cities: Lagos and Nairobi", *Civilizations*, Vol. 17, No. 2: 1967: 186–221.

—— "The Socio-political and Economic Foundations of Social Problems in African Urban Areas: An Exploratory Conceptual Overview", *Civilizations*, Vol. 22, No. 1: 1972: 18–34.

Hart, J. K. "Informal Income Opportunities and Urban Employment in Ghana," *The Journal of Modern African Studies*, Vol. 11, No. 1: 1973: 61–89.

Heeren, J. (ed.) "The Urbanization of Djakarta", Ekonomi dan Keuangan Indonesia, *Jakarta*, Vol. 8, No. 11: 1955: 696–736.

Herrle, P. "The Informal Sector: Survival Economy in Third World Metropolitan Cities", *Economics*, Vol. 26, 1982: 109–26.

Hidayat "The Urban Informal Sector Survey of Java: Some Preliminary Findings", Colloquium on Rural-Urban Relations and Development Planning in Asia, Nagoya: UNCRD, Mimeo, 1977.

—— "Sektor Informal dalam Struktur Ekonomi Indonesia", *Profil Indonesia*, Jakarta: Lembaga Studi Pembangunan, 1979, 35–51.

—— "Menuju Kebijaksanaan Tepat Guna Dalam Menunjang Peranan Sektor Informal" presented at Seminar on Population Growth, Urbanization and National Urban Policy prepared by the Ministry of Population and Environment, Mimeo, Jakarta, 15–18 October 1986.

Hidayat, et al. (eds.) *Penelitian Sosial Ekonomi Golongan Usaha Kecil di Sektor Informal Kotamadya Bandung*, Bappeda Tingkat 1, Bandung: Persatuan Wartawan and Fakultas Ekonomi Universitas Padjadjaran, 1978.

Hill, H. and Mubyarto "Economic Change in Yogyakarta", *Bulletin of Indonesian Economic Studies*, Vol. 14, No. 1: 1978: 29–44.

Hill, H. "Dualism, Technology and Small-Scale Enterprise in the Indonesian Weaving Industry" in Fox, J. J. et al. (eds.) *Indonesia: Australia Perspectives*, Canberra: Research School of Pacific Studies, Australian National University, 1980, 333–48.

Hollnsteiner, M. R. "The Case of 'The People Versus Mr Urbano Planner Y Administrador" in Abu-Lughod, J. and Hay, R. (eds.). *Third World Urbanization*, Chicago: Maaroufa Press, 1977, 307–20.

Hugo, G. J. "Population Mobility in West Java, Indonesia", Ph.D Thesis, Canberra: Australian National University, 1975.

Hugo, G. J. et al. *The Demographic Dimension in Indonesian Development*, Singapore: Oxford University Press, 1987.

Hughes, J. *The End of Sukarno—A Coup that Misfired: A Purge That Ran Wild*, London: Angus & Robertson, 1967.

Hull, T. H. and Mantra, I. B. "Indonesia's Changing Population" in Booth, A. and McCawley, P. (eds.) *The Indonesian Economy During the Soeharto Era*, Kuala Lumpur: Oxford University Press, 1981, 262–88.

Huntington, S. P. and Nelson, J. M. *No Easy Choice: Political Participation in Developing Countries*, Cambridge (Mass.): Harvard University Press, 1976.

Ibrahim, M. A. "The Growth of Indonesian Industry: A Sectoral View", *Prisma*, No. 6, June: 1977: 28–36.

—— *Employment, Incomes and Equality: A Strategy for Increasing Productive Employment in Kenya*, Geneva: ILO, 1972.

Jay, R. R. *Javanese Villagers: Social Relations in Rural Modjokuto*, Cambridge, Mass.: M.I.T. Press, 1969.

Jellinek, L. "The Life of a Jakarta Street Trader" in Abu-Lughod, J. and Hay, R. (eds.) *Third World Urbanization*, Chicago: Maaroufa Press, 1977, 244–56.

—— *The Life of a Jakarta Street Trader—Two Years Later*, Working Paper No. 13, Melbourne: Centre of Southeast Asian Studies, Monash University, 1977.

—— "Circular Migration and the Pondok Dwelling System: A Case Study of Ice-Cream Traders in Jakarta" in Rimmer, P.J. et al. (eds.) *Food, Shelter and Transport in Southeast Asia and the Pacific*, Canberra: Research School of Pacific Studies, Australian National University, 1978, 135–54.

—— "The Pondok System and Circular Migration" in Jellinek, L. et al. *The Life of the Poor in Indonesian Cities*, Melbourne: Centre of Southeast Asian Studies, Monash University, 1978, 1–16.

—— "Underview: Memories of Kebun Kacang, 1930s to 1980s" in Abeyasekere, S. (ed.) *From Batavia to Jakarta: Indonesia's Capital 1930–1980*, Melbourne: Centre of Southeast Asian Studies, Monash University, 1985, 25–90.

—— "Three Petty Entrepreneurs—The Wheel of Fortune" in Pinches, M. and Lakha, S. (eds.) *Wage Labour and Social Change*, Melbourne: Centre of Southeast Asian Studies, Monash University, 1987.

—— "The Changing Fortunes of a Jakarta Street Trader" in Gugler, J. (ed.) *The Urbanization of the Third World*, New York: Oxford University Press, 1988.

Jellinek, L. Manning, C. and Jones, G. *The Life of the Poor in Indonesian Cities*, Melbourne: Centre of Southeast Asian Studies, Monash University, 1978.

Johnson, J. H. et al. (eds.) *The Structure of Nineteenth Century Cities*, London: Croom Helm, 1982.

Johnson, R. et al. *Business Environment in an Emerging Nation*, Evanston: Northeastern University Press, 1966.

Juppenlatz, M. *Cities in Transformation*, St. Lucia: Queensland University Press, 1970.

Kahn, J. "Imperialism and the Reproduction of Capitalism: Towards a Definition of the Indonesian Social Formation", *Critique of Anthropology*, No. 2: 1974: 1–35.

Kahn, J. "Economic Scale and the Cycle of Petty Commodity Production in West Sumatra" in Bloch, M. (ed.) *Marxist Analysis and Social Anthropology*, London: Malaby Press, 1975, 137–58.

Karamoy, A. "Analisa Kebutuhan Pengusaha Kecil dan Ekonomi Lembah di DKI Jaya", *Widyapura*, Vols. 1, 7 and 8: 1977: 1–11.

Karamoy, A. and Sablie, A. "The Communication Aspect and Its Impact on the Youth of Poor Kampungs in the City of Jakarta", *Prisma*, No. 1, May: 1975: 60–9.

—— *Kota Pradja Djakarta Raya, Republik Indonesia*, Jakarta: Kementerian Penerangan, 1952.

Koentjaraningrat "The System and Spirit of Gotong Royong", *Prisma*, No. 6, June: 1977: 20–25.

Krausse, G. "The Kampungs of Jakarta, Indonesia: A Study of Spatial Patterns in Urban Poverty", Ph.D Thesis, Pittsburgh: University of Pittsburgh, 1975.

Kroef, J. M. van der "The City, its Culture and Evolution" in Kroef, J. M. van der *Indonesia in the Modern World*, Bandung: Masa Baru, 1954, 133–88.

—— *Laporan Hasil Survey Profile Pedagang Kaki Lima di DKI Jaya*, Jakarta: Fakultas Ekonomi, University of Indonesia, 1976.

Lebrun, O. and Gerry, C. "Petty Producers and Capitalism", *Review of African Political Economy*, No. 3, May–October: 1975: 20–32.

Legge, J.D. *Indonesia* (3rd ed.) Sydney: Prentice-Hall, 1980.

Leiserson, M. et al. *Employment and Income Distribution in Indonesia*, Washington D.C.: World Bank, 1978.

Lewis, O. "Urbanization without Breakdown: A Case Study", *Scientific Monthly*, Vol. 75, No. 1: 1952: 31–41.

Lewis, O. *The Children of Sanchez: Autobiography of a Mexican Family*, Harmondsworth: Penguin Books, 1961.

—— "The Culture of Poverty", *Scientific American*, Vol. 215, No. 4: 1966: 19–25.

—— *La Vida: A Puerto Rican Family in the Culture of Poverty—San Juan and New York*, New York: Random House, 1966.

—— *A Death in the Sanchez Family*, New York: Random House, 1969.

—— *Five Families—Mexican Case Studies in the Culture of Poverty*, London: Souvenir Press, 1976.

Lewis, W. A. "Economic Development with Unlimited Supplies of Labour", *Manchester School of Economic and Social Studies*, Vol. 22, No. 2: 1954: 139–91.

Lewis, W. A. "Unemployment in Developing Countries", *The World Today*, Vol. 23, No. 1: 1967: 13–22.

Liebow, E. *Tally's Corner: A Study of Negro Streetcorner Men*, Boston: Little Brown, 1967.

Lloyd, P. *Slums of Hope? Shanty towns of the Third World*, Harmondsworth: Penguin, 1979.

Logsdon, M. "Leaders and Followers in Urban Neighbourhoods: An Exploratory Study of Djakarta, Indonesia", Ph.D Thesis, Boston: Yale University, 1975.

Lomnitz, L. *Networks and Marginality: Life in a Mexican Shanty Town*, New York: Academic Press, 1977.

—— "Laporan Sementara Hasil Penelitian Golongan Berpenghasilan Rendah DCI, Jakarta", Mimeo Jakarta: LP3ES (Lembaga Penelitian Pendidikan dan Penerangan Ekonomi dan Sosial), 1972.

Lubis, M. "Jakarta Kota Penuh Kontras", *Prisma*, No. 5, May: 1977: 32–44.

MacEwen, A. M. "Differentiation among the Urban Poor: An Argentine Study" in de Kadt, E. and Williams, G. (eds.) *Sociology and Development*, London: Tavistock Publications, 1974, 197–226.

Mackie, J. *Problems of the Indonesian Inflation*, Ithaca: Cornell Modern Indonesia Project Monograph Series, 1967.

Mahasin, A. "Human Rights: from Cultural Argumentation to Social Stratification", *Prisma*, No. 13, June 1979: 86–105.

Mangin, W. "Latin American Squatter Settlements: a Problem and a Solution", *Latin American Research Review*, Vol. 2, No. 3: 1967: 65–98.

—— "Squatter Settlements", *Scientific American*, Vol. 217, October: 1967: 21–9.

—— "Poverty and Politics in Cities of Latin America" in Bloomberg, W. Jr. and Schmandt, H. J. (eds.) *Power, Poverty, and Urban Policy*, Urban Affairs Annual Reviews, Vol. 2, Beverly Hills (Calif.): Sage Publications, 1968, 397–432.

—— (ed.) *Peasants in Cities: Readings in the Anthropology of Urbanization*, Boston: Houghton Mifflin, 1970.

Manning, C. "Pockets of Privilege Amidst Mass Poverty: Wages and Working Conditions in Indonesian Industry" in Jellinek, L. et al. *The Life of the Poor in Indonesian Cities*, Melbourne: Centre of Southeast Asian Studies, Monash University, 1978; 17–31.

Manning, C. et al. *Struktur Pekerjaan, Sektor Informal Dan Kemiskinan di Kota: Sebuah Studi Kasus di Diraprajan, Yogyakarta*, Yogyakarta: Pusat Penelitian Kependudukan, Universitas Gadjah Mada, 1984.

Marzali, A. "Impak Pembangunan Pabrik terhadap Sikap dan Mata Pencarian Masyarakat: kasus Krakatau Steel", *Prisma*, No. 3, April: 1976: 30–45.

Mayer, P. *Townsmen or Tribesmen*, Cape Town: Oxford University Press, 1961.

Mayhew, H. *London Labour and the London Poor* (4 volumes), London: Griffin, Bohn, and Company, 1861.

Mazumdar, D. "The Urban Informal Sector", *World Development*, Vol. 4, No. 8: 1976: 655–79.

McGee, T. G. *The Southeast Asian City: A Social Geography of the Primate Cities of Southeast Asia*, London: Bell and Sons, 1969.

—— *Hawkers in Hong Kong: A Study of Planning and Policy in A Third World City*, Hong Kong: Centre of Asian Studies, University of Hong Kong, 1973.

—— "Beach-heads and Enclaves: The Urban Debate and The Urbanization

Process in Southeast Asia since 1945" in Yeung, Y. M. and Lo, C. P. (eds.) *Changing South-East Asian Cities: Readings on Urbanization*, Singapore: Oxford University Press, 1976, 60–75.

—— "The Persistence of the Proto-Proletariat: Occupational Structures and Planning for the Future of Third World Cities", in Abu-Lughod, J. and Hay, R. (eds.) *Third World Urbanization*, Chicago: Maaroufa Press, 1977, 257–70.

—— "From 'Urban Involution' to Proletarian Transformation: Asian Perspectives", paper presented at the twelfth Annual Conference of the Canadian Council for Southeast Asian Studies held at Lakehead University, Thunder Bay, Ontario, 5–7 November 1982.

McGee, T. G. and Yeung, Y. M. *Hawkers in Southeast Asian Cities: Planning for the Bazaar Economy*, Ottawa: International Development Research Centre, 1977.

McNicoll, G. and Mamas, S. G. M. *The Demographic Situation in Indonesia*, Hawaii: East West Population Institute Papers No. 28, 1973.

McVey, R. (ed.) *Indonesia*, Southeast Asia Studies, Yale University, New Haven: HRAF Press, 1963.

Meadow, P. and Mizruchi, E. H. (eds.) *Urbanism, Urbanization and Change: Comparative Perspectives*, Reading (Mass.): Addison-Wesley, 1969.

Mears, L. A. "Economic Development in Indonesia through 1958", *Ekonomi dan Keuangan Indonesia*, Vol. 14, Nos. 1 and 2: 1961: 15–58.

Mears, L. A. *The New Rice Economy of Indonesia*, Yogyakarta: Gadjah Mada University Press, 1981.

Milone, P. D. *Urban Areas in Indonesia: Administrative and Census Concepts*, Research Series, No. 10, Berkeley: Institute of International Studies University of California, 1966.

Mintz, S. W. "The Role of the Middleman in the Internal Distribution System of a Caribbean Peasant Economy", *Human Organization*, Vol. 15, No. 2: 1956: 18–23.

—— "Internal Market systems as Mechanisms of Social Articulation" in Proceedings of the 1959 Annual Spring Meetings of the American Ethnological Society, Seattle: Washington University Press, 1959, 20–30.

—— "Men, Women and Trade", *Comparative Studies in Society and History*, Vol. 13: 1971: 247–69.

Moir, H. and Wirosardjono, S. *The Jakarta Informal Sector*, Jakarta: ILO/Leknas/LIPI, Mimeo, 1977.

Moser, C. "The Dual Economy and Marginality Debate and the Contribution of Micro Analysis: Market Sellers in Bogota", *Development and Change*, Vol. 8, No. 4: 1977: 465–89.

Nas, P. (ed.) *The Indonesian City: Studies in Urban Development and Planning*, Dordrecht: Foris, 1986.

Nelson, J. "The Urban Poor: Disruption or Political Integration in Third World Cities?" *World Politics*, Vol. 22, No. 3: 1970: 393–414.

Noormohamed, S. "Alternative Approaches to Low-Income Housing: A Case Study of Jakarta", Ph.D Thesis, Canberra: Australian National University, 1981.

Nugroho Notosusanto and Ismail Saleh *The Coup Attempt of the "30th September Movement" in Indonesia*, Djakarta: Pembimbing Masa, 1968.

Oshima, H. "Perspectives on trends in Asian Household Income Distribution: an Overview with Special Reference to Indonesia", *Ekonomi dan Keuangan Indonesia*, Vol. 30, No. 1: 1982: 91–120.

Pahl, R. E. (ed.) *Readings in Urban Sociology*, Oxford: Pergamon Press, 1968.

Palma, G. "Dependency: A Formal Theory of Underdevelopment or a Methodology for the Analysis of Concrete Situations of Underdevelopment?", *World Development*, Nos. 6, 7 and 8: 1978: 881–924.

Palmer, I. *The Indonesian Economy Since 1965: A Case Study of Political Economy*, London: Frank Cass, 1978.

Papanek, G. F. "The Poor of Jakarta", *Economic Development and Cultural Change*, Vol. 24, No. 1: 1975: 1–27.

——(ed.) *The Indonesian Economy*, New York: Praeger, 1980.

—— "Income Distribution and the Politics of Poverty" in Papanek, G. F. (ed.) *The Indonesian Economy*, New York: Praeger, 1980, 56–66.

—— "The Effect of Economic Growth and Inflation on Workers' Income" in Papanek, G.F. (ed.) *The Indonesian Economy*, New York: Praeger, 1980, 82–120.

Papanek, G. F. and Dowest, D. "The Cost of Living 1938–1973", *Ekonomi dan Keuangan Indonesia*, Vol. 13, No. 2: 1975: 150–181.

Peattie, L. R. *The View from the Barrio*, Ann Arbor: University of Michigan Press, 1968.

Perlman, J. E. *Myths of Marginality: The Urban Squatter in Brazil*, Berkeley: University of California Press, 1976.

Pinches, M. D. "Anak-Pawis Children of Sweat: Class and Community in a Manila Shanty Town", Ph.D Thesis, Melbourne: Monash University, 1984.

Pinches, M. and Lakha, S. (ed.) *Wage Labour and Social Change*, Melbourne: Centre of Southeast Asian Studies, Monash University, 1987.

Polle, V. F. L. and Hofstee, P. "Urban Kampung Improvement and the Use of Aerial Photography for Data Collection" in Nas, P. (ed.) *The Indonesian City: Studies in Urban Development and Planning*, Dordrecht: Foris, 1986, 116–36.

Portes, A. and Walton, J. *Urban Latin America: The Political Condition from Above and Below*, Austin: University of Texas Press, 1976.

Portes, A. and Walton, J. *Labour, Class and the International System*, New York: A Sumimic Press, 1981.

Praginanto, "Pak Parto Pengusaha Warung Tegal", *Galang*, Vol. 1, No. 1: 1983: 44–7.

Prawirasuganda, A. "Adat Perkawinan di Tanah Pasundan", *Tjidschrift voor Indische Taal-, Land- en Volkenkunde*, Vol. 84: 1950: 209–79.

Quennell, P. (ed.) *Mayhew's London*, London: Bracken Books, 1984.

Ramedhan, E. "The Disco Way of Life in Jakarta: from Subculture to Cultural Void", *Prisma*, No. 6, June 1977: 16–20.

Reader, D. R. *The Black Man's Portion. History, Demography and Living Conditions in the Native Locations of East London Cape Province*, Cape

Town: Oxford University Press, 1961.

Reissman, L. *The Urban Process: Cities in Industrial Societies*, Glencoe: Free Press, 1970.

Ricklefs, M. C. *A History of Modern Indonesia*, London: Macmillan, 1981.

Rimmer, P. J. et al., (eds.) *Food, Shelter and Transport in Southeast Asia and the Pacific*, Canberra: Research School of Pacific Studies, Australian National University, 1978.

Roberts, B. R. "Politics in a Neighbourhood of Guatemala City", *Sociology*, Vol. 2, No. 2: 1968: 185–204.

―― "Protestant Groups and Coping with Urban Life in Guatemala City", *American Journal of Sociology*, Vol. 73, No. 6: 1968: 753–67.

―― *Organizing Strangers: Poor Families in Guatemala City*, Austin: University of Texas Press, 1973.

―― *Cities of Peasants: The Political Economy of Urbanization in the Third World*, London: Sage, 1978.

Roeder, O. G. *The Smiling General: President Soeharto of Indonesia*, Jakarta: Gunung Agung, 1969.

Rowntree, B. S. *Poverty: A Study of Town Life*, London: Macmillan, 1910.

Sadli, Moh. "Indonesia's Experience with the Application of Technology and its Employment Effects", *Ekonomi dan Keuangan Indonesia*, Vol. 21, No. 3: 1973: 147–60.

Sajogyo, "Garis Kemiskinan dan Kebutuhan Minumun Pangan" Menado: Laporan Seminar Nasional HIPIIS periode 1975–1977, Mimeo, 1977.

Sannen, Ad. M. H. "Mandur and Tukang: The Functioning of Informal Subcontractors and Building Workers in the Construction Sector of Bandung", in Nas, P. (ed.) *The Indonesian City: Studies in Urban Development and Planning*, Dordrecht: Foris, 1986, 220–37.

Santos, M. "Economic Development and Urbanization in Underdeveloped Countries: The Two flow Systems of the Urban Economy and their Spatial Implications", Toronto: University of Toronto, Mimeo, 1972.

―― "Spatial Organization in the Third World: Two Urban Fields", Toronto: Department of Geography: University of Toronto, Mimeo, 1973.

Sapiie, S. "Study Rumah Murah di Jakarta", Jakarta: Department of Public Works and Electric Power, 1972.

Sartono, Kartodirdjo *The Pedicab in Yogyakarta—A Study in Low Cost Transportation and Poverty Problems*, Yogyakarta: Gadjah Mada University Press, 1981.

Sethuraman, S. V. *Urbanization and Employment in Jakarta*, Geneva: World Employment Programme, ILO, 1974.

Silaban, B. and Djazuli, A. *Kelompok Migran Sirkuler Di DKI Jakarta*, Jakarta: Pusat Penelitian Masalah Perkotaan dan Lingkungan, DKI, 1978.

Smail, J. R. W. *A Study in the Social History of the Indonesian Revolution*, Ithaca: Cornell Modern Indonesia Monograph Series, 1964.

Soedarno "Mobilitas Tenaga Kerja Antara Desa dan Kota Studi Kasus: Pengemudi Becak di Jakarta Timur", Jakarta: Pusat Latihan Penelitian Ilmu2 Social, Universitas Indonesia, 1976.

Soekotjo, R. "Berberapa Masalah Angkutan Kota—Suatu Kasus Transportasi di Kota Padat Penduduk", *Prisma*, No. 2, April 1974: 53–62.

Soemarno, S. "Jakarta Bukan Hanja bagi Jang Berduit", *Prisma*, No. 5, May 1977: 53–5.

Southall, A. (ed.) *Urban Anthropology: Cross-Cultural Studies of Urbanization*, London: Oxford University Press, 1973.

Sritua Arief, *Indonesia: Growth, Income Disparity and Mass Poverty*, Jakarta: Sritua Arief Associates, 1977.

Stedman-Jones, G. *Outcast London: A Study in the Relationship Between Classes in Victorian Society*, Harmondsworth: Penguin, 1971.

Steele, R. M. "Origins and Occupational Mobility of Lifetime Migrants to Surabaya, East Java", Ph.D Thesis, Canberra: Australian National University, 1980.

Steer, A. "Indonesian Urban Services Sector Report", Washington D.C.: World Bank, Mimeo, 1983.

Suharso and Speare, A. "Migration Trends" in Booth, A. and McCawley, P. (eds.) *The Indonesian Economy During the Soeharto Era*, Kuala Lumpur: Oxford University Press, 1981, 289–315.

Sullivan, J. "Back Alley Neighbourhood: Kampung as Urban Community in Yogyakarta", Working Paper No. 18, Melbourne: Centre of Southeast Asian Studies, Monash University, 1980.

Sullivan, J. "Rukun Kampung and Kampung: State-Community Relations in Urban Yogyakarta", Ph.D Thesis, Melbourne: Monash University, 1982.

Sullivan, N. "Masters and Managers in Sitiwaru: Men and Women in a Yogyakartan Urban Kampung", Ph.D Thesis, Melbourne: Monash University, 1983.

Sumardi, M. and Evers, H. (eds.) *Golongan Miskin di Jakarta*, Jakarta: Pusat Pembinaan Sambu-Daya Manusia, 1980.

Sundrum, R. "Consumer Expenditure Patterns: An Analysis of the Socio-Economic Surveys", *Bulletin of Indonesian Economic Studies*, Vol. 9, No. 1: 1973: 86–106.

―― "Manufacturing Employment 1961–1971", *Bulletin of Indonesian Economic Studies*, Vol. 9, No. 1: 1975: 58–65.

―― "Change in Consumption Patterns in Urban Java 1970–1976", *Bulletin of Indonesian Economic Studies*, Vol. 13, No. 2: 1977: 102–16.

―― "Income Distribution, 1970–76", *Bulletin of Indonesian Economic Studies*, Vol. 15, No. 1: 1979: 137–41.

Sundrum, R. and Booth, A. "Income Distribution in Indonesia: Trends and Determinants", in Fox, J.J. et al. (eds.) *Indonesia: Australian Perspectives*, Canberra: Research School of Pacific Studies, Australian National University, 1980, 455–85.

―― *Rapid Economic Growth in Indonesia: 1968–81*, ? , 1987.

Sunindyo, Saraswati "Kampung Sawah, Studi Eksploratif Tentang Perkampungan Liar di Jakarta", B.A. Thesis, Jakarta: University of Indonesia, 1981.

Sunuharyo, B. S. "Analisa Biaya Hidup di Jakarta", in Sumardi, M. and Evers, H. (eds.) *Golongan Miskin di Jakarta*, Jakarta: Pusat Pembinaan Sumber-Daya Manusia, 1980, 73–88.

Surachman, Samiun "Perantau Pengemudi Becak dan Gambaran Masa Depan Mereka: Kasus di Kota Magelang", presented at Seminar Population

Institute, Yogyakarta: Gadja Mada University, Mimeo, 1978.

Suryo, Djoko "Social and Economic Life in Rural Semarang under Colonial rule in the Later 19th Century", Ph.D Thesis, Melbourne: Monash University, 1982.

Sutter, J. O. *Indonesianisasi: Politics in a Changing Economy, 1940–1955* (4 Volumes), Southeast Asia Program Data Paper No. 36, Ithaca: Cornell University, 1959.

Swasono, Wir Edi (ed.) *Entrepreneurship in Indonesia*, Jakarta: Faculty of Economics, University of Indonesia and Bappenas, 1976.

Swianieswicz, S. "Tendencies to Development and Stagnation in the Indonesian Economy", *Ekonomi dan Keuangan Indonesia*, Vol. 11, Nos. 1 and 6: 1958: 78–98.

Tan, T. K. (ed.) *Sukarno's Guided Democracy*, Brisbane: Jacaranda Press, 1967.

—— "Sukarnian Economics" in Tan, T. K. (ed.) *Sukarno's Guided Democracy*, Brisbane: Jacaranda Press, 1967, 29–45.

Tan Kim Swee, "A Study of Kongsi Houses Housing Immigrant Men", Singapore: University of Singapore, 1963.

Temple, G. "Migration to Jakarta: Empirical Search for a Theory", Ph.D Thesis, Madison: University of Wisconsin, 1974.

Temple, G. "Migration to Jakarta", *Bulletin of Indonesian Economic Studies*, Vol. 11, No. 1: 1975: 76–81.

Tesch, J. W. "The Hygiene Study Ward Centre at Batavia: Planning and Preliminary Results 1937–1941", Dissertatie, Leiden: Leiden University, 1948.

—— "Living Conditions of Municipally Employed Coolies in Batavia 1937" in Wertheim, W.F. (ed.) *The Indonesian Town: Studies in Urban Sociology*, (Volume 4), The Hague: Van Hoeve, 1958: 85–224.

Todaro, M. P. *Internal Migration in Developing Countries: A Review of Theory, Evidence, Methodology and Research Priorities*, Geneva: ILO, 1976.

Tokeman, V. E. "An Exploration into the Nature of Informal-Formal Sector Relationships", *World Development*, Vols. 6, 9 and 10: 1978: 1067–75.

—— "Competition between the Informal and Formal Sectors in Retailing: The Case of Santiago", *World Development*, Vols. 6, 9 and 10: 1978: 1187–98.

Turner, J. C. "Uncontrolled Urban Settlements: Problems and Policies" in Breese, G. (ed.) *The City in Newly Developing Countries: Readings on Urbanism and Urbanization*, New Jersey: Prentice-Hall, 1969, 507–34.

—— "Barriers and Channels for Housing Development in Modernizing Countries" in Mangin, W. (ed.) *Peasants in Cities: Readings in the Anthropology of Urbanization*, Boston: Houghton, Mifflin, 1970, 1–20.

—— *Housing by the People: Towards Autonomy in Building Environments*, London: Marion Boyars, 1976.

University of Indonesia, "Pola Management Pada Sejvnlah Pedagang Kecil Eceran Mengenai Latar Belakang Kebudayaan di DKI Jakarta Raya," Jakarta: Fakultas Ilmuz Sosial, University of Indonesia, 1977

University of Indonesia, *Caporan Hasil Survey Profile Pedagang Kaki Lima di DKI Jaya* Jakarta: Fakultas Ekonomi, University of Indonesia, 1976.

Waworoentoe, W. *Hawkers and Vendors in Bandung*, Bandung: Institute of Technology, 1974.

Wertheim, W. (ed.) *The Indonesian Town: Studies in Urban Sociology* (Volume 4), The Hague: Van Hoeve, 1958.

—— "Urban Characteristics in Indonesia" in *East West Parallels: Sociological Approaches to Modern Asia*, The Hague: Van Hoeve, 1964, 165–85.

Whyte, W. F. *Street Corner Society: The Social Structure of an Italian Slum*, Chicago: University of Chicago, 1943.

Williams, J. B. "Sadikin Closes Jakarta", *Insight*, Hong Kong, February 16–20 1973.

Wilson, M. and Mafeje, A. *Langa: A Study of Social Groups in an African Township*, Cape Town: Oxford University Press, 1963.

Wirth, L. "Urbanism as a Way of Life", *American Journal of Sociology*, Vol. 44, No. 1: 1938: 1–24.

Yueng, Y. M. "The Marketing System in Singapore" in Yueng, Y. M. and Lo, C. P. (eds.) *Changing South-East Asian Cities: Readings on Urbanization*, Singapore: Oxford University Press, 1976, 153–64.

Yueng, Y. M. and Lo, C. P. (eds.) *Changing South-East Asian Cities: Readings on Urbanization*, Singapore: Oxford University Press, 1976.

Index